Changing Research and Practice: Teachers' Professionalism, Identities and Knowledge

Changing Research and Practice:
Teachers' Professionalism, Identities and Knowledge

Edited by

Michael Kompf, W. Richard Bond,
Don Dworet and R. Terrance Boak

 The Falmer Press

(A member of the Taylor & Francis Group)
London • Washington, D.C.

UK   Falmer Press, 1 Gunpowder Square, London, EC4A 3DE
USA   Falmer Press, Taylor & Francis Inc., 1900 Frost Road, Suite 101,
       Bristol, PA 19007

First published in 1996

A catalogue record for this book is available from the British Library

Library of Congress Cataloging-in-Publication Data are available on request

ISBN 0 7507 0585 X cased
ISBN 0 7507 0586 8 paper

Jacket design by Caroline Archer

Typeset in 10/12pt Times by
Graphicraft Typesetters Ltd., Hong Kong.

Printed in Great Britain by Biddles Ltd, Guildford and King's Lynn on paper which has a specified pH value on final paper manufacture of not less than 7.5 and is therefore 'acid free'.

Contents

Contents

Introduction

Michael Kompf

My first contact with the International Study Association on Teacher Thinking (ISATT) was at the 1986 meeting in Leuven, Belgium where I co-presented a paper with Professor Alan Brown, my then PhD supervisor at the Ontario Institute for Studies in Education (University of Toronto). Leuven was memorable for its beauty, dignity and age. ISATT was memorable for feelings of validation, positive regard and the kind interest, friendship, approachability and humor shown by all in attendance.

During the winter that followed, Alan visited my small farm and we went for a walk in the woods to observe whatever wildlife that happened to be about. Months later I was shown a terse note Alan had penned to a colleague about the visit: 'We saw tracks and made more.' During our walkabout, we followed the delicate tracks left by deer and rabbits, and made large clumsy marks in the snow, obliterating most traces of other paths with our progress. Alan's observation stuck and has served as a metaphorical guide for research and thinking about research: We see tracks and make more. We leave large and small indications of having passed this way or that. I returned to the woods after Alan's departure and was easily able to follow the trail. I left yet another set of tracks.

ISATT members saw tracks and made more during the 7th biennial meeting held at Brock University in St Catharines, Ontario, Canada from 30 July to 3 August in the summer of 1995. ISATT was founded by educators and learners concerned with the underpinnings of teachers' knowledge, and during its twelve-year history, has provided a forum and opportunity for a wide range of voices. Meetings have hosted an impressive list of speakers and presenters representing the leading edge in educational thought and practice. Equally impressive is the ever-growing list of new scholars and voices who have found their presence welcomed and their career progress facilitated through contact with ISATT.

The 1995 meeting, the first to be held outside of Europe, was no exception to previous encounters of the ISATT type. Five inspiring keynote addresses (Elliot Eisner, Ingrid Carlgren, Cecilia Reynolds, Jean Clandinin and Ivor Goodson) provided a springboard for approximately 150 delegates, representing twenty-two countries, to offer more than ninety papers in a variety of formats. All presenters were invited to submit papers to be considered for inclusion in this collection. What follows are papers chosen by the editors as best representing the intellectual spirit of ISATT and the diversity of those in attendance. Would that two or three volumes were possible!

The structure of the 1995 meeting provided conceptual guidelines for this collection in that, each meeting day consisted of a focal keynote speaker followed by participant papers which extended the central theme. Thus the three sections which follow address the conference theme of 'Changing Research and Practice' by focusing on 'Teachers' Professionalism', 'Teachers' Identities', and 'Teachers' Knowledge'. Each section begins with an overview by one of the editors. In addition to the theme keynote papers, the opening (Elliot Eisner) and closing (Ivor Goodson) keynotes of the conference are included as conceptual bookends to an insightful and challenging collection of papers.

The overall theme of the ISATT gathering, and the title of this book, has to do with Changing Research and Practice. The choice of this turn of phrase indicates not only an observation that research and practice are changing, but also that thinking teachers can actively bring about change in the ways in which research and practice are contemplated and carried out. The papers presented throughout the gathering showed aspects of both interpretations of the conference theme. In addition, the structured, semi-structured and casual conversations which took place underscored the congenial, collegial and constructively critical spirit of ISATT. According to an ISATT information brochure:

> 'Teacher thinking' is understood as encompassing several perspectives: teachers' thoughts, conceptions, practical theories, 'voice' etc.; teachers' intentions, thought processes and cognitions, personal practical knowledge; teachers' thinking as an aspect of professional actions; teachers' thinking and action as influenced by contextual factors in their structural, cultural and social environment.

ISATT's collective works show much evidence of lifelong learners and scholars who have not only responded to educational change, but have also anticipated, initiated and brought about critical change in research, teaching and learning practices. Each of the six conferences have produced a superior volume of readings (Halkes and Olson, 1984; Ben-Peretz, Bromme and Halkes, 1986; Lowyck and Clark, 1989; Day, Pope and Denicolo, 1990; Day, Calderhead and Denicolo, 1993; Carlgren, Handal and Vaage, 1994). In addition, the numerous papers sponsored through *Teaching and Teacher Education*, and now through our own journal *Teachers and Teaching*, we are aware that in putting together this collection, we stand on the shoulders of giants.

As part of the ISATT publication legacy, one of our main, and most difficult, editorial tasks has been the responsibility of ensuring representativeness as regards inclusion and breadth of appeal. Readers will find papers from graduate students, teachers and seasoned veterans of academe. All contributions reach out in the language of practice and theory by describing, interpreting and encouraging innovative and insightful thinking about teaching. The observations and challenges issued by the many contributors speak to lived experiences which center on the many forms of engagement in teaching practice. Of singular importance is the teachers' engagement with self. The continuous and continual process of 'being' and 'becoming' in teaching practice, as all of us change through the accumulation of experience and age, reminds us that, although we may come from far-flung places, we are not alone in our queries, conundrums and quests.

The advantages of international contributors are evident in both the process and content of the works represented in this collection. While the psychological comfort provided by the discovery of common issues, approaches and understandings is encouraging and validating, attending to differences is more to the advantage of the learning practitioner. Specific principles of practice, and how teachers think about, and respond to, such principles, may be influenced by cultural, social, legislative or fiscal circumstances. These forces are only rendered more complex as thinking teachers respond to the epistemological crises and shifting paradigms within their own professions. For many teachers, the thoughts and actions associated with learning are intensely personal and represent a vocational commitment.

Central to any dynamic commitment is a thoughtful and reflective orientation which fosters ongoing critical examination of beliefs and practices. Critical examination requires open-mindedness and a willing predisposition to engage with other perspectives. As such, the ways of being and becoming which define the thinking teacher cross definitional boundaries and are well represented in ISATT's cultural mosaic. Such projects as ISATT '95, or this collection, do not come about without the encouragement, assistance and support of many individuals. The families and support systems of the editors provided patience and time, and tolerated the busyness of organizing and hosting ISATT '95. John Bird was tireless in his organizational dexterity. Lesa Hom and Rahul Kumar provided gracious technical support. Terry Boak showed trust and commitment by volunteering Brock as the site for ISATT '95. To the membership of ISATT, a debt of gratitude is acknowledged for understanding and accepting the torturous routes that editors and conference organizers must travel. To all of the contributors, we extend our thanks for agreeing to share your thoughts and words both at ISATT '95 and in this volume. To the reader: We invite you to see tracks and make more. Surgite!

Michael Kompf, Brock University, 2 February 1996

References

BEN PERETZ, M., BROMME, R. and HALKES, R. (Eds) (1986) *Advances of Research on Teacher Thinking*, ISATT, Lisse/Berwyn, Swets and Zeitlinger/Swets North America Inc.

CARLGREN, I., HANDAL, G. and VAAGE, S. (Eds) (1994) *Teachers' Minds and Actions: Research on Teachers' Thinking and Practice*, London, Falmer Press.

DAY, C., CALDERHEAD, J. and DENICOLO, P. (Eds) (1993) *Research on Teacher Thinking: Towards Understanding Professional Development*, London, Falmer Press.

DAY, C., POPE, M. and DENICOLO, P. (Eds) (1990) *Insights into Teachers' Thinking and Practice*, London, Falmer Press.

Michael Kompf

HALKES, R. and OLSON, J.K. (Eds) (1984) *Teacher Thinking: A New Perspective on Persisting Problems in Education*, ISATT, Lisse, Swets and Zeitlinger.
LOWYCK, J. and CLARK, C. (Eds) (1989) *Teacher Thinking and Professional Action*, Leuven University Press.

Part I

Teachers' Professionalism: Overview

W. Richard Bond

Defining such a concept as 'teachers' professionalism' in one neatly encapsulated expression is extremely difficult and quite likely impossible as professionalism in any occupational context must be expressed in many ways. In its most elementary form professionalism may mean nothing more than: displaying in one's public (and private) life types of behaviors likely to meet with the approval of the community in which one practices one's professional skills. Thus, one behaves in a 'professional' manner. Perhaps it is in this form many years ago that professionals such as church ministers and physicians were simultaneously kept in their place, but were able to maintain positions in society which denoted that they were somehow 'better' than the masses to whom they ministered in the course of their duties.

Over time, the status of 'professional person' and the simultaneous attempt to define and describe those elements which make us so has led to the realization there are many more dimensions to professionalism than the simple matter of socially acceptable conduct. For example, autonomy and the assumption that professionals are highly autonomous. It is unlikely that a person off the street would walk into an operating room from the street and, leaning over the operating table, suggest surgical techniques to the surgeon from a zero knowledge base. Nor would that person walk into a courtroom and argue with a judge over a courtroom procedure or point of law. Again, it is unlikely that a similar person would walk into a classroom and instruct a teacher on pedagogical techniques, although I'm sure a great many individuals would like to do so. People in the aforementioned occupational groups are generally regarded as competent to practice without interference, except, perhaps from their own professional and statutory bodies, or in the event of infringement of a law. By and large, they are autonomous.

Further, it is now accepted that autonomous, professional people may also have monopolies in certain kinds of knowledge. Such is indicated by prolonged and intensive periods of preparation for the professions — usually much more than for most less-professional occupations. For almost all professionals it is necessary to acquire quantities of complex and esoteric knowledge developed by others, and frequently, in turn, to generate new knowledge for others to use.

The combination of autonomy and access to knowledge and information enables professionals to exercise a great deal of flexibility in the practice of their professions. They may rely on their own professional judgment. The more fortunate ones may even command high salaries. Even the less fortunate ones may earn higher than average incomes. And with these *privileges* there are accompanying *obligations* to exercise high levels of commitment and responsibility to the client group.

While the elements of professionalism I have described may contribute to an overall understanding of what is meant by professionalism, they are by no means comprehensive. Those of us in the professions are frequently beset with the problem of trying to identify professionalism that we may practice our skills to the best of our ability, fulfill our obligations to our client groups in particular, society in general and to know who we are. Within the context of education (as a noun), the following educators examine the ways in which teachers' professionalism may be known, and how, in turn, we may know ourselves.

Elliot Eisner (Stanford, USA) has posed a number of questions — and provided some answers — in his examination of the question 'Is "The Art of Teaching" a Metaphor?' The manner in which he addresses his question includes highly abstract as well as more concrete definitions related to both the art and practice of teaching, which, while being connected are not necessarily the same thing. Furthermore, he includes discussion on artistry, metaphor and imagination in explaining the meaning of art. Such discussion might seem to be a far cry from the realities of teaching and professionalism in teaching, but he provides a discussion which sets the imagination racing and provides the backdrop against which the other chapters in this section of the book are played out.

In 'Professionalism and Teachers as Designers', Ingrid Carlgren (Goteborg, Sweden) examines notions of what it is that teachers *should* do as compared with what they *actually* do. She compares the importance of the social versus the didactic dimension and identifies that it is the tacit rather than the explicit elements of socialization and behaviors which define professionalism in teaching. She also includes the increasingly important concept of reflection as an important tool in identifying professionalism.

In 'Becoming a Trained Professional', Margaret Olson examines conflicting versions of teacher education and the ways in which these may contribute to teacher identity. In her case study of Susan she relates the confusing and contradictory problems a student teacher faces in attempting to form her own professional identity, and describes Susan's feelings as she recognizes the differences between her own and others' expectations and the realities of professional practice.

Per Laursen in 'Professionalism and the Reflective Approach to Teaching' has written with his theoretical underpinnings also anchored in reflection, but emphasis is more on how *others* view teachers as professionals rather than how teachers may view themselves. His perspective, then, is more social and general than the highly focused descriptions of some of the other contributors. He identifies the difficulties in determining the position of teachers in the professional spectrum, particularly in light of teachers' knowledge base and current European discussion, and proposes further development of the reflective approach as a means by which professionalism may be defined.

In the final chapter in this section of the book, Pam Denicolo uses George

Kelly's personal construct theory as the theoretical basis for her paper entitled 'Productively Confronting Dilemmas in Educational Practice and Research' and draws upon student research in defining professionalism. Her focus on addressing dilemmas in research and practice identifies that this is something that only teachers can do to help students develop, and that this activity in itself bespeaks professionalism within the context of education. Further, the highly idiosyncratic nature of adjustment and development is supportive of Kellyian theoretical underpinnings, indicating also that such activities are part of a lifelong process. By association, our professional identities must gradually emerge over time.

The authors of these chapters have provided readers with kaleidoscopic views of educating, teachers, teaching and professionalism. Their varied thoughts, notions and understandings of what it means to be involved in the process of educating may provoke many more questions than they provide answers. Together they help place into perspective the complexities of identifying the profession, the concept of professionalism within the context of the teaching profession, and defining professional identity.

1   Is 'The Art of Teaching' a Metaphor?

Elliot Eisner

One of the ironic features of research on teaching is the general neglect of the role that artistry plays in its practice. I say ironic because if teachers are asked to characterize the nature of their work they are much more likely to describe it as an art or a craft than as the application of a science, or even a technology. Yet if you consult the most recent *Handbook of Research on Teaching* you will find that that four-and-a-half pound tome which has 880 entries in its index has no entry devoted to the art of teaching. To be sure there is an entry on the teaching of art — something I care about deeply — but nothing on artistry in teaching. Both the editor and the authors neglect it, despite the fact that teachers don't.

The authors and editors of the Handbooks — three have been published — are not alone. Journals such as the *Educational Researcher*, the *Journal of Teacher Education*, and *Teaching and Teacher Education* apparently receive few contributions and hence give little space to artistry in teaching, the topic I intend to address this morning.[1] I want to acknowledge at the outset the fact that a number of authors have written about artistry in teaching. Gilbert Highet's *The Art of Teaching*. Published in 1950, was among the first. Louis Rubin has written *Artistry in Teaching*, and, of course, Nate Gage has given us *The Scientific Basis of the Art of Teaching*. But as you must know Gage's fine book is essentially about teaching's scientific basis rather than about artistry in teaching.

Donald Schön has given us his insightful *The Reflective Practitioner*, a book that is sensitive and wise but not in conventional terms a research study of artistry in teaching. A scholar who uses artistically grounded research methods is Sara Lawrence Lightfoot, but her book *The Good High School* is not as much about teaching as about schools. Studies of artistry in teaching are rare.

To begin it might be well to speculate about why a concept which teachers warm to would be scarcely mentioned among those who work in schools and departments of education in universities. Part of the explanation might have to do with the position that education occupies on university campuses. In the academic pecking order education is a low-status field. And on many campuses so too are the arts. Universities give their garlands to theory and theory is the darling of the sciences. The arts traffic too closely to crafts and crafts are thought to be more manual than mental. To make artistry central to the study, preparation, or practice of teaching is to marginalize theory and to reduce teacher preparation to apprenticeship. Better to keep one's distance. But there are other reasons as well.

Artistry not only does not enjoy the privileged place of science, artistry is regarded as unteachable. Those blessed by the muse are thought to be gifted and gifts are possessions that are not widely shared. Being artistic, whether in painting or in teaching, is a talent and since so few have it, it cannot be the basis for building the largest of our professions. So what we have when we try to explain why artistry in teaching is neglected in research on teaching are the following. First, intellectual respectability demands, it seems, a scientific understanding of the practice of teaching; at its best teaching is to emulate medicine. Teaching will have, as Nate Gage has so eloquently reminded us, a scientific basis. Second, artistry depends upon talent. Talent is a gift bestowed on only a few. You can't build a profession of millions of teachers on so rare a personal trait. Third, even if artistry is present in teaching, it is undependable. It is science, not art, that discovers regularities and makes prediction possible — even control. Fourth, because it is a gift, it is believed that artistry cannot be learned; it's more than a teachable and learnable skill. To create a profession of teaching demands a scientific foundation, something that leads to learnable principles and procedures.

Everything that I have said so far pertains to the status of artistry in the study of teaching and to some of the reasons for its neglect. But is it true, as I implied, that teaching really is an art, or at least at its best is an art? When we speak about the art of teaching are we speaking literally or metaphorically? When we talk about painting or dancing as arts we use the term art in its literal form. Clearly painting and dancing are art forms. Is teaching? Is talk about the art of teaching simply suggestive or connotative or does it denote? And what difference does it make anyway? Why worry about the matter? To answer these questions we need to examine the meaning of metaphor and the meaning of art in order to determine what these notions mean for our understanding of teaching, especially its improvement.

I spoke of metaphor and suggested a distinction between the literal and the metaphorical. What is the difference? One answer provided by Suzanne Langer, one of the major American aestheticians of this century, is that a metaphor is simply a way of saying something one way and expecting it to be understood to mean something else. To say that this man is a bull while the other a fox is to say something about their respective personal qualities through forms that are not to be taken literally but which, nevertheless, reveal some ineffable common structural features of each. Metaphors, for Langer, are at the very core of our conceptual life. They are fundamental to the beginnings of science and are basic to art itself. Indeed, since, according to Langer, art addresses the ineffable life of feeling, it must rely upon metaphor and the structural properties of form to reveal that life. Langer's aim is epistemological. What she is telling us is that metaphors create illusions that call our attention to the objective features of ineffable states of affairs. To say that teaching is an art is to use a metaphor to reveal a truth.

Lakoff and Johnson's view of metaphor shares similarities with Langer's, but goes beyond hers. For Lakoff and Johnson our conceptual life, in the main, is ineluctably metaphorical and, even more, our comprehension of metaphorical meaning depends not only on the grasp of individual metaphors, but upon an entire network of metaphorical connections, something like a metaphorical field. For example the term 'teaching', Lakoff and Johnson would argue, is metaphorically rooted. To grasp the meaning of teaching we must have an experiential base. Our experience, in turn, is shaped by an array of cultural metaphors: in our culture teaching suggests putting into others something they do not have. In a sense, when we teach we are engaged, one way or another, in filling a container. Lakoff and Johnson's point is that we understand our experience by virtue of something else. The something else they mean is what culture 'gives us' to understand.

Perhaps the most vivid example of that principle in the domain of teaching is to be found in Plato's use of the parable of the cave. In Book Six of *The Republic* Socrates tries to teach Glaucon an entire conception of reality through a story about light, shadows, and men in weights and chains. Plato apparently knew, long before Lakoff and Johnson, that we come to understand one thing through another. What Plato, Langer, and Lakoff and Johnson share is their conviction that metaphor is a powerful instrument of cognition. To speak metaphorically is the only way we can speak, because it is the only way we can think. In the end Langer and Lakoff and Johnson part company: Langer's views are closer to philosophical realism. But for both formulations, as I said, metaphor makes it possible to grasp what we wish to understand. We must not forget what we wish to understand: teaching. Our task is to look at teaching from the vantage point of art.

Let us proceed on our journey to explore the meaning of 'art'. Even If we accept the broad view that Lakoff, Johnson, and Langer share, namely, that a metaphor is a means through which we experience and understand one thing in terms of another, we still confront the problem of knowing in our particular case what the term art refers to when we talk about teaching being one. What can we mean by art? And how does that meaning apply to teaching?

Before taking you on a brief Cook's Tour regarding the meaning of art I want to say something about the phrase, 'The work of art'. It is a phrase that has at least two distinct meanings. When we say 'work of art' we can mean the work of *art* that is, the object created — a painting by Matisse, the Parthenon, Beethoven's Ninth Symphony, or we can mean the *work* of art, the acts of artistry that are performed by someone or some group in the course of doing one's work. The teacher is more likely to be engaged in the latter than in the former. That is, like a dancer or an actor the art — if art there be in teaching — is in the performance. When the performance is finished so too is the work.

Let's take a brief look at a teacher in action. The teacher, John Keating, is on film. The film is a movie. The movie is *The Dead Poets Society*. The question we might ask is, 'Is artistry displayed in John Keating's teaching? If so, where? And what are the likely educational consequences of his artistry, if artistry there is?'[2]

Let's turn now to the meanings of art. One conception of art, a conception advanced by John Dewey, argues that art is, at base, a special form of experience that in its rudimentary form can be had in any transaction between a sentient organism and the environment he or she inhabits. Art is not merely the sole property of an object or performance or process executed by someone we call an artist;

art is a form of life that results from the interaction between the viewer and the work. And what is the nature of this form of life? First, it is pervaded by an emotional quality that gives it coherence or unity; second, it is bracketed by a beginning and an end, it is a unit of experience that is memorable; third, it has meaning. Its meaning is a meaning that is expressed rather than stated, as are scientific meanings; fourth, its meaning cannot be separated or isolated into component parts, it emerges for the competent 'reader' as an integral pervasive quality of a unified experience. The key point for Dewey resides, as the title of his book attests, in the idea of art as experience. For Dewey a work of art is a work that makes aesthetic experience possible.

Another conception of art is advanced by Suzanne Langer. For Langer a work of art is an apparition that articulates feeling the artist knows, but cannot symbolize or convey in literal terms. Let me quote her directly:

> A work of art presents feeling (in the broad sense I mentioned before, as everything that can be felt) for our contemplation, making it visible or audible or in some other way perceivable through a symbol, not inferable from a symptom. Artistic form is congruent with the dynamic forms of our direct sensuous, mental, and emotional life; . . . They [artistic forms] are images of feeling, that formulate it for our cognition. What is artistically good is whatever articulates and presents feeling to our understanding. (Langer, 1953, p. 25)

What we get with Langer is a conception of art that is embodied in a symbol or, as she called it later, an apparition that expresses the ineffable and therefore contributes to the enlargement of human understanding as it pertains to those matters that discursive statement cannot address. Again she writes: 'An artist, then, expresses feeling, but not the way a politician blows off steam or a baby laughs and cries. He formulates that elusive aspect of reality that is commonly taken to be amorphous and chaotic; that is he objectifies the subjective realm. A work of art expresses a conception of life, emotion, inward reality. But it is neither a confessional nor a frozen tantrum; it is a developed metaphor, a non-discursive symbol that articulates what is verbally ineffable — the logic of consciousness itself' (p. 26).

Another conception of art is advanced by Sir Herbert Read, poet, pacifist, philosopher, art historian. For Read art is a form created by human beings through the use of imagination, a form whose proportions and structures echo the proportions and structures that he believed existed in nature. Read even believed that eventually we would discover the mathematical structure common to all of nature and inherent in all of the arts. For Read, as for Plato, mathematical proportion was the bench-mark of art: Art exists in relationships. To create art the perception of those relationships and the imagination needed to create them must come into harmony.

Another conception of art is advanced by Ellen Dissenyake. For Dissenyake, an anthropologist, art is what she calls, 'making special'. The major function of art, for Dissenyake, is to assist in the survival process and survival is more likely if there is community. Community is furthered when a group has the opportunity to celebrate and to share. The arts help build community by providing the objects and ceremonies that contribute to the glue culture needs to hold together. In its present day form it is found in the choreography of church celebrations and in the special events that families and communities share: weddings, burials, thanksgiving, civic festivals.

She argues further that what we regard as art today is, unfortunately, the result of capitalism, commodification, and war; the west has brought home the spoils of conquest and displays them in museums. Art now serves status functions, art becomes an investment, a sign of being cultured. But If you scratch deeply enough you will discover that art has a deeper function to perform. It performs a biological function; it helps keep a culture whole.

I have not exhausted by any means — nor will I try — the theories or conceptions of art that have been advanced by critics, aestheticians, art historians, and anthropologists. But regardless of the partial nature of my descriptions what should be clear is that any conception of artistry in teaching must take into account a conception of art. Put another way, it is not possible to talk meaningfully about the art of teaching without some notion of the meaning of art.

Let's turn now to teaching. My conception of teaching is broad. It includes what Jackson refers to as 'pre-active teaching', those activities that teachers engage in prior to their entry into the classroom and it also includes 'inter-active teaching', those activities that take place within the classroom. In addition, my conception of teaching does not require that students learn what the teacher has intended to teach in order for the teacher to be said to have taught. Put another way, as I am using the term, teaching does not necessarily entail consequences. Teaching is a process that teachers engage in, whether or not they are successful.

I use this broad conception of teaching because it affords me the opportunity to include a wide and diverse array of tasks that teachers perform without determining if students are learning what the teacher intends. What are these tasks and in what forms, if any, does artistry emerge within them? I shall identify four: Curriculum planning, explaining, interpersonal relationships, and assessment.

Consider the planning of curricula. Within the constraints of either a state framework or a set of commercially produced curriculum materials, teachers make choices about the organization, pace, and modification of lessons so that they fit the achievement levels of the class or of individual children. This often requires the creation of new materials or the design of new activities that better suit the student and the educational purposes of the teacher. This surely is a task that when done well requires the use of the imagination and the composition of a form — the new lesson — that works for the teacher's students. It is a task that cannot be resolved merely or solely through the use of recipes, rules, or algorithms. It is, it seems to me, a task of art. It requires skill, technique, judgment, and vision. And even when teachers do not recognize the artistry in their work, it is, never-the-less, there.

Of course, any task can be done artlessly — even painting. But to the extent to which the achievement of artistry is a virtue, the task of designing a unit of work for a student or a class, at its best, can be viewed as a work of art. Following Sir Herbert Read we can say that the teacher's work taps both imagination and perception, imagination in the process of conception and perception in the process of organization. The teacher like the painter is creating an image that fits their respective purposes.

Consider a second aspect of teaching, explanation and its close cousin, narrative. Is artistry involved here? Explanation and narrative share, in Wittgenstein's terms, a 'family resemblance'. They both use discourse to convey meaning, the former to account for a state of affairs, the latter to relate a story, often with a moral purpose in mind. Explanation and narrative also have other features in common. Both require the teacher to put himself or herself in the place of his or her students in order to 'hear' his or her own explanation or story from their perspective. It is important to be able to craft the tale in ways that makes for clarity, that sustains interest, and that reaches a conclusion without losing the audience through extraneous details, or tangents, or that fails to come to closure. And this requires not only the ability to empathize with the student, but to have a feel for language and for its pacing, its connotative meaning, its spin. I have often thought that if I had only two data points to use to select teachers, I would try to determine if they could tell a story and if they could give directions to a lost motorist. To tell a story they have to build a plot. To help a lost motorist they have need to be able to hear their directions from the motorist's perspective. Both tasks require forms of thinking and feeling about which I am speaking.

Both explanation and narrative require the creation of a diachronic form, a form that sustains attention over time, that requires the use of the imagination, and that serves an educational purpose. At its best the story evokes a feeling that is perhaps best described as aesthetic; we are moved by what we hear just as we are moved, when the text is really good, by what we read. Great teachers like great books show us new vistas. The experience they help make possible approximates the aesthetic qualities of life that Dewey writes about in *Art as Experience*. Art, Dewey argues, exists not only in experience with what we call works of art, it exists on a continuum that begins with the most rudimentary aspects of life. The shaping of an explanation like the shaping of a story would surely count for Dewey as a candidate for art.

The aspects of teaching I have described so far — curriculum planning and explaining — are simply locales in which the artistic features of teaching can, in principle, emerge. I do not claim that artistic features are always present. Indeed, they may be rare. The question is do these features *when they are present* count as instances of artistry in teaching? While you are thinking let me turn to a couple of other locales in which artistry in teaching may emerge. One of these is in the domain of the interpersonal. The other is in the process of assessment.

By 'interpersonal' I mean those interactions within a classroom in which a teacher engages a class or an individual in a discussion or dialogue or debate. What must the teacher know how to do in order to make such events productive? One thing the teacher must know is when to be silent. Another is how to provide the space students need to become engaged and to secure a sense of ownership of the process. How do you as a teacher know when to intervene? How do you decide whom to call upon? When is it time to pull major points together? How and when do you bring things to closure?

In many ways good discussions are like jazz improvisations; you don't necessarily know who is going to play what, but when you hear it you have to follow on to make the music flow. Responses to the 'music' of classroom discussion are often a matter not of reflective practice — reflection here is much too slow — but a matter of instantaneous response to the qualitative immediacy of the events themselves. Such responses seem instinctive, but they really are result of considerable experience. The artful often appears effortless.

It seems to me that theory in such circumstances plays only a marginal — even a negligible — role in inter-active teaching. This does not mean that the teacher's performance is mindless, it is not. It means that the teacher's actions are directly responsive to qualitative matters, much the way a painter or dancer feels the rightness, the qualitative necessity to move one way rather than another; the qualities of the configuration demand it and when those moves are really right, when they really work, the result is a performance that has aesthetic quality.

If my characterization of only one aspect of the process of teaching is only partially right, the practice of teaching is substantially an art, at least when it is well done. In the circumstances I have described the teacher is no mere rule follower, no bank clerk who is utterly constrained by approved procedure. The teacher in the dynamics of classroom discussion is tuned into the proceedings, improvising when necessary, changing direction when needed, modulating tone of voice, distributing opportunities for students to participate, judging time, keeping several pots and three fry pans on the fire while making sure that what's in them does not burn.

In a sense the point I am making pertains to the importance of being nonreflective in teaching, if reflection connotes pause, meditation, personal deliberation. For much of teaching immediacy is demanded: Reflection is too slow, a line too late is dead.

To talk about teaching in these terms is to risk implying that teaching is no more nor less than acting or dancing or playing tenor sax in a jazz quintet. This is not the case. Teaching includes forms of action and reflection that are not found in any of these fields, just as these fields include forms of action and reflection not found in teaching. I am not trying to 'reduce' teaching to these arts; I am trying to identify the features of teaching in which artistic features and artistic modes of thought are not only present, but when teaching is at its best, salient. A teacher who invests everything to make a lesson or a curriculum unit special is 'making special' in Dissanyake's terms a form that engages and unifies a class. The unit or project contributes to the creation of community.

Thus far I have talked about three aspects of teaching: curriculum planning, narrative and explanation, and interpersonal relationships. I turn now to the fourth and final aspect of teaching that I will address; assessment or evaluation. Is there artistry in these areas? If so, where?

Artistry is normally thought of as a form of physical creation; the making of something, a poem, a pot, a painting, a play. But artistry can also be thought of as achieving an appreciation of the qualities and meaning of things or ideas already made. The connoisseur of Chinese ceramics experiences and interprets the quality of the glaze and if really sophisticated identifies the location of the ancient kiln in which the vessel was fired. In short, the connoisseur is engaged in a searching constructive process intended to awaken him or her to the subtle but significant features of the object under consideration. As a result, interpretation and appraisal follow.

Connoisseurs of Chinese ceramics would be the first to tell you that even with the vast amount of information they possess, their work is more art than science. In the end they must rely on refined sensibility to experience qualities that the rest of us find hard to see. Assessment in teaching has similar features. Teachers, must be tuned into the subtle but significant qualities of classroom life; the tempo of a lesson, the comportment of a troubled student, the amount of time Scott can go without guidance, the need that Helen has for a hug — and for how long. There is no scientific theory that is adequate for making these judgments, yet teachers make them daily. Does the ability to read situations such as these constitute artistry? Is appreciation an art? Is artistry involved in reading meaning in what is implicit and qualitative? Dewey went so far as to say that for someone to appreciate a work of art, he or she had to go through the same operations psychologically that the artist went through in creating the work. For Dewey appreciation is a creative act.

My point here is that the assessment of students depends in large part, if not entirely upon the sensitivity of the teacher to the unmeasurable. The unmeasurable is qualitative and directly experiential. The measurable is symbolic. Consider the difference between heat and temperature. One is a qualitative experience, the other is a measurement. Teachers base their assessments on their experience and they put these experiences into patterns that allows them to make sense of what they have experienced. They are geared more to heat than to temperature. Perception, organization, interpretation, and assessment appear to be the pattern they use to understand what is happening.

The tasks or aspects of teaching I have described employ forms of thinking that depend upon the intelligent use of the sensibilities to read the often subtle array of qualities unfolding in the classroom. They depend upon the use of imagination to envision aims that have educational value. They require the skillful application of techniques that have become so automatic that they need not consume the teacher's attention; substantive matters can be addressed rather than mere method. They also demand a willingness to surrender to impulse and to yield to a sense of rightness in their work, even when not a part of the teacher's intention. And they require a willingness to take risks.

The problematic situations the teacher confronts are often ill structured. Conferring order while being open to chance and to the 'happy accidents' that may emerge in the course of one's work are also an important part of artistry in teaching. Artistry requires a willingness to shift destinations in flight when greater gains or a more satisfying journey is likely. These, it seems to me, are some of the cognitive skills and personal dispositions that artistry in teaching entails. The locations for their expression are in the tasks I have described — and in a host of others I have not.

If these tasks or aspects of teaching are, as I have claimed, locations for art in teaching then to talk about the art of teaching is to talk about a 'real' aspect of teaching. The phrase, 'the art of teaching' is a metaphor intended to convey features of teaching for which we have no name. As Langer says, we use metaphor to mean one thing when we say another and we expect to be understood.

Is teaching an art? The answer seems to me to be, 'It can be'. Teaching like most other human activities can be artless or artful. We prefer the later to the former. But the question of utility remains. What is the value of regarding teaching as an art? What does it buy us? The last section of my remarks addresses this question.

I shall have five points to make about the utility of recognizing artistry in teaching. First, recognizing artistry in teaching provides us with a way of thinking about teaching — a metaphorical field — through which to see and reflect upon features of teaching that we might not have seen or thought about before. When teaching is conceived of as the practice of an art we are more likely to seek out its artistic features, we are more likely to pay attention to form in teaching, to consider style, tempo, the way a lesson crescendos in a teaching episode, to look for expressivity in the performance of both teachers and students. Art and artistry, if we follow Lakoff and Johnson, are metaphorical concepts embedded in a metaphorical field. This field brackets our perceptions, it defines the world in particular ways. The absence of artistry in our conception of teaching leads to its absence in our discussions and research on teaching and keeps a potential window closed. When that window is closed we cannot secure the vision that the presence of the concept not only permits, but invites. Thus, the first benefit we receive from regarding teaching as an art is a fresh view of what teaching entails.

A second benefit from recognizing artistry in teaching is paradoxical. On the one hand the very presence in our consciousness of the artistic aspects of teaching makes it possible to develop theory that in principle can account for its presence and its effects. A theory of artistry in teaching is intended to do what theory does — explain and when possible predict and control. On the other hand our recognition of the presence of artistry in teaching is also very likely to increase our awareness of the limitations of theory. Artistry, if it's anything, is ideographic. Theory is nomothetic. It traffics in regularity. Theory idealizes. The consequences of recognizing artistry in teaching is to arrive at a paradoxical point in which both the lure of theory construction and an awareness of its limitations operate at the same time. I do not regard this state of affairs as disastrous; in intellectual life it comes with the territory.

A third benefit from recognizing artistry in teaching is that it invites the use of forms of feedback to teachers that are normally given to those in the arts. The feedback I speak of is in the form of the critique. Critiques in the arts are intended to increase awareness of the qualities of a work of art. 'The aim of criticism,' wrote Dewey, 'is the re-education of the perception of the work of art.' This re-education begins with the critic's refined perception which is then transformed and rendered publicly to help others see what has transpired in the course of teaching. This critical rendering exploits the capacities of language in all its forms — poetic, literary, figurative, literal — to reveal and interpret what the critic has seen. Artistry here too comes into play in the rendering of the work.

For teachers such feedback goes well beyond reports written on the basis of commando raids into their classrooms, tallies calculated from check-off sheets, or decontextualized admonitions about the features of good teaching or about 'what works'. It is more than logs provide and much more than factual descriptions can reveal. Criticism itself is a demanding art that depends upon a highly differentiated sensibility in some domain and a thorough understanding of the context in which the work is created. I have described this approach to assessment in detail in my book *The Enlightened Eye*. It is truly sad that we have created schools and sustained professional norms that discourage the provision of constructive educational criticism; all of us could benefit from sensitive observation and interpretation of our teaching. The recognition of artistry in teaching might help us overcome the isolating character of schools and mechanistic approaches to the study of teaching.

A fourth potential consequence of viewing teaching as an art is that it may increase our readiness to accept differences in the ways in which teachers teach and in the destinations toward which individual teachers wish to travel. Both bureaucracies and technologies have a tendency to standardize processes and outcomes: Goals 2000 is an encomium to the standardization of aims just as the assembly line pays homage to routine as essential to its successful operation. Artistry courts surprise. It welcomes initiative. It celebrates imagination. The values related to artistry may be just the sort we need to reduce the attrition rate among teachers; we lose about half of the incoming cohort five years after they start their careers. Artistry acknowledged and prized might encourage teachers to make their professional lives interesting by thinking of themselves as being engaged — when they are at their best — in the practice of an art.

A fifth potentially productive outcome is related to the fourth, namely the creation of a professional ambience that has less tolerance for over-simplified solutions to educational problems. The 'solutions' I speak of are old ideas like teacher-proof curricula, or five steps to effective teaching, or incentive or choice programs that see the answer to educational problems located in competition among schools. The theory seems to be: If capitalism is good for our economy, it must be good for our childrens' schools.

Artistry does not reduce complexity, it has a tendency to increase complexity by recognizing subtlety and emphasizing individuality. It does not search for the one best method. It puts a premium on productive idiosyncrasy. It is a crucial compliment to getting it down to a science. In the vernacular, 'getting it down to a science', means, ideally, getting it down to errorless procedure. A procedure becomes errorless when there are no surprises. When there are no surprises, there is no problem. When there is no problem, there is neither challenge nor growth. Artistry in teaching as a pervasive concept goes beyond routine, invites risk, courts challenge, and fosters growth.

Let me bring my remarks to a close by returning to the question that serves as the title of my paper. The question that I asked at the start of this paper was: 'Is the art of teaching a metaphor?' Insofar as metaphor resides at the core of our thinking, insofar as it lives at the root of our conceptual life, sure it is. How could it not be? But what if we turn the question around and ask, 'Is teaching an art?' The answer to that question depends on what the teaching is that we are considering. Teaching can be an art when teachers are artists, that is, when their teaching is artful. Teaching is artful when it has some of the characteristics I described earlier.

Artistic performance in teaching is a quality of work we ought to cherish and try to foster. Conceiving of teaching at its best as an art does not require us to give up the scientific sources that are helpful in its pursuit. It does remind us that science does not tell the whole story and that the quintessence of performance, *even in the conduct of science itself*, is found in its artfulness.

How we can further artistry in teaching is a question that I believe could lead to a rich research agenda for any group concerned as we are with teacher thinking. To what extent, if any, do teachers regard themselves as being engaged in an art when teaching? Can they identify their artful moments if given the opportunity to see videos of themselves teaching? Where and under what conditions do artistic forms of thinking emerge in their work, both pre-active and inter-active? Where do their satisfactions reside in the course of their work and to what extent are those satisfactions aesthetic in character? To what extent, if any, do students recognize artistry in teaching at any level of schooling? Does it make a difference in their experience? And does the kind of feedback given to performing artists help improve teaching? The current research climate is hospitable to such a research agenda. The time to pursue it is now. And if not now, when? If not us, who? And so my friends, *Carpe Diem*! Seize the Day!

Notes

1 Editor's Note: Elliot Eisner's chapter is drawn from his opening keynote address at the ISATT '95 gathering.
2 At this point in the address a short video clip was shown from 'Dead Poets Society' in which a novel approach to class interactions and teacher demeanor is enacted by Robin Williams in the role of John Keating.

Reference

LANGER, S.K.K. (1953) *Feeling and Form: A Theory of Art*, New York, Scribner.

2   Professionalism and Teachers as Designers[1]

Ingrid Carlgren

Introduction

In the mid 1980s, talk about teachers as professionals started among central bureau-crats and politicians in Sweden. After several decades of denying teachers' know-ledge (i.e., when teachers were seen as problems rather than problem solvers) they were now considered (as professionals) to be the solution to many of the problems at hand. From a situation in which teachers were attributed almost no knowledge, they were suddenly ascribed knowledge of everything important for school deve-lopment. Not until 1990 did teacher unions start to discuss professionalism (in 1995 one of the unions started a campaign: 'Teachers' Lift Sweden'). Thus the discussion of teachers as professionals was top–down and not initiated by teachers. This aspect must be kept in mind when discussing teacher professionalism. The discussion may reveal more about the changing relation between the State and the teachers than about the quality of teachers' work.

When we talk about 'teachers as professionals' different aspects, meaning and concepts may come to mind. One could be 'teachers' professional knowledge' — what it is, how it is organized, how it can be developed etc. Another aspect is the 'professionalization of teachers', that is the process by which an occupation becomes a profession in the sociological sense (including such as professional autonomy, a long university education, control of the development of professional knowledge etc.). Or another aspect could involve 'teacher professionalism', refer-ring to the quality of teachers' work.

In the following I will mainly address the issues of teachers' professional knowledge and professionalism — and especially focus on designing of school prac-tice as a growing aspect of teachers' work (i.e., my focus is not on teachers' teach-ing). The reason for this is that I consider the design aspect to be a forgotten and mis-recognized aspect of teachers' work.

Teachers do much more than teach. Teacher professionalism therefore cannot be reduced to an issue of the quality of teaching. Just as teachers' work is some-thing complex and manifold — so is the meaning of teacher professionalism. The growing design aspect of teachers' work involves new demands on teachers. To use the theater as a metaphor: teachers are not only expected to be performers, directors, stage designers, stage hands and illuminators — they now also have to be script writers. These multiple roles carry consequences for teachers' professional knowledge as well as the meaning of teacher professionalism. Additional implications may be seen for any discussion of teachers as reflective practitioners.

I will start by considering teachers' work and the teaching profession — with focus on an historical perspective (i.e., how it has changed). Thereafter I will discuss teachers' professional knowledge — mainly in relation to the discussion of professional knowledge as tacit knowledge. Concerning the issue of teacher professionalism, I will focus on the epistemological questions and especially the meaning of the idea of the reflective practitioner. I will also consider the relationship between so called 'theory' and 'practice'. Finally I will discuss some consequences for teacher education by considering designing school practice as part of teachers' work — besides teaching. While I will be addressing these issues with Sweden in mind, there are probably many similarities and important differences across all countries.

The Teaching Profession

What is a teacher? How are teachers perceived? We have become used to thinking about the teaching profession as something that does not change, and teachers as conservative and unwilling to change. We have learned to see teachers and teaching as entities that 'never change'. I do not think this perspective is accurate. There are many aspects to the construction of this perception. One example is the role of educational research which has contributed to the mis-recognition of the teaching profession (Lortie's work for example).

One way to understand this is by accepting that everyone has ideas of what school ought to be. When schools and schooling do not correspond to utopian schemes teachers are blamed. When schools are evaluated, more preoccupation is noted with what it is not, than with what it is. All 'real' schools fall short when compared with utopian visions — and they all seem to be the same. In the search for deviations from the visions the differences between schools have not become visible — neither have the changes.

Quite contrary to this common view, I think that the teaching profession is always changing. Even though it may look like the same on the surface (classrooms, lessons, tasks, homework, grades and so on) there are qualitative changes beneath the surface: the content of the lessons, the ways of working, the relations between teachers and pupils, the materials to work with and so on. The compulsory school teacher has been an agent for modernity with the task of bringing about changes — among people as well as in the school's own practice. Teachers have had an important function in the modernization of society.

As a result of societal changes, the aims and purposes of schooling change. Most notably, during the second half of this century there has been a permanent process of school reformation. As a result, there also occurs permanent ongoing redefinition of teachers' tasks and competencies. In these ways teachers' work is characterized by 'ruptures' rather than continuities. Teachers' knowledge therefore will often be out of date. Every reform thus implies a loss of competence from the teacher's perspective.

There are important differences between teaching and more traditional crafts. The lack of stability and continuity make the accumulation of knowledge difficult (this is an explanation other than Lortie's). I now treat teachers as one occupational group. From an historical perspective, this century has seen different groups of teachers come to work in the same institution, still uncertain as to whether it is possible to talk about one teaching profession.

There are two main teacher traditions: First, the primary school teachers (grade 1–6) emerged during the nineteenth century and is the group which best corresponds to what I previously called 'modernity agents' or 'modernity missionaries'. The second tradition involves grammar school teachers. These teachers have a longer history in ways closer to what can be called a 'craft tradition'. This distinction exists because the grammar school teachers' work has not been connected with social reforms in the same way as the primary school teachers' work. The two traditions are still alive, although integrated in 1988 into one form of teacher education for compulsory school teachers. These teachers are now prepared to teach grade 1–7 or 4–9. Since the State took responsibility for mass education (in Sweden in 1842), and the occupation group of primary school teachers was created, quite a lot has happened. I will outline some of the changes that have influenced the work of teachers over the last 150 years.

The overall development from a pre-industrial to a post-industrial society during the past 150 years forms the background for most of the changes (although the relation between school and society is not one-dimensional). Some aspects of importance for schools and the teaching profession are: the enormous expansion of available information; secularization and the crisis of tradition; the division of labor and the growing demand for formal education in more and more occupational areas; the separation of manual and intellectual work; the development of the Welfare State and together with that the rise of central bureaucracies — the growth of science and belief in objectivity (devaluing of the subjective judgment); societal planning and social engineering (with centrally produced general solutions to be implemented locally.

Throughout all of the foregoing, teachers were out, and experts (another name for researchers) were in. The growth of educational research and the postmodern crisis, including the impossibility of steering and central solutions, and the need for local solutions to specific situations, brought teachers back in as experts.

Along with change in society, the commissions of schools change. Moral and religious upbringing were important in the past. Religion was the most important school subject during the nineteenth century, only to be replaced during this century by the fostering of the citizen (local geography and history in the first half of this century and later civics became an important school subject). Now towards the end of the century, the fostering of the autonomous and reflective individual is appearing strongly as an aim of education; together with the concept of school as a melting-pot in the circumstances of growing multi-culturalism. These changes influence the relations between teachers and pupils in significant and meaningful ways. The teacher cannot uphold his or her authority by leaning on tradition or on the authority of the school. Instead, there is pressure to develop authority as a person (something which give the teachers a constant strain). There is also a need to reorganize the ways of working in school.

The teaching task, from a more narrow meaning, has changed as well. Even if schools are still expected to teach the three R's: the meaning of these activities has changed. The task and implications of reading are not the same today as 100 or 150 years ago; the same can be said about writing. The ways of knowing and the kinds of knowledge to be developed in school have changed as well. While schools used to have important functions as transmitters of information and certain facts, the teaching task has become more complicated (e.g., the transmission of higher-order cognitive skills).

Another aspect of this discussion has to do with the organization of the school system. Up to the 1960s, when the compulsory comprehensive 9-year school was established in Sweden, there was a 'parallel school system', with different forms of schooling for different groups of people. Later, upper secondary schools, to-gether with the vocational training programs, were all integrated into one, upper secondary school. This creation of an undifferentiated school system gave rise to many difficulties, especially for lower secondary subject teachers with a grammar school tradition.

The ways in which schools are steered have also been altered. When the great comprehensive school reforms were implemented, the central bureaucracy grew and steering was carried out by rules and detailed prescriptions. This period culmin-ated during the educational technology era (in the end of the 1960s and begin-ning of the 1970s). Since that time there has been a gradual change towards local involvement and decentralization. Today there is so called 'goal steering' together with a marketization of education (just like in the rest of the western world — a voucher systems, schools opting out, great local freedom but a centralized control of the results). As a consequence there are new demands on teachers to accomplish quite a lot of curriculum development at the local level as well as locally designed evaluations. Goal steering require teachers that know how to interpret goals and develop local curriculum.

Around the turn of the century a professionalization movement of primary school teachers in Sweden occurred. Demands for a better education and the estab-lishment of pedagogy as a university discipline were among the issues that were pushed. A special push came from female primary school teachers who were not from low social origins. Primary teachers as a group were behind the idea of a 'common basic' school for all children. Many of them were quite active in the progressive movement (introducing activity pedagogy of different kinds). The first influences came from Europe and later from the United States. Collaborations be-tween teachers and researchers were occurring and teacher unions arranged summer courses where teachers could meet researchers and get into contact with the growing psychological research. They were also taking part in the planning of the comprehensive school reforms.

In 1950, however, after the parliamentary decision about reforms, the school minister declared that from now on teachers were not in need of research or theory: instead they needed detailed prescriptions for their work and practical solutions to the individualization problems. The content and forms of the summer courses were altered as new groups were in charge of them. At the same time pedagogy as a university discipline became established and were involved in the growing educational research. Most of the researchers that were employed did not have a teaching background. Quantitative methods and psychology were strong.

After some time teachers became one of the objects for educational research and 'teacher development' an important issue for researchers as well as bureaucrats. I will not go further into this except to point out that during the period 1950 to around 1980, a deprofessionalization of teachers occurred. The training of teachers has been considered important from the start of the compulsory school. Seminars to train primary school teachers were established quite early and, from the beginning, were criticized for quality.

One prominent aspect of these institutions has been that: new teachers were trained to do what they would later have their pupils do. Although this tendency is not prominent any more, there are still remnants. The issue of how to develop competence for change has been important in all teacher education reforms. The meaning of this has, of course, changed. After World War II there was a great belief in developing a scientific attitude. This is not to say that the teacher was seen as a scientist, but was rather seen as someone who was acquainted with scientific work. Later (around 1965) the teacher was more seen as a technician. During the 1970s, the politically correct teacher with the 'right' views on man, learning and knowledge was constructed. And during the 1980s a great belief in didactics as the basis for teacher professionalism emerged and now the discourse is about reflective practitioners and professionalism.

All these changes have had a profound impact on teachers' work including: forms for instruction; ways of working; content of schooling; ways of relating to the pupils; and not including how teachers are seen by others and by themselves. What I want to emphasize now is the change from following rules and syllabuses to the designing of local curricula and activities designed to realize goals. This trend is combined with demands for accountability, which in turn, ask for visualization and communication of what's being done in school and why.

After the latest reform the teachers are expected to develop local 'workplans'. The centrally developed plans do not include the allocation of time over the years, or how to organize for example integration between subjects and so on. Based on the overall aims of the National Curriculum, and the quality of mind that the different school subjects are supposed to develop, teachers must decide locally on how to organize teaching and the selection of content and ways of working. Even though there are still syllabuses, they have a new form and function — formulating what qualities that should be developed through the subject rather than what should be taught.

Teachers' Professional Knowledge

In Sweden, the character and structure of professional knowledge have been discussed for approximately fifteen years. The discussion started with the computerization which occurred in some professions (e.g., civil servants at social insurance offices) and was extended to other occupational groups, especially those that were expected to be scientificated (e.g., nursing and preschool teaching).

The main debate has been about whether it is possible in principle, and whether it is sensible (even if it is possible) to formulate professional knowledge based on experience, context and that which is in persons, and is to a large extent pertaining to the senses (the experienced practitioner knows by seeing, sensing, smelling, hearing and so on . . .). This debate has been very much influenced by the Wittgensteinian thinking and has been developed by Kjell Johannesen and Tore Nordenstam, two philosophers in Bergen, Norway. They started to use the expression 'knowledge by acquaintance' to designate the kind of knowledge to which they referred. Wittgenstein himself gave the following example: you recognize a flute when you listen to it. You can't do that without having heard a flute before. It is impossible to learn to recognize a flute by for example reading a book about it . . . it takes experience.

However, teachers' professional knowledge has not been discussed in terms of 'tacit knowledge' (which in Sweden by the way is translated to 'silent' knowledge; whether it is silent because it is not formulated, or because it has been silenced is generally not distinguished). One reason for that can be the prominent status that has been given to didactics as *the* type of teachers' professional knowledge during the 1980s. But, the reason may also be related to a *disrespect* for teachers' professional knowledge which has been looked upon as either nonexistent or 'wrong'. Teachers should do and know something else than that which they do. When doctors say they cannot cure a certain form of cancer no one doubts them. If teachers say they cannot teach certain things to certain children, those teachers are considered to be in need of further education.

This disrespect can also be connected to the many school reforms — and to the 'ruptures' in the teaching profession, which in that way is very different from a traditional craft — such as for example the making of violins. The reforms establish new aims and goals for teachers' work as well as new conditions. This makes it hard to lean on previous experience — teachers' previous knowledge by acquaintance become useless. Tacit professional knowledge in 'rupture' professions seem to be paradigmatic. Knowing how to accomplish silence in a classroom is, for example, something completely different than knowing how to get the children to talk. As a teacher you may be very good at teaching although paradigmatically wrong (one aspect of teacher professionalism is therefore to be paradigmatically correct; one of the reasons for the high sensitivity for fashions?). Therefore, for many teachers there will be a contradiction between what should be and what they know to be. In an interview study we did some ten years ago — concerning how teachers looked upon teachers' work they were very elaborate about what it should be and found it very difficult to describe what it actually was. Their language was developed to express ideals rather than realities.

The dilemma between what should be and what is, is very salient in the teaching profession. However, it can be seen as a more general question of stability and change in professions which are characterized by ruptures. How can experience accumulate in 'rupture' professions? Is continuity in teachers' professional development at all possible? Is it a matter of the ways of knowing? Are other ways to organize professional knowledge necessary in order for it to survive? Is there a need for more formal knowledge as compared to the practical and mainly tacit experience-based knowledge?

However, the contradiction between what is considered that teachers should do, and what they actually do, corresponds to an opposition between teachers' tacit knowledge, and the formal, theoretical knowledge about teaching and learning. What teachers do, is not in accordance with learning and teaching theories. This discrepancy has long been explained by teachers' 'wrong' ways of thinking about teaching and learning (although nowadays it is more commonly understood that the problem is more complicated). Another aspect of why learning theories do not fit what teachers do in classrooms is that they are not grounded in classroom practice. If formal knowledge is not grounded in, or integrated with, tacit experience-based knowledge, the contradiction will remain. To see classroom work from the perspective of learning theories or didactic models leads to a very narrow understanding — which excludes many of the dimensions that teachers have to cope with in their work, especially the social dimensions including organization and control of classroom work that have been lacking in pedagogical theories and didactic models. As a result the social dimensions are suppressed in teachers' consciousness, but they cannot be abolished from teachers' work and therefore they force their way into consciousness as for example the so-called 'hidden curriculum'.

While social dimension can be described as the forgotten or hidden dimension, the didactic dimension is the 'official' aspect of teachers' work. This leads to a *misrecognition* regarding teachers' work where social questions have been interpreted as pedagogical (e.g., recitation and piloting) instead of seeing them as accomplishing a balance between the social and the pedagogical dimensions of teachers' work they are understood as examples of teachers' poor teaching.

Even though there has been quite a lot of research done concerning the social dimension, it has not been integrated into the didactic theories. Perhaps integration would lead to a lessening of the gap between 'thinking and acting' or 'theory and practice' in teachers' work: and between the hidden and the official curriculum. The development of learning theory in a 'situated learning' direction seems promising in that it is easier to combine with analysis of classroom practice 'as it is'.

What about the design aspect of teachers' work? By making the teachers responsible for the designing it is hoped that solutions will be developed that better correspond to what is possible. The gap between the ideal and reality is expected to diminish. However, to a large extent, teachers lack experience of design work and therefore tacit knowledge in that area. It is somewhat paradoxical that the political rhetoric around the latest reform is built on teachers' professional knowledge as the guarantee for school development. But the meaning of reform is that teachers are expected to do things they have never done before (i.e., once again they lack in competence that are needed under the new conditions). They are asked to rely on their professional knowledge for questions and issues with which they have little or no experience.

But have teachers not always planned their work? Yes — but there is a reason to call the 'planning' that is asked for 'designing', in that it involves new aspects. Much of teachers' planning has been of a character that is either what can be called 'cake planning' (plan to have all the ingredients) or 'activity planning' (plan the activities and in what order). Of course there are some design elements in this, but on the whole it is similar to 'following a book'. The new situation calls for another kind of planning — the teachers have to design the school practice as a certain kind of practice which is to develop certain ways of being and knowing among the students. This includes selection and organization of content as well as ways of working. Teachers are even asked to design their own school subjects . . . This kind of planning (which can be called 'goal planning'?) is not common among teachers. Especially not in a collaborative form. Therefore it is a new kind of practice that is asked for. A practice involving development of the meaning of the goals, realization of those meanings and development of organization and content of the classroom work corresponding to the intended meanings.

This is, however, not what teachers do. Instead they do activity-planning, i.e., they transform the goals into activities and plan the order of those activities, regardless of this I think it is interesting to think about whether the coming of a designing practice as part of teachers' work is a way to establish greater continuity in teachers' professional knowledge — if it will lead to a reformulation of the professional knowledge that will make it more constant. A prerequisite for that is that all dimensions in teachers' work will be considered in the designing — and not just those that are recognized in pedagogical theory and didactic models.

Teacher Professionalism

Professionalism is about the quality in teachers' work and indicates different aspects of teaching. Examples include keeping up an ethical code and to be ethically aware, or doing what's right under the circumstances or using one's professional knowledge in the best way. Sometimes the tacit knowledge of a professional group is equated with professionalism. However, the concept of tacit stupidity exists as well as the concept of tacit wisdom. Tacit knowledge is not good in, and of, itself. Even if tacit knowledge is a necessary condition for doing a good job it is not enough. I think Max Van Manen comes very close to a description of professionalism with his concept of 'pedagogical tact'. Similar to professional knowledge, it is organized as tacit knowledge but not in an explicit and formulated way. It has a quality in it that corresponds to the idea of teaching and being pedagogically oriented.

One aspect of professionalism relates to how professional knowledge is organized and used. Traditionally quality in this sense has been perceived as a systematic relationship between 'theory' and 'practice'. However, such a view is closely connected with a technical rationality building on a certain way of understanding theory as well as practice. Theory is seen as mirroring reality, a 'true description' which is developed through research and scientific work. Therefore, good practice should be based on theory. Practice is perceived as applied theory. Theory has to do with research and thinking, while practice is about acting.

I think we need other ways of seeing 'theory' and 'practice'. First, theory *and* practice are involved in research in addition to teachers' work. It becomes a question about two kinds of practices and two kinds of theories — both containing thinking as well as acting. While theory is about seeing, practice is about doing. Seeing and doing represent two different ways of knowing — and result in different kinds of knowing. While research aims at developing theory other practices aim at other things (e.g., developing good schooling and learning environments). (This can be illustrated by the famous Chinese saying: 'The fish doesn't know it is swimming in water until it jumps out of it' — when the fish swims in the water it is practically knowing — but it must jump out of the water to be theoretically knowing.)

As an alternative to the technical rational way of seeing these things Schön postulated the idea of 'the reflective practitioner'. (It is not easy to talk about reflection, since it is such an overused concept, but I have to do it. It is interesting how concepts become fashion and how the meaning of concepts thereby are extended to incorporate everyone's favorite ideas. Reflection has come to mean everything that is good — it means everything and therefore nothing. The question is: should we accept that it is overused and look for new concepts that may become the next fashion — or should we fight for certain ways of using the concepts — reclaim their meaning. I suggest the latter — and that we should fight the tendencies to use words for conjuration rather than expressing meanings. Language is a too important tool to be destroyed by being used as decoration only.)

I think there are still important insights to be gained from Schön's ideas of the reflective practitioner — which gave reflection another meaning than that which is commonly held. Although Schön has been seen as belonging to the Deweyan tradition (which of course he does — in a deeper sense in that they are both pragmatists). I think the way he is different from Dewey is more interesting. One way to describe the difference is to connect it to the differences between 'theory' and 'practice' (i.e., between seeing and doing). While Dewey was concerned with theoretical thinking and cognitive activities Schön is concerned with practical thinking and reflection in the action. While both deal with seeing things 'as' something, as an important aspect of reflectivity — the meaning of this differs. For Dewey this meant an abstraction of meaning connected to a mental effort and a matter of conceptualizing and formulating. For Schön, on the other hand, it is a matter of building on a repertoire of examples in ways that are very close to Wittgensteins 'family resemblance' (i.e., to see a situation as similar to other situations). The aim is not conceptualization or formulation. It is a non-cognitive reflection-in-action.

Both Schön and Dewey distinguish between reflective and non-reflective practice. Schön's distinction between knowing-in-action and reflection-in-action is related to acting while Dewey's distinction between apprehension and comprehension refs to the cognitive acting or theorizing. Apprehension is when understanding is direct — the thing and the meaning is one. Comprehension is delayed understanding — the meaning has to be looked for and abstracted in order to understand 'the thing'.

This is, I think one aspect of the idea of the reflective practitioner that has not been analyzed enough. Another aspect is Schön's focus on virtual practices. His prototype is the architect who designs buildings but does not build them. It is a design profession built on the practice of sketching — with the possibility of erasing a line that is wrong — and go back and forth in the drawing and sketching. The back-talk from practice is in this case a back-talk in a virtual world; a simulated world.

In a discussion about the teaching profession — whether it is possible for the teacher to be reflective-in-action or not, it is somehow taken for granted that the teacher's actions are in the classroom. But classrooms are not a virtual world, but are rather a real world that does not 'talk' back in simulated ways. The real world rather hits back. It is impossible to erase in the classroom. In the real world the practitioner is constrained by what has been called the practical imperative. She cannot try out an idea and then change her mind. She has to do the right thing at the right moment. And when it is done it cannot be undone.

It is rather notable that the design aspects of the teacher's planning work has not been perceived as a practice involving actions. Instead it has been seen as something that is before action in which, to a large extent, the plans have been made by others. Teachers have been seen as the doers, as those who realize what others have planned. But that is changing. It is becoming more obvious that teachers spend more and more time planning and designing — together with others.

Planning is a practice which involves acting as well as thinking. Unlike classroom practice it is, or at least can be, a simulated practice. Teachers' planning can be seen as analogous with the architect's sketching (but not what I earlier called cake planning or activity planning). In these kinds of planning the function of language is pointing to certain activities rather than expressing meaning. 'Goal-planning', however, requires other kinds of planning activities: To think about the purposes of schooling and relate the different activities to those purposes; to think about the meanings of the activities — and to try out different ways of designing the school practice; to plan a local curriculum is to design a practice where the students will be able to develop in accordance with the syllabus goals as well as the overall aims.

The process of designing can, however, be done in very different ways — reflective as well as non-reflective. The non-reflective way to do it is for example to take the school subjects for granted, including the ideas of lessons, classes, teachers, students, courses etc.. To use such taken-for-granted 'natural' categories in planning is knowing-in-action. It involves questions like: How do we distribute the time between different subjects over the years? Shall we have single or double lessons? Should we integrate the science subjects? Is it better to have the craft lessons spread out over the nine years or not? In this kind of planning it is taken for granted that there are teachers, pupils, lessons, subjects and so on.

Unlike the foregoing, a reflective designing practice would involve reframing of different kinds. For example: Must all weeks look the same in school? Are there other means than lessons to reach the goals? Is it necessary to have lessons to reach the goals of physical education?

However, it does not seem as though the increasing planning activities in schools are very reflective. Local curriculum is developed mainly because it is asked for. Instead of seeing this planning as a worthwhile practice in itself — it is seen as something to be done for others, something that does not have very much to do with the 'real' work of teaching.

In the teaching profession, thinking and reflection is to a very large extent embedded in classroom practice. To develop the designing practice as a part of reflective practice requires that the purposes and meanings of the activities in school be separated from the contexts in which they are embedded. Through liberating the content or the meaning from the forms it will become easier to think about classroom practice outside of the classroom and to escape from the contextual prison that the professional knowledge is embedded in.

How can this be done? Teachers cannot sketch like architects. Or can they? What is the equivalent of the architects sketch in teachers' work? What are the tools for reflection-in-action that can be used in the teaching profession?

In many practical areas, models of practice are used for simulation. We have had a lot of models in education as well (e.g., Bob Stake's evaluation model). For a model to be useful in reflective practice it must be combined with conceptual thinking and not just be seen as a mirror of reality. If seen as a mirror a model can never become as good as real practice — but if it is seen as a model with which one can play around, it can be useful in reflective design of practice. I think the most valuable tools are conceptual tools (e.g., concepts and metaphors). Through this the meaning of practice is thereby abstracted and can be dealt with separated from the special forms in which it is found. To take a somewhat silly example: a teapot is a thing and a concept — in a way a concept captured in a form. But you do not need a teapot to make tea (the idea of a tea-pot) and you do not have to use the tea-pot for making tea (something which Picasso demonstrated when he turned it upside down and made an elephant of it).

To relate to schools: you may not need science lessons to realize the aims of the science subjects in school. You may not even need science content.

Some Consequences for Teacher Education

I will end this paper by discussing some consequences for teacher education. I wonder if there is any other institution so despised as those who deliver teacher education. While I do not intend to go into all the problems discussed about teacher education, teacher education, as a whole, has been seen as a failure ... and as having little or no impact on teachers' exercising of their profession, when compared to experiences made before and after formal education (Jordell, 1987). The small effects that can be noticed are wiped out after a short time (Lacey, 1977).

One thing, however, is certain: the criticisms of teacher education have a history as long as teacher education itself. There are old antagonisms between teacher training, colleges and universities. This antagonism has not disappeared after the incorporation of teacher training into the universities.

I see a problem of practice in teacher education. The scope of students' practical experience (practice) in the education of compulsory school teachers in Sweden is a half year out of three and a half to four and a half years. Although this part is very much valued by students, it is still considered to be a significant problem by most teacher educators. The main problem is: students' experience of teaching is counteractive to the rest of the teacher education programs. This 'problem' expresses very clearly the problematic (complex of problems) I have discussed earlier in terms of teaching as a 'rupture' profession. In traditional crafts, the most important thing is to transmit mainly tacit professional knowledge — and this is best done through apprenticeship learning. In the education of teachers it is the success of this transmission that is considered to be the problem. It is only the professional knowledge of paradigmatically correct teachers that is accepted. Very few practicing teachers are accepted as masters. Therefore different measures have been taken to interfere with the practical experiences that the teacher students have. The different forms of 'reflective discussions' of students' practical experiences is one example.

I think that viewing teachers as designers make it possible to discuss the practice-problem in new ways. If design work is seen as part of a teacher's work and practice, then teacher students must have practical experience of planning as designing. In order to develop teacher professionalism they need to get experience of reflective planning practice.

What's new about that? Planning, and teaching of planning models, has always been an important part of teacher education. But mainly as a preparation for 'practice' — not *as* practice. I have observed a shift of focus. The practice of planning is as important as the practice of teaching — and it can be done within teacher education. It can be designed as learning experience for the students which they cannot get in schools. They can develop competencies that schools are lacking, but are in extreme need: to complete local work plans because of frustration in the schools over these plans. (This past year, I have come into contact with a few schools that develop and sell local plans to other schools.)

To develop a competence as designers of school practice — the teaching of planning has to change. It has to be 'real' practice, where the plans are discussed as such (i.e., with reflective back-talk as part of the planning), so students have experiences of naming and framing as well as reframing; where students get used to formulating and discussing the meaning of things, (i.e., they get used to using the language as a reflective tool — and not just to point to activities in which the meanings are embedded). This pointing-function of language is typical of practical traditions where the knowing is in the action and not in the talking. In short it could be said that students need to be acquainted with the practice of theorizing.

If it is true, that the tools are concepts and formulated meanings, then Schön's view of reflection-in-action may merge with Dewey's more conceptual view namely to be reflective-in-conceptualizing action! Finally, if anyone has formed the impression that I think reflection is the most important thing in teachers' work — they are wrong. I have only been talking about one aspect of being a teacher.

Note

1 Editor's Note: Ingrid Carlgren's chapter is based on her keynote which opened the 'Teachers Professionalism' portion of the ISATT '95 gathering.

References

JORDELL, K.O. (1987) 'Teachers as reflective practitioners? On the teaching profession in light of Donald Schön's view of professionals as reflective practitioners', in STROEMNES, L. and SOEVIK, N. (Eds) *Teachers' Thinking: Perspectives and Research*, Tapir.

LACEY, C. (1977) *The Socialization of Teachers*, London, Methuen.

3   Becoming a Trained Professional[1]

Margaret R. Olson

Abstract

By exploring Susan's dilemmas of becoming a 'trained professional' I uncover some of the underlying epistemological tensions and mixed messages of professional practice which pervade teacher education programs and shape preservice teachers' images of professionalism. Through Susan's stories of trying to develop her own professional authority while being a character within the institutional narratives of her teacher education program, I explore interwoven, tacit and conflicting versions of institutional narratives in which Susan struggled. These versions have become sacred stories (Crites, 1971) embedded within present teacher education institutions (both universities and schools) and they implicitly shape the ways in which individuals construct their images of professionalism. Here I show how technical rational and apprenticeship versions of teacher education perpetuate images of teacher preparation as training and inhibit the development of professional authority through Dewey's (1938) version of reflective inquiry.

Personal and Institutional Narratives

Education students become experienced through a variety of situations and relationships in their teacher education programs. University teachers, cooperating teachers, student peers, and students that they themselves will be expected to teach are all part of the context in which education students construct and reconstruct their narrative knowledge of teaching and learning. Each individual the student encounters is authoring his or her own narrative of experience within his or her construction of what education means. Each narrative of experience is constructed within unique but shared contexts and by unique individuals. For example, each cooperating teacher constructs and reconstructs his or her narrative of experience within a context different from each university teacher and each teacher education student. Each individual focuses attention on different kinds of experience, values different kinds of knowledge, and encourages different kinds of teacher–student relationships depending upon the moral stance of his or her own personal/professional narrative. To add to the complexity, teacher education takes place in institutional contexts that are embedded within historical traditions based on socio-cultural views that shape epistemological orientations. Because these institutional contexts are also continuous and interactive, they can be thought of as institutional narratives that both shape and are shaped by individuals and other institutional contexts.

Here, I describe three different versions of teacher education which are tacitly interwoven and lived out as institutional narratives in our teacher education practices. I then show the confusion and frustration Susan, a preservice teacher, experienced as she tried to make sense of these conflicting versions in order to develop her own professional authority as a teacher.

Contexts of Teacher Education

Apprenticeship, inquiry, and technical versions of teacher education have evolved from historical beginnings in the late nineteenth and early twentieth centuries. These versions have become sacred stories (Crites, 1971) embedded within present teacher education institutions implicitly shaping the ways in which individuals construct their unique images of professionalism in teaching.

The apprenticeship version described by Dewey valued 'imitation of model behavior, mastery of essential skills, and acceptance of routine procedures as the basis of action' (Patterson, 1983, p. 6). This version, prevalent in the normal schools, values the transmission of practical knowledge from those who know to those who do not. The intention becomes one in which the novice is expected to learn from the experts who have 'more' experience. It is a prevalent way of constructing knowledge about teaching. In this version, experience is seen as a body of practical knowledge which can be transmitted to others to practice. This is a story of practice makes perfect. Patterson (1983) describes the normal school as reinforcing the apprenticeship model of teaching and states that 'the influence of the normal school has been pervasive and in harmony with maintaining the status quo' (p. 3).

The ways in which emerging universities in America were shaped by the 'intellectual hegemony of Positivism' (Schön, 1983, p. 34) during the late nineteenth and early twentieth centuries led to technical rationalism as a sacred story of professional education. Faculties of education soon became part of these institutions, drawing needed clientele to the universities (Urban, 1990). The tensions between practical relevance and theoretical abstraction are played out in present institutional narratives both within universities and between universities and schools. However, both are versions of knowledge as hierarchically constructed where becoming a teacher involves the accumulation of theory and practice. The apprenticeship and technical rational versions of teacher preparation are parallel stories, each focusing on certainty, prediction, and control. The more one can know and the more practice one has in implementing what one knows, the better teacher one can become. Here, perfection seems possible with enough theory and enough practice. These two versions lead preservice teachers to wonder if they 'know enough' to be able to teach.

Dewey's notion of the laboratory school is foundational to the inquiry orientation in teacher education. Patterson (1983) describes this orientation as involving 'problem identification, intelligent judgment, and imaginative application of knowledge with appropriate ensuing analysis and evaluation, the results of which influence subsequent behavior' (p. 6). In this version, teacher education is ongoing and is always open to reconstruction as we inquire into practice in order to tell, live, retell, and relive more informed stories of educative practice. Even as Dewey (1938) emphasized the importance of learning through inquiry as well as the integral nature of the knower and the known, the pervasiveness of positivism as a means of abstracting generalizable objective theories about teaching soon became the dominant sacred story of technical rationalism.

While the sacred story of technical rationalism has been questioned (Schön, 1983), the hierarchical organization built up by the epistemology of positivism leaves little space for other stories to be heard. At present, the sacred stories of apprenticeship, technical rationalism and inquiry are tacitly interwoven and lived out in individuals' practices within the contexts of teacher education. Education students must author their emerging teaching narratives within these implicit sacred stories.

Education students need to develop relationships with, and to be evaluated by, individuals who are living different narrative constructions of teacher education. These narratives are tacitly lived out in practice rather than spoken about. Not only are students evaluated as learners but as teachers as well, based on the particular narratives that are authored by their cooperating teachers and university teachers. When different sacred stories are being lived, the resonance of meaning necessary for understanding is not present.

Introducing Susan

There are many ways to tell about Susan's experiences. A version told of Susan by an observer could be of the model student graduating with distinction, receiving a scholarship, being an executive member of two student council groups, and having time for home, family, and friends. This version would tell of glowing practicum reports and her ability to think carefully and critically about educational issues. In fact, this version would be the canonical (Bruner, 1986) version of the perfect student, perfect woman — the cover story (Crites, 1979) many of us have learned to tell as the story for which to strive.

The stories Susan chose to tell me focused on her continual dissatisfaction with her program, her professors, and herself. These were stories of disillusionment, disconnection and dissension — stories of frustration and confusion, of fear and anxiety. Brown (1991) and Gilligan (1991) have helped me begin to make sense of these two seemingly incommensurable stories — the cover story I (and others) could see and tell about Susan, and the stories Susan told me about herself.

The teacher education program in which Susan was situated was one focused on the importance of reflective practice. Faculty members worked hard to enable their preservice students to develop abilities which would lead them to feel confident in making professional decisions. However, trying to live a version of teacher education as reflective practice which was still implicitly interwoven with technical rational and apprenticeship versions of learning to teach, both by faculty members and preservice teachers, led to many mixed messages of what teacher preparation and teacher professionalism were all about. For example, Susan's particular program was structured in a way that reinforced the technical rational/apprenticeship version with three years of university courses preceding her fourteen-week student teaching term which was followed by a last term at the university.

Here, I revisit some of my earlier research (Olson, 1993) with Susan to explore her dilemmas of becoming a 'trained professional'. I focus on the two terms preceding her practicum term as she was subtly 'cultivated' (Connelly and Clandinin, 1994) into the authorized version of teaching which her program was attempting to prepare Susan and her peers to 'transform' (Connelly and Clandinin, 1994).

Encountering Different Ways of Knowing

I remember how excited Susan was to be finally getting into the third year of her four year BEd program, a year she imagined would pull all the pieces of the previous years together. Susan expected the professional knowledge she would need to know would finally be revealed and would give her the knowledge and thus the confidence she would need to have a successful practicum and to become a good teacher.

Susan had hoped to gain a variety of perspectives which she would be able to fit together in order to have a more holistic picture of what would be involved in teaching. However, the variety of perspectives Susan experienced did not materialize in the way she had hoped. 'Nothing fits. I have a puzzle. It's four different puzzles and I don't even have all the pieces.' Soon after we began to work together, Susan described her experience in the following way. 'I'm finding a lot of classes that are completely disjointed from one another and yet in an elementary school they're all going to have to be integrated into the same thing.' This sense of disconnection continued as Susan struggled throughout her program to construct connections between the conflicting plot lines she was being presented and her own narrative knowing of education.

Susan's encounters with different ways of knowing were not made explicit in her program. Often the authorized story of one way of knowing being explicitly told was implicitly contradicted in the telling. While I present these explicitly as separate dilemmas, for Susan, they were experienced as simultaneous tensions leading to a state of confusion and frustration.

Dilemma 1: Questions and Answers

Susan experienced a continual tension between feeling there were right answers, a view of knowledge she had come to know in her public schooling, and a strong desire to question those answers and imagine different possibilities. Susan was overwhelmed with the incoming information. The time Susan needed to discuss the issues presented was seldom available. Susan also experienced a tension between the certainty she wanted to have in order to feel confident as a teacher and the desire to inquire into the knowledge she was being presented. 'I'm finding it a real crash course in something that I really don't have any perception of yet.' 'Covering the curriculum' did not allow Susan the time she really needed to think about and question underlying issues she became aware of throughout her program.

Susan felt it was important to think carefully about issues and raise questions in order to uncover the lived stories in their contextual complexity. By exploring underlying issues, Susan felt it would be possible to 'see what's really going on', and begin to imagine ways to change present stories and construct better ones. She found little support for this view as others saw her as idealistic or negative. 'I think there's a difference between being positive and being blind. And I find a lot of blind people at this university. I don't see what is so wrong with having high expectations.' Susan often felt alone in trying to penetrate to issues she felt were covered up and ignored by the authorized stories.

> No one wants to make waves. No one wants to be the rebel or the re-volutionary person or whatever and I think if a lot more people were, it might be a better place . . . everywhere. If you're still in perspective and you're not radical, but you have thought carefully about the issue and what it means to you and what it means to everyone else around you, and decided is it worthwhile to fight about or is it worthwhile to let it slide and most people don't even think, don't even get that far. They just think let that slide right off the bat.

Susan struggled between trying to gain the knowledge she felt her professors must have while at the same time feeling shut out when she began to question that knowledge. 'I ask a lot of questions and I really get the impression that they're not overly happy to see your hand up.' When Susan's questions pointed to some of the underlying dilemmas in education, she often felt shut down and ignored as she was told to stick to the curriculum being covered in the present course. 'It's almost like they're impatient. "We just did it and this is the way you do it so why are you questioning my method?"'

While Susan was questioning in order to get a better understanding of the concepts and how they might relate to her future classroom practice, she believed her questions were often heard as a demand for the professors to justify what they were presenting. 'Everyone seems really sensitive to the fact that why are you questioning my knowledge? I'm not questioning *you* personally, I'm just question-ing period.' Susan often sensed her professors had a course to 'cover' that took precedence over her needs and interests as a student. Susan often found questions asked by other students relevant to what she wanted to know. However, these questions were not acknowledged as part of the teacher education course curricu-lum, but were seen by professors as personal questions to be dealt with out of class.

'Well, I'll answer that after class if you want to come and ask me.' And I thought, 'I think everyone in here is quite interested in the answer to that question and it's very relevant, but it didn't fit the plan.' Susan fumed inside, feeling that only certain kinds of things were allowed to be open for discussion.

Susan found herself forced to answer questions and complete assignments on a superficial level to get the marks even when she felt totally confused by the underlying issues she was trying to grapple with. Again, she felt like she was being focused toward learning the authorized stories while focusing on discussing the underlying issues was forbidden or ignored. 'I think that when it comes to teaching you obviously want to look at it as positively as you can or you'd be miserable all the time, but is it realistic to say that what we always do and what we've done in the past has been great?'

Susan began to realize it would be much easier just to do the assignments and not question. Her questions seemed to keep her from completing required assignments. Susan began to think living the story of covering the required curriculum rather than questioning it was what was expected. 'It seems that a lot of my energy is being wasted into thinking about why rather than everyone else just doing it, you know. So I pondered why for this assignment for two weeks when I could have had it finished and been done.'

Dilemma 2: Becoming a Trained Professional

Within the first week of classes, Susan began to have misgivings about having her expectations met. Susan had expected a very different type of 'training program' than what she was receiving. 'In any training program they usually have an artificial test, pilot run and then they put you into the real situation and pull you back out and say "Whoa. You messed up. You forgot about A, B and C and what were the fundamentals there that you didn't do?"' Susan could not make sense of her program which was structured so differently from what she had expected. She was overwhelmed with the diversity of ideas she was being presented and had no idea how to combine these ideas or select an appropriate perspective. 'We're not even learning A, B and C, we're just sort of learning everything all at once and it's all running together and it's not running together and you're trying to make the connection but there is no connection sometimes. You're sort of left.'

Susan was shocked at the flexibility of the curriculum. She had imagined there was a standardized curriculum for each grade level that all children would learn. Seeing the diversity of the curriculum left Susan disoriented, confused, and terrified, as if the rug had been pulled out from under her. She imagined that if students came into her class having received instruction in different areas, teaching would be very difficult. 'I mean that makes your task so much more complex and that's a hard enough thing to do anyway if you have thirty students.' Not only was she now aware that children had individual abilities, but now she realized they might have different curriculum backgrounds as well. She could not imagine how she could teach under such conditions. 'But if you have thirty students coming from fifteen different places, do you have group A, group B, and group C? Group A learned this, group B learned that, group C learned that. How do you teach anything then? Just stumble around in the dark until you find something that works?' In order to be a good teacher, Susan felt she would need to know what she was doing. 'If I'm going in there expecting that I'm going to know half about what I'm doing, how is this going to work?' For Susan, this meant knowing correct procedures and answers. She felt her concern with uncertainty was not addressed within her program.

Susan became more and more concerned as she became aware of how complex teaching is. Susan felt her courses were raising her awareness, but not providing her with the 'background knowledge' she felt she needed. Susan began to realize what she considered to be the professional knowledge of the teacher as expert was fraught with dilemmas and ambiguities she had never imagined during the first two years of her program. She was being awakened to issues without being given any ideas of how to handle them. Since Susan was trying to live and tell a story of teacher as expert, she felt she would be expected to have the answers if she were not to be an impostor in the classroom. 'If I know what I'm doing and I know my area well, I'm a confident person. But I can't see how they're expecting everyone to be confident in something they know nothing about. Yet they're not providing me with the information that's going to give me the confidence that I will need.' Rather than being presented a package of professional knowledge, Susan felt the cover had been lifted as it had on Pandora's box and she was left to deal with the resulting dilemmas and uncertainties on her own. However, closing the cover would destroy any hope of resolving the issues of which Susan had become aware.

Susan was continually frustrated by trying to construct new stories of teaching and teacher education. She was afraid she would become the kind of teacher she did not want to be. Alternate possibilities did not seem to be encouraged. Susan seldom found what she considered to be examples of the stories she was trying to construct. She also felt discouraged by others who insisted on living a story of security. For Susan, the conventional story provided only the false security of covering up what she did not know and left her feeling like an impostor.

She struggled to articulate this tension in the following way. 'I don't want a recipe. It would be lovely to have one. . . . But at least if I had a *standard* recipe and then create my own from here. Here's the basic ingredients and this is how they connect. I don't feel like I'm getting basic ingredients. I feel like I've been turned loose in Super Store (laugh) and told to "Make something that is good"'. Since Susan had no idea what to choose or how to combine the choices she might make she felt incapable of constructing a meaningful program for her future students. 'How about Kraft macaroni? That's what I'm going to get. A recipe lesson plan I'm sure. That's how I feel right now. But I didn't want to go out there being the "safe teacher" the one that follows the way it's always been done, because I don't agree that the way it's always been done is the best way. But if it gets to the point of whether I'm going to be able to survive in the classroom or not, then I might choose the safe way. Or when it gets so overwhelming then it's easier for my sanity to go to the safe way.'

Susan was also getting the message from her professors to stick with what was familiar. 'And it seems like that's what they're teaching us. . . . Pick a safe lesson plan, pick a safe subject. . . . Pick something you know about.' Susan saw little space or support for the risks involved in exploring new possibilities.

Susan ended the term still having the feeling that her expectation of becoming a 'trained professional' would not be realized. 'I had expected to go through four years of university training coming out being a trained professional and I won't be a trained professional. I'll be an amateur (laugh) you know. An apprentice really.'

Dilemma 3: Putting Theory into Practice

Susan knew the theoretical concepts she was receiving in her university courses would look very different in lived classroom situations, but she could not imagine how to effectively bring these theories to life. Susan knew she was getting only part of the story. While she felt that within herself 'the awareness is there', she had a terrible sense of foreboding. 'I have this terrible feeling though that I'm going to go out into the school and have these expectations [laugh] and get tuned into the real world [laugh]. This is how you thought they would work, well this is how they work!' Connections between the abstractions of paradigmatic knowing and the contingencies of narrative knowing were missing. 'There's been no conceptual, this is the concept, what do you think of this concept, how would it work in your classroom? How would it not work? What are the difficulties you would see? What if you had someone like this in your classroom, how would you modify your lesson etcetera to suit the needs of this child?'

Susan described her course work at the university as 'completely artificial. There's nothing in here that is true to the real classroom except that we're all students but at this level we're all responsible for our marks, we're responsible for attending class. It's not even the same ball game. I feel like the environment is so artificial.' Susan had no image of a classroom full of children to help her contextualize the concepts she was supposedly learning in her class. 'Even if you could get in with four or five teachers and stick with them for a month, and have these lectures on activities, ideas. How to present them, how to put them into a developmental thing.'

Susan was also aware she needed to consider 'developmentally appropriate tasks', but she could not imagine what these might look like in practice. 'They're assuming that you know automatically what level is appropriate for what or that you're going to discover it as you get into the classroom.' Talking and reading *about* teaching and children did little to help Susan figure out how to work *with* children. Susan's hope to 'discover that now so I have something to work with once I get there' seemed to recede further and further into the distance.

As the term progressed, the sense of disconnection between the information Susan was receiving and her narrative knowing was reinforced. 'I feel like I'm learning about this stuff now, but not having it apply long term. I'm learning about it now, get my mark, get my credit, get my degree, and then I'm going to go out there and learn how to do it. That's how I feel.' Susan also felt that once she started teaching, she would need to 'rely on herself' but did not find spaces in her program to develop the confidence to do so. 'I feel like I'm going to have so much work to do when I'm finished this. I'm going to know where the resources are and how to use them, but that's it. From there it's going to be trial and error and if it works it works and if not you're relying on yourself. And that's it.' Susan did not see trial and error as a form of inquiry or reflective practice.

Susan described one class when she was given the opportunity to connect what was being taught to her personal practical knowing.

> We had a practical application writing sort of seminar. How to write. How to do a writing lesson and it was good. We went through it and did it ourselves. We talked about how you would present it to students. We did it ourselves. Did it in partners just like it was suggested. Shared our ideas in the class and we went through the process ourselves. So it really got you thinking well, yes I agree, maybe I'd do that a little different. From my experience in doing it I felt this way and in order for my students to feel better about that I would maybe change this. It really gave you something to work with.

Susan often could not visualize the abstract descriptions she was being given being enacted in practice. 'We're getting all the "should" and "why you should" and "it's better for the learner", you know, but the how is lacking there. I try to visualize every lesson that I do as being presented to *my* class, but I'm just having a hard time thinking of myself here and myself there because it's different and I can't visualize that to myself.'

Susan's emphasis on learning *how* was an expression of her need for the practical experience that would help her make sense of the theory. She could not imagine the personal relationships in a situation she had not experienced. 'Well [she] said for this lesson, picture, visualize your students. Sort of make them personal to you and I'm having a really hard time doing that.'

Dilemma 4: Relevance and Imposition

Susan began the term hopeful she would have the opportunity to reflect critically on personal and professional issues in teaching. She wanted to hear a variety of perspectives in order to clarify or expand her own knowing. However, in many of her classes, there was little opportunity for conversation about issues Susan found relevant as her professors tended to focus on telling Susan what they felt she needed to know. She spoke of 'telling' as a 'one-sided conversation'.

Susan was pleased some of her courses 'seem to be thinking courses which I like'. She hoped these courses would 'get you to sort of think about who you are and why you are who you are. And how you are will affect your teaching'. Susan appreciated it when her views were asked for, listened to, and discussed. She described how she felt it was important to take time to think about her own values and become aware of 'your biases. And it's good too because how many times do you really sit down and think about yourself that way. Usually you're so busy thinking a hundred things.' Susan hoped her university courses would provide the opportunity to 'really evaluate yourself carefully' since she knew once she started teaching there would be little opportunity to take time to think.

While Susan felt she was 'ready to form my own conclusions, to make my own predictions, to be responsible to know what I would want to know', she felt 'like no one's saying that you do know what you want to look for'. Susan found little opportunity to make her own choices within her courses. 'I think that it's a hard thing, especially at university, to conform to doing what you're told and that seems to be the way all my courses have been this semester. Doing what I'm told, and don't ask any questions because this is, see that's the leader and they have the power. I'm the follower. I have no power, you know.' Susan's image of herself as a follower in her university courses contributed to her continual insecurity about becoming a teacher, who she saw as a leader in the classroom, when she felt she had never been given the opportunity to experience this role in her courses. Susan could not rely on herself until something or someone else validated her ideas.

Finding little choice open to her within her teacher education courses, Susan eventually chose to 'conform to the teacher's agenda' as she became more and more frustrated by having her questions and concerns ignored. 'You get kicked so many times or whatever or shot down so many times that you think what is the point? Why am I going to set myself up for feeling horrible for the next three hours? Why ask the question? and get snubbed, and feel like "Ohhh that makes me mad." Why do that? So there you go. You're conforming to the expectations of the teacher's agenda.'

The pressure of multiple assignments gave her little time to think about what she was doing. Each course had its own separate agenda, expectations, and assignments. Near the end of the term, Susan 'had eleven assignments and [was] going nuts.' There seemed to be no time to reflect on her assignments or herself as a teacher. 'With all these assignments coming up I really haven't had a moment to sit down and carefully look them over and say "This is what I need to do".'

Susan was receiving a pervasive message that summarized the conflict she was experiencing. 'We want to promote lifelong learning. Your assignment is due on Monday. And that's it. Your assignment's finished.'

Shifts in Knowing

During her second term, Susan struggled with trying to make connections between what she valued as a student and what she felt she was expected to do as a teacher. As a student, Susan valued having time to explore the process of coming to know in her own way, appreciated having choices and having her ideas acknowledged. While she wanted to provide this for her students, she was also learning to tell a teaching story of clear objectives, and well planned lessons. She was learning to teach as she had been taught, even though, as a student, she resented this type of teaching. Susan could not imagine how she could evaluate what her students had learned if she was not clear about what she expected them to know. While Susan wanted her students to construct their own knowing, she worried about her responsibilities as a teacher to keep her students focused and to cover the required curriculum.

Knowing What to Expect

In order to feel comfortable and confident, it was important for Susan to be prepared and being prepared involved knowing what to expect so she could plan. Feeling she needed to know what to do before she actually started teaching was a continual tension for Susan.

Susan felt her professors were assuming she already had clear concepts in areas where she felt she had minimal experience. Susan also found each professor had different expectations and she needed to figure out each one individually. 'I found that every class has sort of expected that you've taken it somewhere but every professor has a different idea of what his expectations for a lesson plan are. And I can't find that out from another class. I have to find it out from him.' However, Susan felt, since each professor seemed to have different expectations about what lesson planning was, 'it would almost be better for them to show you all these styles. And then you can look at that professor and evaluate his teaching, if it worked for you. If this lesson plan makes sense to you, would you use it? Then you have a repertoire of skills at least rather than is there one right way to do it.'

However, one thing that seemed to be a common message from all Susan's courses was that as a teacher she would be expected to have a clear idea of where she was going. Lessons were to be planned, taught, and evaluated. 'A lot of the books, the literature I am reading is saying you should have a mental script. OK, so I can understand why you would want that because at the end, if you didn't have any idea of what answers you were expecting you wouldn't know what you'd taught and the kids wouldn't really know what they learned.' Susan could not imagine evaluating her teaching or her students' progress unless she had specific expectations in mind ahead of time. 'Unless you had a clear expectation in your mind, I don't see how you could reflect back and see if it was successful or not.' 'I think that if you're going to make the lesson meaningful to your students, well you'd better have it clear in your head, from the onset, that this is what you want them to learn. If it goes a different direction, then you'll be able to understand why it went that way. If you didn't have any expectation or understanding in the first place then it's just another hour that you've filled.'

Susan struggled with the tension of meeting the interests and needs of individual students while at the same time keeping a focused lesson. She could 'see so many contradictions'. She knew if she had specific goals for the lesson 'then I have a hidden agenda to my lesson, right. I'm asking this question and the kids who catch on to my style of teaching are going to go "oh, she wants this answer".' This was 'going on the other side of what I've read to say if you are expecting an answer then your kids will catch on very quickly how to please *you*, not how to *learn*. How to please you with their responses.'

Susan was not able to resolve the tension between constricting her students' learning with a pre-planned lesson which would provide her with a sense of certainty in what she would expect to happen, and allowing the students to explore their interests which would lead Susan to a sense of uncertainty because she would not know what to expect. 'I know what I would like my class to be like but I don't know if I'll have the skill to get in there and do it this way without having it go fifty directions and then turn around at the end of the day and say, 'If I'm going to keep a job [laugh] and I'm going to keep my sanity, I better get some organization happening here because now I have fifty other potential lessons and where do I go?'

Learning to Think

As Susan thought about her own public schooling experience, she realized that while she did well and got good marks, she had not learned to think for herself. Susan felt

> university teaches you to think which is a crime because shouldn't you have learned that through twelve years of school? And the knowledge that you picked up and all the facts that you memorized, but you don't remember now anyway was a real waste of time because we could have taught you how to find out the resources, how to look through them, how to think about it, how to apply a strategy that would help you and then you should be competent in pretty well any setting.

Susan valued having time to think but was often disappointed in the time allowed for thinking about learning within her classes. 'When I have come across some course that I really connected with they helped me to think . . . and I haven't come across a lot of profs that seem to value that. They automatically think you should know how to do that. Well you're not being a teacher then are you. You're transmitting all this. And what is your job and what are you supposed to be *training* me to do?'

Susan also found when students were encouraged to be reflective, 'nobody went past the surface meaning of the question which I thought at this level they would.' When I asked Susan what she meant by being reflective, she described reflection in the following way. 'Thinking about why and what and other ways and the rationale behind, like the why we do it, and the rationale behind the why.'

Susan imagined training and education to be the same thing. 'Like now they're training us to teach with an integrated subject approach versus trying to train you to teach math, science, so I think of that as training, or education. It's the same thing. I mean them as the same.' She expected to be presented with 'general rules and procedures'.

Susan also wanted time to think about what the theories might mean to her. However, Susan felt

> there doesn't seem to be enough *thinking* going on in a lot of what I'm doing. I can go through all these activities and not even think about them. Which is what everyone in our group seems to do. Quick get it done and talk about whatever. But I said, 'What do you think would be *learned* by this activity?', then I start thinking, well if I couldn't *explain* what I think they're going to learn, then what would be the point? Wouldn't they just be doing a worksheet? Here's worksheet number two. Here's worksheet number three. Oh, you're done? Do some more [laugh].

I'm Learning!

Susan knew from her own experience that she needed time to 'play around with something' before she could feel she had learned something about it. 'I think that that happens every time you learn something.' Susan had decided to take a science curriculum course this term since she felt incapable of teaching science. In her science curriculum course she was finally able to experience a kind of learning that made sense to her. Early in the course Susan found her professor open to questions and able to respond from a practical as well as a theoretical point of view. 'My professor gave us our stuff and sort of made it like a game. The object of the game is to get the light bulb to light. And once you've gotten it, find as many ways as you can to get the light bulb to light.' In this class, Susan was able to make connections between her narrative knowing from previous experience and the task the professor had set. 'I asked about an open and a closed circuit, like I was thinking electrician things. I said, "But what about a switch?" So my professor brought us a switch! And I'm thinking, "What a good teacher!", you know. Not "well we'll do switches, well it'll probably work like this." The professor said, "I'll see if I have one, I'll try and find one for you.".' By being encouraged to test out her own ideas, Susan felt 'like "I'm *learning*! *I'm learning*!" Not just that I made it right because I was told why it lit. We had to find out on our own why we thought it lit.' Susan could begin to imagine this kind of learning happening in her own classroom. 'I thought with kids, what an excellent way to do it because you'd obviously be curious'. Susan described this type of lesson as 'training because we went through it ourselves'.

Susan appreciated the way her professor recognized her as someone whose ideas were worthy of pursuing by asking an open ended question. 'I hated science because I always felt stupid. I could never do it the right way. I felt really smart at the end of that class because I had come up with the switch, and it worked.'

Susan felt the approach in this class really opened up her own learning. 'You don't ever really have a closure in that class and I *like* that. We have a closure in the fact that we call it linking. So you're linking up your knowledge and trying to make it understandable to yourself with the help of your teacher if you need it and maybe you don't. Or with the help of your students, your peers.' The kinds of 'closure' Susan experienced in this class allowed her to make connections between what she felt she had learned and what she would still like to know. 'It's not "OK that's it for electricity and tomorrow we're going to do meal worms", which is what my other class was exactly . . . Instead of inviting them to be creative you're shutting the door in their faces and saying "It's done, it's over and that's the end." And you got the right answer, pat yourself on the back.' This course provided a sense of accomplishment and future direction for Susan.

Susan could see connections between this approach to science and language learning.

> This language program, philosophy, goes right into science and now you play and you did your replay, so I want you to write what you did and some kids will never in that year get above a level of being able to say first I poured the water into the cup. Then I added the color. Then this happened. But that will come. I think that it's developmental . . . Try and challenge them in a different way then. If you've written how you did it. But what does that mean? But that goes into whole language, language learning again. That's writing and it's for a different purpose and it's reading and it's spelling and it's grammar and it's punctuation.

Susan

> 'got a lot out of that class and I'm not scared of teaching science any-more and I was petrified before.' [She could now see science as a starting point to build the rest of her curriculum around.] 'I can see it being really valuable. Like I can see science being, rather than some subject that you only teach because it's in the curriculum, I can see it as being a real strong point to build a lot of your other subject areas around. Science and then into phys ed and then into art and into language and then into math. I can see this being a real strong subject for that.'

However, while Susan could imagine using a constructivist approach to build a curriculum for her students and to enable them to inquire into and make connections in their own learning, she did not seem to see this approach as a way to inquire into her own teaching.

Note

1   This work has been supported by the Social Sciences and Humanities Research Council of Canada.

References

BROWN, L.M. (1991) 'Telling a girl's life: Self-authorization as a form of resistance', in GILLIGAN, C., ROGERS, A.G. and TOLMAN, D. (Eds) *Women, Girls and Psychotherapy: Reframing Resistance*, Binghamton, NY, Harrington Park Press, pp. 71–86.

BRUNER, J. (1986) *Actual Minds, Possible Worlds*, Cambridge, MA, Harvard University Press.

CONNELLY, F.M., and CLANDININ, D.J. (1994) 'Telling teaching stories', *Teacher Education Quarterly*, **21**, 1, pp. 145–58.

CRITES, S. (1971) 'The narrative quality of experience', *Journal of the American Academy of Religion*, **39**, 3, pp. 292–311.

CRITES, S. (1979) 'The aesthetics of self-deception', *Soundings*, **62**, pp. 107–29.

DEWEY, J. (1938) *Experience and Education*, New York, NY, Macmillan.

GILLIGAN, C. (1991) 'Women's psychological development: Implications for psychotherapy', in GILLIGAN, C., ROGERS, A.G. and TOLMAN, D. (Eds) *Women, Girls and Psychotherapy: Reframing Resistance*, Binghamton, NY, Harrington Park Press, pp. 5–32.

OLSON, M. (1993) 'Narrative authority in (teacher) education', Unpublished doctoral dissertation, University of Alberta, Edmonton, Alberta.

PATTERSON, R.S. (1983) 'Go, grit and gumption: A normal school perspective on teacher education', McCalla Lecture, Faculty of Education.

SCHÖN, D.A. (1983) *The Reflective Practitioner: How Professionals Think in Action*, New York, Basic Books.

URBAN, W.J. (1990) 'Historical studies of teacher education', in HOUSTON, W.R. (Ed) *Handbook of Research on Teacher Education*, New York, Macmillan, pp. 59–71.

4 Professionalism and the Reflective Approach to Teaching

Per F. Laursen

Abstract

There is a close relationship between the conception of the knowledge-base of teaching and the social position of teaching as a profession. This point is illustrated by a short sociological/historical analysis of the development of theories of teaching and the social position of teachers. During the last ten to fifteen years there has been a permanent struggle concerning the status of the teachers. During the same period the knowledge-base of teaching has become dominated by the 'reflective' approach. A revision of the reflective approach is recommended if it is going to support the development of teachers' professionalism.

Introduction

D.A. Schön introduced his concept of the reflective practitioner in 1983 as a way of restoring confidence in the professions. His intention was to propose a more correct and more trustworthy theory of professional knowledge and thereby raising the status of the professions. Looking at Schön's endeavour from the viewpoint of the teaching profession he has been both successful and unsuccessful. He has been successful as far as the 'theory' of the reflective practitioner has become the absolutely dominating approach to teaching and to teacher education. But he has been unsuccessful as far as confidence in the profession has not been restored; on the contrary attacks on the professionalism of teachers have become even harder than before.

Of course Schön cannot be given any responsibility for the renewed attack on teachers' professional status. I will try to answer the question why the success of the reflective approach in teacher education and in theory of teaching have not resulted in the intended restoration of confidence in the profession. I will argue in this chapter that it is necessary to reform the reflective approach if it is going to be an effective support of professionalism. The aim of the paper is to propose ideas for the further development of the reflective approach.

Schön's basic idea was correct: There is a close relationship between the conception of the knowledge-base of a profession as teaching and the social position of teaching as an occupation/profession. The point can be illustrated by a sociological/historical analysis of the development of theories of teaching and the social position of teachers.

This paper is based on a very general look at teacher education and the knowledge-base of teaching. The material is drawn from history and present discussions in Europe and North America. Of course there are important differences between countries and cultures concerning both history and the present situation. Still there seems to be some general traits in common. Both in Europe and in North America there are struggles concerning the professional status of teachers and uncertainty about the knowledge-base of teaching. These general traits are the theme of the paper and I consciously — and probably also unconsciously — ignore many important differences.

History of Teachers' Status and Knowledge-base of Teaching

Teaching as a separate occupation is about 200 years old. During the first 100 years the knowledge-base of teaching was 'prescriptions' normally written by people outside the occupation (e.g. priests and civil servants) telling teachers in detail how to teach. Most applications of the prescriptive approach were based on religion, political ideology or philosophical anthropology; 'consequences' for educational practice were deduced from these ideologies (Laursen, 1994).

From the beginning of this century teachers reached a semi-professional status independent of the priesthood. From about the same time the knowledge-base of teaching was constructed by psychologists and educators as a theory of teaching methods. It was dominated by a 'rationalistic approach' telling teachers how to plan their lessons and select teaching methods.

This rationalistic approach was developed early in this century in context of behaviorism. The behaviorists tried to transform theories of learning into methods for efficient teaching. E.L. Thorndike was the great pioneer of this movement. The endeavour has, to some degree, been successful but the behavioristic theories are still limited to teaching methods — they say little or nothing about aims and content of instruction.

The rationalistic solution to this problem was to focus on a more abstract 'scheme of thinking' (Taba, 1962, p. VI). The fundamental principles of this scheme were suggested by R.W. Tyler (Tyler, 1949) who recommended that the teacher make decisions concerning the following four areas when preparing lessons:

1 purpose;
2 selection of learning experience;
3 organization of learning experience; and
4 evaluation.

Concerning the social status of teachers this scientifically more valid knowledge-base meant that teachers gained more autonomy. Especially in the 1960s this gave rise to optimism concerning the future development towards a recognition as true professionals.

The Struggle over Professionalism and Reflective Approach

Proponents of the professionalization movement probably in the 1960s viewed the future as being quite straightforward: Teaching was going to grow both in its scientific knowledge-base and in its social prestige and thereby attaining the desired professional status. The development has been quite different. Instead of the gradual acknowledgment of professional status professionalization has become the focus of both social and political struggle and of academic discussion.

The causes of this development are of course manifold. Among the most important are:

- There has been a loss of public confidence in the professions in general. Not only the new and less well established professions but also the most prestigious, the medical profession, have come under attack during recent years (Labaree, 1992, p. 126). Part of the background of this may be a general trend of the 'late modern' or 'postmodern' cultures to distrust any kind of authority.
- Some conservative governments have directly attacked the professional status of teachers and other groups. Well known is especially the case of the conservative British government whose proposal of school-based teacher training clearly has been part of a strategy to undermine the professional status of teachers (Beresford-Hill, 1993, p. 84). The neoconservative market-economy-ideology opposes professionalism because professional status normally is associated with monopoly of a certain group on certain positions. And because conservatives prefer the market instead of professional judgment to settle issues.
- Many other groups than teachers strive for recognition as professionals, e.g., nurses and social workers. The strategies of the different groups have been almost identical: They have argued that their job have become more important and more complicated and that they need prolonged training of a more scientifically based character and that they need more autonomy in performing their jobs. The hope has been that professional status and better salaries would follow.

  Movement towards professionalization being such a general phenomenon has contributed to a trend of inflation in the value of professional status. Early in the century being professional meant being at the top level of our society. Today it means being like many others.
- Sociologists have become much more sceptical towards professionalization. The classical functionalistic sociologist T. Parsons viewed professionalization

as almost identical with progress in civilization and modernization (Parsons, 1968). Modern sociologists are much more sceptical and tend to view professionalization as a strategy of the professionals taking care of their own interests in prestige and salary (Bourdieu, 1989). Although the arguments for professionalization, of course, are always on behalf of students, clients or patients.

As especially stressed by Abbott (1988) the results have been that today professional status cannot be acquired once and for ever. Instead professionalization must be viewed as an ongoing struggle without any single path that can guarantee a group to reach the preferred status as full professionals. Many groups strive for recognition as professionals, strong forces oppose them and the struggles are open-ended. Teachers, unions and maybe especially teacher educators have argued in favor of professionalization and the argument has — in short — been that the technical competence of teachers should be offered in exchange of status, autonomy and salary (Labaree, 1992, p. 148).

The rationalistic approach to theories of teaching had for decades claimed to be able to develop this competence by making scientifically based teaching possible. However the research seemed more to undermine this claim than to support it. Especially two results questioned the belief that scientifically based classroom practice was developing:

Firstly several empirical studies of teacher education and socialization — among them the now classical study by Lortie (1975) — showed that teacher training does not have much impact on the ways teachers actually teach. Instead new teachers use as models the good teachers they have experienced during their long career as pupils. These models seem to be more influential than theories of teaching. In accordance with this tendency teachers do not seem to appreciate their theoretical based training in teaching methods and curriculum planning (Jacobsen, 1989).

Secondly several studies of teacher thinking have compared the way teachers plan their courses against the 'Tyler rationale' of the rationalistic approach to teaching. The results indicate that more experienced teachers do not plan according to the Tyler-tradition (Clark and Peterson, 1986, pp. 263–6). Teaching practice is only to a modest degree a rational process aiming at clearly defined purposes. Clark and Peterson argue that planning of teaching is 'selection, organization and sequencing of routines' (p. 260).

In the 1980s proponents of the professionalization movement were caught in a dilemma: They had argued that in exchange of status, salary and autonomy they could deliver scientifically based teaching practice. But at least part of the research itself seemed to show teaching instead as a routinized activity to which personal experiences and preferences are more important than research results. And simply to extend training and raise graduation requirements seemed not to be able to change this.

D.A. Schön and the reflective approach promised a way out of this dilemma. It seemed to propose a new epistemology of practice that at the same time would be both scientifically valid and close to the daily practice of teaching and the way teachers think about it. This is probably the explanation of what has been called 'the Schön shock' (Eraut, 1995), the sweeping popularity of the reflective approach during the 1980s and the first part of the 1990s.

Twelve years after the introduction of the reflective approach there seems to be good reasons to reconsider critically the hopes and intentions connected with the popularity of the approach.

Firstly it is obvious that the reflective approach has not been able to restore confidence in the knowledge-base of teaching and in the status of teaching as a profession. Part of the background may be that Schön's diagnosis of the crisis of confidence was wrong. Schön's analysis said that the reason of lack of confidence was that the 'technical rationality' was a misleading epistemology of practical professional knowledge.

The analysis of Abbot and others shows instead that there are more general social and cultural causes behind the confidence crisis. Today any kind of special social status and any kind of expertise is critically questioned. Even the most perfect knowledge-base of teaching could not have secured the teaching profession a safe status as fully recognized professionals.

Secondly the reflective approach has become inefficient as a part of the strategy of the professionalization movement. The view on teacher education in the reflective approach has become too close to the view on teacher education embedded in the conservative attacks on teachers' professional status. As said by one of the critics of the reflective approach its main impacts on teacher education have been the twin ideas (a) that they should 'learn on the job' — that is, during the school practice, and (b) that they should think a bit about a number of fashionable social topics (racism, sexism, special needs, language, governmental demands on the curriculum, and so on) (Wilson, 1991, p. 116).

At the same time one of the main points — if not *the* main point — of the attacks on teachers' professionalism was the idea of school-based teacher training. Both in Europe and in USA this idea has been closely connected with general attacks on teachers' status as professionals and on the monopoly of educated teachers on the teaching positions (Beresford-Hill, 1993, p. 84). Of course proponents of the reflective approach would add that there is an important difference between their view on learning during school practice and the conservative idea of school-based teacher training. While the latter is an apprenticeship — like training in mastering the traditional routines of the classroom the former is primarily a critical reflection on these routines.

Still the struggle on professionalism is a struggle about general social and public recognition. And to the public the view on teacher education of the reflective approach must look as being closely related to the view of the conservative attack on professionalism. Both views are part of a general move towards 'the practical' (Wilson, 1991, p. 118).

Thirdly it should be noted, although it is not part of the main point of this paper, that there has been much theoretical-based critique of the reflective approach. To name but a few it has been critized of being vacuous (Wilson, 1991), of ignoring problems of social reproduction in the educational system (Laursen, 1995), and of ignoring the speed of the decision-making in the classroom (Eraut, 1995).

Discussion: Reflection in Favor of Professionalism

It is fairly obvious that the professional status of teachers is still threatened and that the reflective approach (as we have known it until now) is problematic as the knowledge-base of teaching to be recommended by the professionalization movement. In this situation there seems to be three possible strategies:

1   teachers could give up the claim to be professionals;
2   teacher education could abandon the reflective approach; and
3   the reflective approach could be developed favoring professionalism.

The first strategy, to give up professionalism, has been proposed by Labaree (1992). He feared that professionalization would result in 'rationalization of the classroom' (p. 144) meaning enhancing the influence of teacher educators and technical theories and increasing the political distance between teachers and parents. In my view giving up professionalism is a dangerous strategy. The conservative attacks on professionalism and on teacher education show that if teachers lose or give up the struggle for professionalism the result will be less qualified teachers, more routinized teaching and a free flow of market economy into the educational sector.

The second strategy, to abandon the reflective approach to teacher education, has been proposed by Wilson (1991). He favored a return to teacher education stressing introduction to 'the relevant disciplines of education (philosophy, psychology, sociology, etc.)' (p. 116). This seems to me also an impossible strategy. There are reasons for the popularity of the reflective approach and one of them is of course problems of the more traditional approaches to teacher education of which 'introduction to the disciplines' is one. A second important reason is that being reflective and critically examining one's practices is an important general cultural trend (Giddens, 1984 and 1990) that cannot be ignored by teachers. Of course it is possible to abandon the label 'reflective approach' and abandon some of the versions of teacher education using that label. But to oppose reflection as a trait of teacher education seems to be to give up an important part of what it today must mean to be a competent teacher.

The third strategy, to develop the reflective approach in a way that supports professionalism, seems to me to be the only recommendable strategy. Lately there has been several publications advocating reformulations of the reflective approach. To mention but a few P.Tomlinson (1995) has argued that a much clearer conception on teacher competence is needed and Korthagen and Wubbels (1995) have shown that it is possible to give the concept of reflection a more distinct and operational content the impact of which can be empirically tested in evaluating teacher education.

Looking at these contributions from the viewpoint of professionalization the main points are:

- It is necessary to develop a more clear, distinct and operational concept of teacher competence and of reflection. The most persistent critique of the reflective approach has been that the word reflection is used in many — and often unreflective! — ways (Bengtsson, 1995).
- If reflection is going to mean more than 'thinking a bit about a number of fashionable social topics' (Wilson, 1991) analysis of teaching must be at the heart of it. Therefore the reflective approach cannot be such a radical rupture with the traditions of teacher education as the critics seem to fear. The conceptual tools for analysis of teaching and life in classroom cannot be found anywhere else but in the disciplines of education.
- The aim of analyzing teaching is to become aware of alternatives. While the apprenticeship-like versions of school based teacher training aim at the mastery of a limited number of teaching skills the characteristic of the reflective approach should be the creative aspects of teaching. Teacher education must pay attention to creativity as a central trait of human action (Joas, 1994).
- Most modern theories of teaching stress that good education is learning-oriented as it is said in Korthagen and Wubbels' first point about qualified teaching (Korthagen and Wubbels, 1995, p. 54). Still it is known from research on teacher thinking and practice that teachers are not much aware of the learning of students (Marton, 1994, p. 35). Educating teachers to be in contact with the learning of students is one of the most important challenges to teacher education.

Conclusion

To support the development of teachers' professionalism the reflective approach to teaching must stress:

- a clear, distinct and operational concept of teacher competence and of reflection;
- conceptual tools for the analysis of teaching;
- the creativity of teaching; and
- teachers' awareness of the learning of students.

References

ABBOTT, A. (1988) *The System of Professions*, Chicago, University of Chicago Press.

BENGTSSON, J. (1995) 'What is Reflection?: On reflection in the teaching profession and teacher education', *Teachers and Teaching*, **1**, 1.

BERESFORD-HILL, P. (1993) 'Teacher education, access and quality control in higher education', *Oxford Review of Education*, **19**, 1.

BOURDIEU, P. (1989) *Outline of a Theory of Practice*, Cambridge, Cambridge University Press.

CARLGREN, I., HANDAL, G. and VAAGE, S. (1994) *Teachers' Minds and Actions: Research on Teachers' Thinking and Practice*, London, Falmer Press.

CLARK, C.M. and PETERSON, P.L. (1986) 'Teachers' thought processes', in WITTROK, M.C. (Ed) *Handbook of Research on Teaching*, (3rd ed.), New York, Macmillan.

ERAUT, M. (1995) 'Schön Shock: a case for reframing reflection-in-action?', *Teachers and Teaching*, **1**, 1.

GIDDENS, A. (1984) *The Constitution of Society*, Cambridge, Polity Press.

GIDDENS, A. (1990) *The Consequences of Modernity*, Cambridge, Polity Press.

JACOBSEN, B. (1989) *Fungerer Læreruddannelsen?*, København, Undervisningsministeriet.

JOAS, H. (1994) 'The creativity of action: Pragmatism and the critique of the rational action model', in CARLGREN, I., HANDAL, G. and VAAGE, S. (1994) *Teachers' Minds and Actions: Research on Teachers' Thinking and Practice*, London, Falmer Press.

KORTHAGEN, F.A.J. and WUBBELS, T. (1995) 'Characteristics of reflective practitioners: Towards an operationalization of the concept of reflection', *Teachers and Teaching*, **1**, 1.

LABAREE, D. (1992) 'Power, knowledge, and the rationalization of teaching: A genealogy of the movement to professionalize teaching', *Harvard Educational Review*, **62**, 2.

LAURSEN, PER F. (1994) 'Teacher thinking and didactics: Prescriptive, rationalistic and reflective approaches', in CARLGREN, I., HANDAL, G. and VAAGE, S. (1994) (op. cit.).

LAURSEN, PER F. (1995) 'A sociological critique of the theory of the reflective practitioner', in PARÉ, C. (1995) *Better Teaching in Physical Education?: Think About It!*, Trois-Rivières, Universitée du Québec à Trois-Rivières.

LORTIE, D.C. (1975) *School-Teacher*, Chicago and London, The University of Chicago Press.

MARTON, F. (1994) 'On the structure of teachers' awareness', in CARLGREN, I., HANDAL, G. and VAAGE, S. (1994) (op. cit.).

PARSONS, T. (1968) 'Professions', in SILLS, D.S. (Ed) *International Encyclopedia of the Social Sciences*, New York, Macmillan and The Free Press, vols 11 and 12.

SCHÖN, D.A. (1983) *The Reflective Practitioner*, New York, Basic Books.

TABA, H. (1962) *Curriculum Development*, New York, Harcourt, Brace and World.

TOMLINSON, P. (1995) 'Can competence profiling work for effective teacher preparation? Part I: General Issues', *Oxford Review of Education*, **21**, 2.

TYLER, R.W. (1949) *Basic Principles of Curriculum and Instruction*, Chicago and London, The University of Chicago Press.

WILSON, J. (1991) 'Teacher education', *Oxford Review of Education*, **17**, 1.

5   Productively Confronting Dilemmas in Educational Practice and Research

Pam Denicolo

Introduction

One of the frustrating things about espousing a 'personal construct' philosophy, or indeed any of a range of phenomenological approaches to research, is that it behoves one to take into account an astounding variety of possible interpretations or alternative constructions of reality. Holding to the tenets of these approaches does not compel one to agree with all the options or to rate them all equally, but it does present an *embarras de choix* on which to base personal selection to inform decision making. How much easier it would be to return to childlike belief that there is an answer to every problem as long as one conforms to a simple set of rules and obtains the relevant information from experts and books.

Few of us are very old before we discover that rules are not simple, nor is there only one set, that experts frequently disagree and sometimes 'don't know'. As we grow we increasingly find ourselves having to make urgent decisions in a field of uncertainty and in the face of contradictory evidence. It is a particular type of such difficult decisions, dilemmas in the professional lives of educators, which forms the focus for this paper.

History and Context

The stimulus for addressing this topic has both a long history and a recent impetus. No doubt like every reader, my autobiography could be represented by a series of critical, difficult choices made, for instance from a selection of science rather than arts subjects at school, psychology rather than chemistry at university, to an education department rather than a psychology one at work. *Post hoc* rationalization does not completely erase the pain of the deliberation nor some cogitation about what would have happened if . . . However, pragmatism, optimism and a liberal lacing of calvinistic socialization combined to form my intuitive theory that confrontation with life's conundrums contributes positively to development. Thus it was with a sense of 'rightness', a fitting into context (Goodman and Elgin, 1988,

p. 158), that I recently undertook the simultaneous supervision of two PhD projects, one concerned with investigating the value of conflict in undergraduate education (Maund, 1994) and one exploring how young adults might benefit from a more overt, pronounced addressing of dilemma in their studies (Miller, 1994).

Linda Maund ably described her work in another paper presented at the Brock conference (Maund, 1995), while I am indebted to Patrick Miller for allowing me, for this paper, to draw on his thesis and the ideas with which we conjured during many a lengthy debate.

It is said that once alerted to something, we see it all around us. These research endeavors certainly made me more sensitive to the dilemmas which impinge on our professional lives and are addressed in educational literature. Both of these will be drawn on in this paper to illustrate the pervasiveness of dilemma in education, from the pupil's, the teacher's, the teacher educator's and the researcher's perspectives. Built on these will be the premise that grasping the horns of dilemma, recognizing its existence and resolving, if incompletely, its tensions, helps hone the skills of the learner/practitioner.

Dilemmas or Problems?

The foregoing has been predicated on the assumption that dilemmas are something different in kind to problems, although the terms may be used interchangeably in colloquial discourse. Indeed, some orthodox philosophical views, for example, monism and deontic logic (Kant, 1969; Gowans, 1987) contend that true dilemmas do not exist, that purported dilemmas result from spiritual ignorance, an uninstructed conscience or from inadequate information combined with lack of rigour in thinking. A summary of the monist argument might be that since God is the source of all moral law, implications of contradictions in the latter would mistakenly imply confusion in the former. A wayside pulpit, quoted in Hare (Hare, 1981, p. 25) puts the deontic principle succinctly: 'If you have conflicting duties, one of them isn't your duty.'

We may agree that dilemmas *ought* not to exist, and yet we continue to experience them. From a phenomenological perspective they suffuse our lives, particularly as we come to accept the relative nature of knowledge (Perry, 1968). For centuries literature, which arguably mirrors life, has presented many examples, admittedly of the most dramatic kind, of the conflicting obligations which confront people. They find themselves in situations in which they cannot avoid evil actions because no guilt free alternative is available:

> for Sophocles' Antigone the choice was between family duty, burying her brother, and civic duty, avoiding honouring a traitor;
> Aeschylus has Agamemnon caught between the human feeling for his daughter Iphigenia and his duty to fellow countrymen to achieve military success;
> Nora, in Ibsen's *A Doll's House* (1958), is torn between duties to her husband and to herself;

the mother in Styron's (1980) *Sophie's Choice* can save from death only one but not both of her children.

Common sense provides further evidence of the universal nature of dilemma, at least in a relatively liberal society, and can be illustrated by the antithetical advice of many proverbs (Billig, 1988, p. 16) — *look before you leap, he who hesitates is lost*. Dramatic dilemmas usually involve a conflict of ethics whereas more everyday versions commonly involve a selection between unfavorable consequences. These are two possible attributes of dilemma.

Miller (1994) reviewed many perspectives in the dilemma/problem debate, from philosophical, psychological, sociological and political ethics viewpoints. He proposed as a working definition that dilemma is a particular type of predicament which occurs when the pressing alternatives available, or serious obligations we face, seem so evenly balanced that it is hard, sometimes impossible, to make a choice. Further, he posited (pp. 30–1) that dilemmas exhibit the following characteristics.

They would all be:

1 everyday occurrences, yet pressing and serious to the participants, not trifling or inconsequential;
2 conflict situations, presenting evenly balanced choices or obligations;
3 conflicts derived from the incompatible demands of either a single principle or a pluralistic ethic;
4 situations which cause unfavorable consequences i.e., leaving some remainder, whichever alternative is selected; and
5 distinguishable from problems in that only the latter leave no remainder and are eliminated when solved.

While some may have a moral dimension, some may have alternative solutions which are perceived as invalid, while the symmetry of others may be disturbed by an ostensible preferred option.

Whether dilemmas are 'real' in some objective sense or exist simply as a construct of the agent, their impact on human activity, in particular in education, make them worthy of study.

Dilemmas as Part of the Curriculum

In the empirical section of his work, Miller (op. cit.) explored with young students (16–19 years) their experiences of situations, the characteristics of which matched with those listed above, and what meaning those experiences had for them. They reported that, while they may not be able to resolve future dilemmas any more quickly or with greater certainty, they had gained much value from the experience, for example, enhanced awareness tempered with caution, self-reliance and independence.

In focus groups, teachers from different disciplines were able to cite examples of distinctive dilemmas which occur in their subject areas. One example from Physical Education was 'whether to have a shot at goal or pass to a team member' and one from Economics was whether full employment or reduced inflation should be sought. Overall though, the teachers unanimously agreed that cross curricular study skills would be enhanced by lessons focussed on the general study of dilemma recognition and resolution.

The research in total suggested that such study would assist in the journey towards mature, relativistic thinking by providing opportunities:

- to adopt different perspectives;
- to try out a variety of arguments; and
- accept the validity of conflicting alternatives.

and would help pupils:

- to learn to live with the consequences of difficult, marginal decisions;
- to come to terms with conclusions that are not cut and dried but are sometimes finely balanced and costly either way; and
- to appreciate the difference between decisions based on blind assurance and those based on a thorough, careful balancing process.

Counter to this, it may be suggested that considering dilemmas in schools is artificial and lacking in emotional involvement but too often education is focussed on finding the answers to defined, closed questions. This is hardly a preparation for the complexity of life after school. Benefits might be derived from weighing alternatives in an environment where a mistake is not too costly (like a flight simulator provided for training airline pilots!)

The description given by Postman and Weingartner (1969) of '*good learners*' could be derived from the advantages suggested by Miller above.

> Good learners prefer to rely on their own judgement . . . are not usually fearful of being wrong . . . recognise their limitations and suffer no trauma in concluding that what they believe is apparently not so. Perhaps most importantly, good learners do not need to have an absolute, final, irrevocable resolution to every problem. (p. 42)

Dilemmas in Teaching Experience

Addressing their experience of teaching in the United Kingdom, the contributors to Bell's (1995) book provided many examples of their struggles and dilemmas when faced with implementing policy directed by central government. These included dealing with the paradoxes inherent in the policies themselves, for instance being given control over, and responsibility for, budgets which contained historical debts and obligations, and disjunctions between means and objectives and between policy and professional values. An example of the former is the presence of a traditional, product based curriculum which is intended, nevertheless, to equip pupils with process skills deemed suitable as future contributions to the world of work and the national economy (Denicolo and Harwood, 1995). The latter is illustrated by the tension between the policy need to be accountable to the taxpayers, including parents, and the professional commitment to meet the individual needs of the taught.

While each contributor to this book conveyed either an overt or covert sense of despair, yet each had some positive recommendations to make to others of their ilk, drawn from what they had learned from coping with these frustrating, dilemmatic experiences.

Apple (1982, p. 63) noted that recognizing inherent contradictions within ideological processes is the first step, exposing them to debate and therefore challenge the second, in releasing the potential for resistance to ill conceived change.

Some others who have addressed dilemmas faced by teachers in their practice include Olson (1982), Lyons *et al.* (1986), Lyons (1990), Barnes (1992), Carter (1992) and Kilbourn (1992). All of these authors recount examples of paradoxes of action since, as Carter (p. 110) noted 'a chosen course of action may simultaneously correct one problem and prompt others'. On a similar theme, Kilbourn suggested that:

> Deeply held views about efficiency (timing, pace etc), ethics (participation, equality, fairness), subject matter (principles of enquiry, knowledge), philosophy of teaching . . . , and rigour (conversation that stays on track cannot all be satisfield within a given interaction. (p. 87)

Olson and Lyons *et al.* also discussed the multitude of demands on teachers' time and energy and the conflicts they face in prioritizing, in managing the urgency of the immediate against the importance of the long term. In her later paper, Lyons provided examples from previous and recent work of practical, moral and epistemological dilemmas derived from:

> the intricate interactions between a teachers knowledge and values, assumptions about knowing, a craft, and relationships. (p. 161)

The issues she exemplified through the vignettes of particular teachers resonate at a general level with most teachers' experience, at least with those in the literature referenced herein.

One such issue concerns the relativism of knowledge, different notions of what constitutes the 'truth' for the teachers themselves, for their pupils, and for those who set and examine the curriculum. Underpinning this is a more fundamental professional tension, between developing understanding and learning skills and helping pupils to pass exams and gain credentials, commitments that are not always in harmony.

Nor yet is there anything but fine professional judgment to be relied upon when attempting to implement rules with justice, attention to individual circumstances and intent. A staff debate in my own experience illustrates this. The rule firmly states that no form of plagiarism is allowed, zero grading resulting for any one piece of work that contains it. The debate concerned a complete essay derived from a former course presented again for a different assessment (teachers have long memories!) and another essay liberally scattered, without attribution, with sentences contained in lecture handouts. The problem was made more complex when the experience and culture of the candidates were considered, yet the rule itself was inflexible.

Presenting the heart searching of one teacher, a black American teaching about apartheid in South Africa, Lyons (1990) raised a common dilemma about dealing with controversial material. The subsuming question in these situations is whether an objective, 'sanitized' version of the various contributing perspectives should be presented or whether one's own commitment to a particular viewpoint should be overt. This is not just a personal ethic issue. In recent years in the United Kingdom, the media have censured teachers both for not adequately accentuating the moral perspective, as if there were only one, and for presenting too overtly a partisan view (e.g., one with liberal or 'leftist' principles).

Barnes (1992) cogently expressed a theme common to all these examples:

> Teachers cannot easily afford the luxury of a detached viewpoint: they have to teach, to make choices, whether or not they have a clear view of where they are heading. (p. 15)

He suggested that, by becoming researchers in their own classrooms, by regarding their professional practice as a source of hypotheses to be tested, they can challenge and develop their 'frame' for teaching. He did, however, suggest that they would benefit in this enterprise of becoming 'extended professionals' were there fewer contradictory institutional and cultural imperatives.

At least currently, there does seem to be a surfeit of paradoxes and dilemmas for teachers to contend with which leads to the question about whether they are adequately prepared for this in their training.

Preparing for Paradox: Initial Teacher Education

Bryan (1995), describing his move from school teaching to tutoring in initial teacher education, recorded his astonishment at the disjunction between the rhetoric of validating bodies, what ought to be, and the reality that was evinced in the training college, between the philosophy espoused by fellow teacher educators and what was possible within the confines of a course within a higher education institution. That situation is further exacerbated by UK government policy which deems that student teachers should spend considerably less time in 'ivory towers' and more time in schools. Bryan represents many educators in abhorring the policy contrast inherent in recommendations that nurses require higher education incorporating informed reflection as a prerequisite for professional development while teachers are required to devote less time to theory and more to 'on the job' practice. Both he and Maguire (1995, pp. 121–2) recognized the 'impossible' job presented to training colleges of producing a reflective, informed and critical teacher through a course of thirty-six weeks, two thirds of which is spent in schools on practice.

In her paper, to which readers are addressed, Maguire provided pertinent examples of the dilemmas faced by student teachers and their tutors and explored the importance of these confrontations to the development of the professional practice of both. She argued that current training policy, with its emphasis on competencies, could well result in teacher education being downgraded from an intellectual challenge to a practical, technical skills training:

> What may get lost in all this may be the interrogation of pedagogy, the tentativeness and questioning which characterise the creative and informed professional teacher. (p. 130)

Ruddock (1992), too, regretted the growing policy of anti-intellectualism in teacher education which encourages teachers to 'learn by doing', rather than by reflection on practice. She believed that it is an important responsibility, inter alia, for teacher educators to help teachers: 'have some constructive experience of what reflective research will yield when applied to the everyday problems and dilemmas of teaching and learning in schools' (p. 163).

Laudable though this is, it is again 'among the other things' proliferating and competing as responsibilities to be borne by teacher educators. These same teacher educators must also devote some time and effort to their own research in order to continue to develop theory and practice. This is addressed in the next section.

Conundrums for the Educational Researcher

In order to be present at a conference, so that we might learn from the experience and expertise of others, requires the resolution of several dilemmas. The time taken to write a paper and attend such a conference has to be abstracted from that available for preparation of next year's courses, for supervising the research-in-progress of others and for conducting our own. Other demands on time, domestic and family, also have to be considered so that in making a choice, even in deciding that it is the right one, a residue of regret for the rejected alternatives still remains.

In pursuing our own research and supporting that of others, choices also abound about what of the many urgent questions in education should be addressed. Should we focus on the problems which intrigue us personally or those which seem a priority among a community of professionals? Will the generation of theory, even if esoteric at the moment, be more valuable than the development and evaluation of suggestions which have immediate utilitarian consequences for practitioners? Positive and negative implications adhere to both poles of each dilemma presented, before the research is even begun.

Previous papers, for example Pope and Denicolo (1986) and Denicolo and Harwood (1995b), have explored the dilemmas inherent in making methodological choices, from appropriate paradigm to research instrument selection, and these will not be rehearsed in detail here but the essence of the conclusions drawn is provided by Patton (1990):

> the art of evaluation (research) includes creating a design and gathering information that is appropriate for a specific situation and a particular decision making context. In art there is no single, ideal standard . . . any given design is necessarily an interplay of resources, possibilities, creativity and personal judgements . . . Research, like diplomacy, is the art of the possible. (p. 13)

Ruddock (op. cit., p. 168) urged that higher education can make a distinctive contribution to teacher education by a commitment to the collaborative kind of action research which is both reflective and emancipatory. Teachers-as-researchers with whom I have collaborated agree with this principle. Let me illustrate their thoughts on this matter by abstracting some of the phrases they used in describing their research activities: 'creative; ownership of direction; transformative; requiring courage and vision; arduous; lonely; challenging; requiring passionate commitment'.

Apparent contradictions abound in this list, yet they all agreed that these were pertinent descriptors of the process: it could not be transformative without being challenging, nor could they own the direction without it being arduous, for example.

Exploration of the meaning that formal versions of such research, for higher degrees, had for teachers led to the recommendation (Denicolo, 1994) that participants, supervisors and researchers alike, should be constantly alert to the balance of benefits and costs associated with such engagement:

- self development;
- professional stimulation, skill development;
- neglect or loss of some previous roles, especially social ones; and
- the pressures of conflicting duties.

The choices made about and during the process of research, no matter how altruistic the intention, no matter how passionate the commitment, may still leave a residue of guilt (e.g., neglected family and friends or other work) or at least a remainder of regret. They conform to the definition of dilemma provided earlier by Miller and, again, those who had to make the choices reported that it was in the making of these decisions and living with the results that they achieved personal and professional development.

Active Learning through Dilemmas Recognition and Resolution: Some Conclusions

From education young pupils may learn only facts and formal problem solving mechanisms which lead them to expect that by accumulating sufficient 'nuggets of truth' and by applying the correct formula that they can solve future personal and professional problems. On the other hand, they may learn that facts are contingent on circumstance, that arguments need to be weighed and alternative perspectives considered. Such learning will stand them in good stead for dealing with the paradoxes to be faced in adulthood. Miller (op. cit.) argued that teachers, by helping pupils to recognize the existence of dilemmas and by encouraging debate on their resolution, can engage them in active learning, as opposed to passive receipt of information, which promotes such relativistic reasoning, dialectic thinking, and reflective moral judgement. Through this process, especially through dealing with post decisional regret, they also gain self knowledge, as Nussbaum (1985) confirms: 'The experience of conflict can also be time of learning and development . . . a progress that comes from an increase in self knowledge and knowledge of the world' (p. 260).

This applies equally well to educators, of pupils, students or teachers, and to educational researchers. As Kelly (1955) suggests, it is only by continually testing and revising our constructs that we learn. It is only in recognition of constructive alternatives that stronger adherence to, or rejection of, our former positions and philosophies becomes possible. Equally, mental and physical skills do not become honed unless they are set against the rock of challenge.

Whilst not advocating that we each should be challenged by the kinds of dilemmas found in classical tragedies, nevertheless it behoves us to give healthy recognition in education to the lives to which we are heir. Nor yet is it productive to regard dilemmas as only choices between negative poles, but rather they could be seen as choices between alternatives which may have positive outcomes as a result of the exercise of that choice.

To avoid such recognition, to discount the contribution of dilemmatic choices to lifelong learning is to become urban ostriches. Instead, acknowledgment that dilemmas pervade our lives, and in doing so promote development, can produce people who are: 'actively inquiring, flexible, creative, innovative, tolerant . . . who can face uncertainty and ambiguity without disorientation' (Postman and Weingartner, 1969, p. 204).

References

APPLE, M.W. (Ed) (1982) *Cultural and Economic Reproduction in Education: Essays on Class, Ideology and the State*, London, Routledge and Kegan Paul.

AESCHYLUS, (1956) 'Agamemnon', in *The Oresteian Trilogy*, translated by VELLACOTT, P. Harmondsworth, Penguin.

BARNES, D. (1992) 'The significance of teachers' frames for teaching', in RUSSELL, T. and MUNBY, H. (Eds) *Teachers and Teaching*, London, Falmer Press.

BELL, J. (Ed) (1995) *Teachers Talk about Teaching*, Buckingham, Open University Press.

BILLIG, M. (1988) *Ideological Dilemmas*, London, Sage.

BRYAN, L. (1995) 'Revisiting classrooms', in BELL, J. (Ed) *Teachers Talk about Teaching*, Buckingham, Open University Press.

CARTER, K. (1992) 'Creating cases for the development of teacher knowledge', in RUSSELL, T. and MUNBY, H. (Eds) *Teachers and Teaching*, London, Falmer Press.

DENICOLO, P.M. (1994) 'Doctoral students: The integration of the research role in professional lives', Paper presented at the 2nd European Conference on Personal Construct Psychology, St Andreasberg, Germany, April.

DENICOLO, P.M. and HARWOOD, A.G. (1995a) *Research in the Social Sciences: A Review of Illusions, Disillusions and Uncomfortable Conundrums*, Faro, University of the Algarve Press.

DENICOLO, P.M. and HARWOOD, A.G. (1995b) *Research in the Social Sciences: A Review of Illusions, Disillusions and Uncomfortable Conundrums*, Faro, University of the Algarve Press.

GOODMAN, N. and ELGIN, C. (1988) *Reconceptions in Philosophy and Other Arts and Sciences*, Indianapolis, Hackett.

GOWANS, C. (Ed) (1987) *Moral Dilemmas*, Oxford, Oxford University Press.

HARE, R.M. (1981) *Moral Thinking*, Oxford, Oxford University Press.

IBSEN, H. (1958) *A Doll's House*, translated by FARQUHARSON SHARPE, R. and MARX-AVELING, E. London, Dent.

KANT, I. (1969) *Groundwork of the Metaphysics of Morals*, translated by PATON, H.J. London, Hutchinson University Library.

KELLY, G.A. (1955) *The Psychology of Personal Constructs*, New York, Norton.

KILBOURN, B. (1992) 'Philosophical, subject matter and classroom understandings', in RUSSELL, T. and MUNBY H. (Eds) *Teachers and Teaching*, London, Falmer Press.

LYONS, N. (1990) 'Dilemmas in knowing: Ethical and epistemological dimensions of teachers' work and development', *Harvard Educational Review*, **60**, 2, pp. 159–80.

LYONS, N., CUTLER, A. and MILLER, B. (1986) *Dilemmas in Teaching*, Unpublished mss, Graduate School of Education, Harvard University.

MAGUIRE, M. (1995) 'Dilemmas in teaching teachers: The tutor's perspective', *Teachers and Teaching: Theory and Practice*, **1**, 1, March.

MAUND, L.C. (1994) 'The role of conflict in the teaching and learning of undergraduates', Unpublished PhD thesis, University of Surrey.

MILLER, P. (1994) 'Perspectives on the recognition and resolution of dilemma within an educational framework', Unpublished PhD thesis, University of Surrey.

NUSSBAUM, M. (1985) 'Aeschylus and practical conflict', *Ethics*, **95**, pp. 233–67.

OLSON, J. (Ed) (1982) *Innovation in the Science Curriculum*, London, Croom Helm.

PATTON, M.Q. (1990) *Qualitative Evaluation Methods*, London, Sage.

PERRY, W.G. (Jnr) (1968) *Forms of Intellectual and Ethical Development in the College Years*, New York, Holt, Rinehart and Winston.

POPE, M.L. and DENICOLO, P.M. (1986) 'Intuitive theories — A researcher's dilemma', *British Educational Research Journal*, **12**, 2, pp. 153–66.

POSTMAN, N. and WEINGARTNER, C. (1969) *Teaching as a Subversive Activity*, Harmondsworth, Penguin.

RUDDOCK, J. (1992) 'Practitioner research and programs of initial teacher education', in RUSSELL, T. and MUNBY, H. (Eds) *Teachers and Teaching*, London, Falmer Press.

SOPHOCLES, (1962) *Three Tragedies: Antigone, Oedipus the King, Electra*, translated by KITTO, H.D.F. Oxford, Oxford University Press.

STYRON, W. (1980) *Sophie's Choice*, New York, Bantam

Part II

Teachers' Identities: Overview

Don Dworet

Several years ago a school superintendent responsible for special education told me that placing a special needs student into a regular classroom should not be a problem because 'a teacher is a teacher' and by definition should be able to teach any type of child. Unfortunately, many of the teachers in his district were quite concerned about this. They believed that they were prepared both professionally and attitudinally to teach only those students who were intellectually and physically capable of learning. Who is correct? Is anyone called 'teacher' an individual capable, willing and able to teach anyone? How teachers view themselves and what factors contribute to this view represent the primary focus for this section.

Teacher 'identities' refers to the different views that individuals have about themselves as teachers in general, and how this view changes over time and in different contexts. Cecilia Reynolds' chapter, based on her keynote address, provides the perspective that our identity as teacher is affected greatly by what surrounds us, what others expect of us, and what we allow to impact on us. The workplace 'landscape' is very pervasive, very demanding, and in most cases, very restrictive. The development from novice to professional brings with it the acceptance of the 'role' of teacher with an implicit understanding that some who accept the title also accept the role. Often the novices' view of what 'teacher' should be conflicts with what they observe and are expected to do. For those who successfully negotiate this dissonance, acceptance of and into the role is easy. For those who wish to maintain a more diverse view of 'teacher' acceptance of the role is often problematic. It is truly the gifted 'gardener' that can develop the landscape, weeds and all, so that all plants receive the sunlight, water and nurturing required for full growth and beauty.

Karyn Cooper and Margaret Olson provide further commentary on the multiple roles that comprise the word 'teacher'. Their chapter reflects the complexity of teacher identity and how 'identity' changes as a result of experience and landscape. Identity is not static but rather quite dynamic, and changes with the circumstances in which teachers find themselves. Cooper and Olson also discuss the difficulty individuals have in confronting the expectations others have of the teacher 'identity' and that those who challenge this identity do so with much difficulty. Though there are different 'identities' there are limits to the range and type these identities may take.

Given the dynamic nature of teacher identity, Janice Martin and Michael Kompf discuss a method which assists teachers in helping them better understand their own identity through journalling and concept mapping. These practices not only assist teachers to better understand how they view themselves but also, through this introspective process, better understand how their interpretation of their identity impacts on students. As demands on teachers change over time, so does their identity. There is little doubt that teachers of the 1990s are facing a much different landscape than teachers of a generation ago.

Maureen Pope and K.W. Yeung provide some information on the student teacher role and the stresses encountered by these individuals as they progress through their student teaching requirements. Concern over practice teaching and not being observed by others is high on their list of concerns. Thought not directly connected to teacher identity, this chapter does provide some insight into the issues faced by developing teachers and the understanding that experienced teachers and faculty counselors have of their role in working with teachers-in-training. Changes in policy regarding who will educate new teachers and whether or not teachers themselves accept this new role as part of their identity is certainly cause for concern. If training new teachers is now part of the landscape in education, how will this additional task affect how teachers view themselves and their responsibility to make room for this additional responsibility?

The final chapter in this section deals with an issue many teachers must confront — their identity as teacher versus a possible competing identity, in this case teacher competing with musician. Joan Tucker describes the experience of an individual originally trained to be an accomplished musician who prefers performing or encouraging others to perform rather than to music class teaching. This is not an isolated incident. It is one which frequently occurs in all schools. Teachers are often asked to teach classes or perform administrative duties which they do not really want to do nor see as part of their individual teacher 'identity'. Some continue to perform well in these other roles and some have much difficulty either in implementing the new role or in obtaining a high degree of personal satisfaction.

What then is teacher identity? Is the superintendent described in the opening paragraph correct? Can this label reflect someone who can be a landscaper under all conditions or are there limitations which inhibit the growth and beauty of the garden. The idea that — a teacher is a teacher is a teacher — is much more complex than the superintendent would have us believe. The chapters which follow provide an excellent framework for examining this issue and offer all of us much to think about.

6   Cultural Scripts for Teachers: Identities and their Relation to Workplace Landscapes

Cecilia Reynolds

I will begin with some personal reflections about the link between identity and landscapes. In the school year 1993/94 I was fortunate enough to have a full year sabbatical, my first, and to spend much of that year travelling in the South Pacific. During that period I had a lot of time to reflect upon my identity. Indeed, my daughter had given me a wonderful quote stating that 'the purpose of a sabbatical was to allow you the time to BE the person you had BECOME'. So, while I was in places like Thailand, Australia and New Zealand, I looked back and reflected upon my experiences and perceptions and thought about my dreams and goals.

I realized through that process, that like most teachers, my everyday surroundings and the fast pace of the school year, had afforded me little time or incentive to do this type of reflection. I realized too, how different the landscapes were in the countries I was visiting from those which surrounded me at home. And it was, to a large extent the act of leaving my usual workworld, of placing myself in unfamiliar contexts that spurred on my reflections about my identity. It was as if I needed this distance and challenge to assist me in not only thinking about who I had become but also in practicing, in these new settings, being that person.

And so it was that over that year, I spent time on beaches and in rainforests, I hiked up mountains and sailed on the ocean . . . that is of course in-between my scheduled conferences and meetings. I also began to spend quite a bit of time in art galleries. I'm not sure exactly why this happened, perhaps it was that I had time to do so, perhaps it was because this seemed to be the sort of thing one did as one travelled . . . Or just maybe, it was because I was looking for something . . . searching for something.

What I found was a renewed appreciation for the link between the art I saw by those who lived in the countries I visited and the beauty of the surrounding landscapes in those countries. If, for example, paintings, sculptures, dances, and symphonies can be viewed, and I believe they can, as expressions of the interior landscapes of people within a culture, then the question arose for me time and again: 'What effect, if any, is there of the elements of the external landscapes where that culture is found?'

My questioning did not start and stop, however, at the doorways to galleries, museums and concert halls. I began also to wonder about artistry of all types, about crafts and knowledges done not only by the celebrated but also by the 'ordinary' people. And, as Eliot Eisner did in his opening address to this conference, I began to wonder about the link between celebrated and ordinary art.

This was most apparent to me during my visit to Northern Australia. I had been to the museum in Darwin and was quite taken with examples of Aboriginal art I had seen, in particular the corkwood dreaming with its intricate dots and designs. The next day I found myself walking along a beach on Cape Tribulation and there in the sand were intricate dots and designs strikingly similar to the artwork I had just seen the day before. The artists in this case, however, had been beetles, sandcrabs and other forms of life busily going about their daily routines, seemingly oblivious to the beauty they left in the sand. Perhaps, I thought, not only are each of us affected by our landscapes, maybe we each, in our own way are able to affect our landscapes.

During my sabbatical travels I began to notice how much the people in the countries I visited fit with their landscapes. How their stature, their speech patterns, their group activities and even the flow of their conversations blended with, and reflected, the spaces around them. They were not existing apart from that space they were an integral element of it. They affected that space and they were affected by it.

On my return to Canada, I began to look at Canadians differently. I began to question how they and I were affected by the spaces of which we are a part. I also began to look at teachers differently. I was working at the time with one of my colleagues, Harry Smaller, on a study of beginning teachers. We had surveyed over 1000 students during their teacher education and then followed up a subgroup of about 300 into the first year following graduation. Finally, we had interviewed an even smaller sample of about sixty three years after graduation.

When I returned from my travels, Harry and I began to analyze the data from that study. Together, we began to question the impact of workplace structures, workplace landscapes if you will, upon teachers. We were curious about how it was that teachers became the persons they were. How their identities related to their everyday worlds. Both Harry and I believed that material conditions were an important part of identity formation and reformation for teachers over time.

I remember once having a somewhat heated discussion with Julie Ellis, a colleague who is now at the University of Alberta, about whether or not it was possible to recognize a teacher in a crowd. My colleague insisted it was not possible. She believed that choosing to teach was a very personal thing and that teachers in the process of teaching more or less drew out of their personalities the various elements that had been there all along but only needed the catalyst of the act of teaching to bring them to the foreground. I, on the other hand, felt that I was sure that I could pick out teachers within any group, let's say at a party or at a restaurant. I felt that there were common traits-mannerisms, the turn of a phrase, the 'teacher's look' — that marked them as part of a group. At the time, we put our differences down to the fact that she was a psychology type and I was a sociology type but, since then, I've come to think it isn't quite that simple. Indeed, our discussion had at its core a difference in standpoints which is often reflected when the topic of teacher identities is raised.

Out of curiosity, as I prepared for this talk, I examined the titles of the sessions for today to see if they could be grouped in any way. Indeed, going from titles alone, it seemed to me that they could and, furthermore, that the groupings revealed some important aspects of today's topic — 'teachers' identities'. While there, of course, are many ways that I could have grouped these, this overhead shows how they can be sorted into two large categories.

On the one hand, there were all these titles that had something to do with the individual . . . On the other hand, there were all these titles that had something to do with groups of individuals . . . I want to make clear that I do not see these two lists as separate from one another. . . . indeed it is the relation between the items on the lists that is my main point this morning. It is interesting, however, to note that we can quite easily come up with a number of ways to describe the two lists. As I have already said, we could think about individuals and groups . . . alternatively, we could describe these as lists of what people deal with when they are alone and . . . when they are together.

If we were George Herbert Mead, the American philosopher, we might consider that one list deals with topics related to the 'I' part of 'self-identity' . . . while the other list deals largely with the 'me' and the 'you'.

If we were the French sociologist Pierre Bourdieu, we might even consider that in one list . . . we have all those things which he calls 'habitus', that is those aspects of ourselves which are part of our individual history and come out of our formative experiences during infancy and also from the whole collective history of our family. . . . while in the other list, we have what Bourdieu calls 'field' — that larger social space ruled by our relationships and the socially constructed organizations in which we find ourselves living out our lives.

If you were me, however, and wanting to write this speech to match the title I came up with many months ago, you might consider that on one list we have 'cultural scripts' . . . those subjectivities available to us to choose from as we play our part and on the other list we have 'workplace landscapes' . . . those conditions which impact upon our performance. What is of interest then is what are the cultural scripts for teachers, what are their workplace landscapes and how do these two areas relate with respect to teachers' identities?

Well in a search for a way to organize this discussion I went to the overall theme of this conference: 'Thinking together . . . Changing research and practice.' What I propose is that we do some thinking about teachers' cultural scripts and see how that thinking leads us to consider changes to our research and practice. And then we do some thinking about teachers' workplace landscapes and look at how that leads to considerations for changes in research and practice.

First of all, I'd like to share my thinking about teachers' 'cultural scripts'. I should begin by saying that I have always had an aversion to any form of deterministic theory about the development of my identity . . . or any one else's for that matter. While I have read about and understand the power of genetics, I basic-ally reject the position that I am merely a biologically programmed replica of my mother. I reject too, the notion that hormones, chemicals and other aspects of my physiology rule in any absolute way who I am and what I can do . . . although, I must admit that the older I get the more respect I have for the limitations of my mind and my body. . . . I recently saw a bumper sticker that said 'Driver suffers from CRA' and in brackets underneath it spelled out that this meant 'Can't Re-member Anything!'

Thanks to writers such as Jane Gallop and Adrienne Rich, I have come to consider the importance of what Gallop calls 'thinking through the body'. I agree with her that for far too long western culture has systematically persuaded us of an immutable split between mind and body, between reason and nature. As Adrienne Rich puts it in her book *Of Women Born*: 'Culture: pure spirit, mind . . . has . . . split itself off from life, becoming the death-culture of quantification, abstraction, and the will to power which has reached its most refined destructive-ness in this century' (Gallop, 1988).

The import of this mind–body split for our discussion today is the part which it has played in theorizing and research traditions in education. The scientific tra-dition of positivism has held that 'reality is fixed and can be observed directly' (Hare-Mustin and Marecek, 1990, p. 27). Constructivism, however, 'asserts that we do not discover reality, we invent it' (Hare-Mustin and Marecek, 1990, p. 27). I like that better.

I like too the notion put forward by Jacques Lacan about the humanist subject as someone whose story can never be fully told since 'at any future point the apparent certainties of the present can be re-visited and re-vised' (Davies, 1993, p. 23). Thus, 'the story of who we take ourselves to be can never be concluded' (Davies, 1993, p. 23).

Like Bronwyn Davies in Australia, I have turned away from traditional socialization theories as adequate explanations of how we become who we are. Those theories focus too strongly on 'the process of shaping the individual that is undertaken by others' (Davies, 1993, p. 13). Instead, I have most recently been working with the notion of subjectification, as put forward in poststructural theory. Here, the focus is on 'the way each person actively takes up the discourses through which they and others speak/write the world into existence . . . Through those dis-courses they are made speaking subjects at the same time that they are subjected to the constitutive force of those discourses' (Davies, 1993, p. 13).

Using this view, teachers, like everyone else, participate in the discourses of which they are a part. They interpret and make sense of their world 'through the storylines of their culture' (Davies, 1993, p. 41). That culture can be argued to provide them with limited choices of appropriate 'subject positions' or 'scripts'. They can do a literal reading of those scripts and/or they can interpret them in new ways. They can accept the scripts available and/or they can search for new and better ones for themselves. Applying this to our data on novice teachers, Harry Smaller and I were able to identify a number of scripts which the culture of teach-ing made available to our new teachers. Among these were:

- the child saver;
- the learned one;
- the super parent/coach/friend; and
- the professional.

Our demographic data on Ontario teachers going as far back as the early 1900s revealed, however, that clearly these scripts consistently had been taken up by only certain 'types' in the overall population. The script for classroom teachers in the elementary schools called for white women of Judeo-Christian beliefs, preferably young and unmarried, definitely virtuous beyond question, and patriotic to the core. The script for secondary school teachers, and administrators at all levels, called for white males of Judeo-Christian beliefs, preferably mature and married, definitely heterosexual, and supportive of the dominant political climate of the day.

What was most troubling for Harry and I, as we examined our data on new teachers in the 1990s, was how little their stories differed in many respects from those of the teachers we had studied in earlier historical periods in Canada. In other words, it appeared to us that scripting and type casting for teachers in our country has been frighteningly static and controlled for over 100 years.

This moves me to the second part of the theme for this conference . . . Changing research and practice . . . because this thinking, this recognition of subjects and cultural scripts reveals how each of us, in attempting to construct our 'selves', does so in ways which are gendered, classed, raced, ethnicized, and so on, by elements of a culture which has many elements which must be questioned. Doing this, however, means that we must move from a positivist to a constructivist perspective because 'whereas positivism asks what the facts are, constructivism asks what the assumptions are; whereas positivism asks what the answers are, constructivism asks what the questions are'. Perhaps for many of you a list of questions will seem very unsatisfying, but it is my view that just such a list is what we need in education at this juncture in time. I am tired of the old questions and their convenient answers.

Following this, I have a number of questions about teachers' identities which I am hoping will be addressed in some of the sessions today. These include:

- What are the boundaries of teachers' dreams and why?
- Why do so many teachers want to be liked?
- When do teachers tell themselves 'You've made it'?
- Can teachers be anything they want to be?

Many of you may be familiar with a film called *Awakenings* which was popular in Canada and elsewhere in the early 1990s. It was about a man who revived briefly from a coma. The doctor in that film was modelled after Oliver Sacks, a real-life physician and author. I want to read a short passage from his most recent book, *From an Anthropologist on Mars* because I believe it is pertinent to this searching for new questions.

> That the brain is minutely differentiated is clear: there are hundreds of tiny areas crucial for every aspect of perception and behaviour . . . The miracle

is how they all co-operate, are integrated together in the creation of a self. This sense of the brain's remarkable plasticity . . . has come to dominate my own perception of my patients and their lives. So much so, indeed, that I am sometimes moved to wonder whether it may be necessary to redefine the very concepts of 'health' and 'disease', to see these in terms of the ability of the organism to create a new organization and order, one that fits its special, altered disposition and needs, rather than in terms of a rigidly defined 'norm'. Sickness implies a contraction of life, but such contractions do not have to occur. Nearly all of my patients, so it seems to me, whatever their problems, reach out to life — and not only despite their conditions, but often because of them, and even with their aid . . . In earlier books I wrote of the 'preservation' of self, and (more rarely) of the 'loss' of self in neurological disorders. I have come to think these terms too simple — and that there is neither loss nor preservation of identity in such situations, but, rather, its adaptation, even its transmutation, given a radically altered brain and 'reality' (Sacks, *The Toronto Globe and Mail*, 1995).

What Oliver Sacks words mean to me is that we should be questioning the 'norms' we may be using. What are we assuming about teachers' realities? What are we failing to acknowledge about the realities of research regarding teachers' identities. How open to change are those realities? What adaptations and transmutations are we all encouraged to undertake by our contexts?

With this in mind, let's turn to 'workplace landscapes' — the second area I wish to focus on with you this morning and the area that roughly describes about half of the papers for today's sessions. Here again, we can begin by 'thinking together' and move on to consider what this means for 'changing research and practice'.

We don't often hear teachers referred to as workers nor are we inclined to describe their classrooms and schools as workplaces. A number of people, however, have recently pointed out that we have much to learn by doing just that. Indeed, Deborah Britzman (1991), in her book *Practice Makes Practice*, introduces the idea that by doing this, we can consider not only the structure of experience but also the experience of structure.

Britzman points out that looming on the landscape of most teachers is the spectre of 'conformity'. Conformity requires 'an adherence to the dictates of social convention and it privileges routinized behavior over critical action. Its centripetal force pulls toward reproducing the status quo in behavior as it mediates our subjective capacity to intervene in the world. Education, when dominated by the discourse and discursive practises of conformity, scripts a mechanistic training' (Britzman, 1991, p. 29).

In our study of novice teachers in Ontario we found evidence of three problems related to the discourse of conformity described by Britzman, and we saw how exposure to workplace landscapes on a sustained basis brought a number of contradictions to the attention of these new teachers. First, our participants had clearly accepted a 'vocationalism' which meant that they saw becoming a teacher as primarily 'an adaptation to the expectations and directives of others and the acquisition of pre-determined skills — both of which are largely accomplished through imitation, recitation and assimilation' (Britzman, 1991, p. 29). At this early stage in their work as teachers, their primary goal was to 'blend in' to their surrounding landscape. To survive 'induction' and to be 'enculturated' as a 'good teacher' according to prescribed definitions and scripts.

What we found in their interviews three years following their teacher education year, was that, those who had found part or full time work in classrooms were shocked by the diversity of the actual landscapes in schools, and they were dismayed by the extent to which those landscapes worked against their being able to perform prescribed teacher scripts as well as they had during rehearsals — those limited opportunities available to them in their teaching practicums.

Secondly, we found evidence that these novice teachers encountered educational psychology as a major edifice in teachers' workplace landscapes, an edifice which had a long shadow. The foundations of that edifice and the language spoken within it were organized around beliefs about the neutrality of knowledge, the primacy of 'facts', the control of behavior, and the objectivity of teachers.

Extended exposure to a variety of school landscapes, however, confused and conflicted these new teachers regarding a number of issues. Many of them began to question previously held beliefs about themselves and about their students. A few expressed concerns about the dominance of a discourse which they now saw as robbing individuals of the 'potential to become something other than what has been predicted'.

The third, and perhaps most problematic area of conformity, however, for these novice teachers was that which revolved around 'efficiency and order' in our schools. Repeatedly, our novice teachers reported that the workplace landscapes they encountered were full of children and young people who did not fit the image of students they had anticipated. Parents too were not always as cooperative as they had expected. These new teachers began to question how they were to maintain order and advance learning when many students fought their attempts to do so and when some parents stood against them. Not surprisingly perhaps, their response was often to blame the children, the parents and even themselves rather than question the dictate for 'efficiency and order' which seemed so clearly a part of the discourse of conformity.

This leads to a number of 'what ifs' in relation to ways that we might be able to transform the dominant discourse of conformity which seems to so adversely affect not only teachers but also students. What if teachers . . .

- came to expect diversity rather than conformity in their classrooms?
- actually worked with one another to solve problems?
- felt free enough to admit that they had problems?
- were encouraged to be reformers, even rebels, and given the necessary supports for their efforts?
- were encouraged to see and deal with the partiality of their own knowledge,

the limits of their ability to control behavior and their subjective responses to their students?
- had a say in the social policies they were asked to implement?
- were treated like professionals rather than children?
- were able to choose when and with whom they wished to collaborate?

Here again, as earlier in my talk, I am suggesting that the act of posing these questions is important — even if we do not believe that we can come up with the 'right' answers. If even some of these 'what if' questions were seriously addressed, then I believe that teachers could begin to consider some new scripts or some ways to rework old scripts.

Teachers might even be able to think in terms of yet another metaphor — that of the landscaper, someone who endeavors to change the lay of the land. As Ingrid Carlgren pointed out in her address for this conference, this is unlikely to work well if teachers merely follow the dictates of an architectural landscaper who never gets down into the dirt. But, it also won't work well if, teachers focus only on their own garden plot and fail to see its relation to the larger overall design of the site.

At the macro level, our educational systems need to be spaces that are both functional and beautiful. We need to make sure that the many different areas which make up our site have sufficient light and that the various structures which are part of the site allow for movement and change over time. We can choose to employ local materials in our constructions or we might want to look outside of our immediate surroundings and import some materials. Our work, however, will ultimately be judged by those who spend the most time at the site because it is they who will know best the amount of upkeep the site requires, how comfortable it is over the long term and how sustainable it is considering the surrounding environment.

In our age of virtual reality, some of us might be tempted to use metaphoric greenhouses so that rare orchids can bloom inside our systems, even when there are arctic conditions outside. We may want to try to irrigate our arid regions, so the unexpected fruit can be gathered. However, like the scientists in the ill-fated fictional *Jurassic Park*, we must never underestimate the power of chaos or the effects of the butterfly's wings.

I don't know about you, but when I think about changing workplace landscapes in schools, I think perhaps it is the image of the gardener, and not that of the architectural landscaper, that comes to mind. Perhaps this is the better image when considering the *local* changes that we might make. In every educational workplace, maybe even the one where you spend much of your time, there are many aspects that are somewhat like the plants and pests found in a household garden. There are hardy perennials that may bloom only once in a while but that keep coming back year after year. There are bright showy annuals. There are leaf hoppers, potato bugs and even slugs. Our school workplaces are also like gardens in that they are periodically at the mercy of changing climatic conditions. They must weather storms, heat waves and sometimes even heavy frosts. Like gardens too, our school workplaces have unruly areas which, despite our best gardening efforts, always seem in need of further attention. There are those pesky weeds, those shady areas, those wet bogs, and those sections that somehow seem to have far too much fertilizer.

As educators, it seems to me, we would do well to listen to the advice of Lorraine Johnson (1995) who writes about gardens in a local Toronto newspaper:

> Gardens, by virtue of the act of gardening are nurtured nature. Gardeners design their gardens with all that this implies. They make choices, they make mistakes, they create beauty, they create failures, but each and every conscious act of putting a trowel in the earth involves a design decision, for better or worse.

Have you ever noticed how a garden can reflect the identity of the gardener? Have you thought about how gardens vary from one country to another — say a French garden as compared to an English garden? Have you noticed how there are certain historical trends or fashions in gardens — from mazes to pools to wildflowers to organic techniques? My point, of course, is that while all these things are worthy of note about gardens and gardeners, they are also important for considerations of teachers and schools and ourselves.

In my address this morning I have focused on two areas . . . 'cultural scripts and workplace landscapes' . . . and suggested that both are useful concepts not only for thinking together about teachers' identities but also for working toward changing research and practice. By examining cultural scripts for teachers, I suggest that we can begin to question a number of taken-for-granted assumptions about the work teachers do and the power they have to effect that work. By considering workplace landscapes, I suggest that we can question the effects of system structures on teachers and their power to change those structures. By considering cultural scripts in relation to workplace landscapes, I suggest that important questions arise and new metaphors and ways of seeing become possible.

References

BRITZMAN, D. (1991) *Practice Makes Practice*, Albany, NY, SUNY Press.

DAVIES, B. (1993) *Shards of Glass*, Cresskill, New Jersey, Hampton Press.

GALLOP, J. (1988) *Thinking through the Body*, New York, Columbus University Press.

HARE-MUSTIN, R. and MARECEK, J. (Eds) (1990) *Making a Difference: Psychology and the Construction of Gender*, New Haven, Yale University Press.

JOHNSON, L. (1995) 'The natural garden, take two', *The Toronto Globe and Mail*, 6 July.

THE TORONTO GLOBE AND MAIL (1995) 'Sack's Secret: To see the gift in affliction', 25 February.

7   The Multiple 'I's' of Teacher Identity

Karyn Cooper and Margaret R. Olson

Abstract

Our research in teacher education and our practice as teachers has led us to wonder how teacher identity develops. Here, we explore contextual factors which elicit differing and possibly contradictory teacher identities. We explore the multidimensional, multilayered and dynamic nature of teacher identity by interweaving theories with stories of our own and other people's experience. We illuminate historical, sociological, psychological and cultural influences which shape teacher identity and endeavor to understand factors which influence the continuous process of teacher identity. We also describe some of the common tensions within individuals as well as between individual and group identities as teachers.

Introduction: Multiple 'I's' of Teacher Identity

We begin by setting a context for conceptualizing self as a process; we then discuss many sources of the self, all of which are in continual interaction. We take a holistic approach to exploring the many facets that contribute to the development of teacher identity. We explore some of the personal/professional interconnections involved in becoming teachers. Stories help us show how the particular and generalizable relate in a dialectic tension as multiple selves are constructed and reconstructed through historical, sociological, psychological and cultural influences which shape how we 'learn' to become teachers. We show how these stories are often discounted within more traditional contexts of teaching and teacher education, leading to fragmentation of self.

Setting the Context: Situating the Self

While we often speak of human beings as having or being a 'self,' our sense of self is much more dynamic, mysterious, complex and multifaceted than any articulation of it can ever be. We do not propose to open an age old debate regarding the nature of our knowledge making systems and the deep tensions between positivistic science and holistic experience. However, it is important to show how rationalistic thought is too reductionistic and simplistic to acknowledge the contextual complexities of self-identity, yet continues to pervade our thoughts, thus becoming influential in shaping teacher identity.

Simplistic views of the self, for example, behaviorist theories developed by Watson in the 1930s, have developed through dualistic notions of knowledge which has led to separation of mind from body. This sense of disembodiment has plagued us since the time Plato wrote *The Republic.* This classical perspective began the divorce between body and mind and the supremacy of rational thought, that is, 'right reason'. The supremacy of rational thought (mind over body) dating back to the Greeks of antiquity continued to rein during the Enlightenment era, exemplified in the famous words of Descartes, *cogito ergo sum.* This dualistic thought that separates reality into pairs of opposites has been held for centuries by western philosophers and is still very much with us today. Johnson (1987, p. x) summarizes this view:[1]

> The world is as it is, no matter what any person happens to believe about it, and there is one correct 'God's-Eye-View' about what the world really is like . . . there is a rational structure to reality, independent of the beliefs of any particular people, and correct reason mirrors this rational structure . . . There is nothing about human beings mentioned anywhere in this account — neither their capacity to understand nor their imaginative activity nor their nature as functioning organisms nor anything else about them.

Many writers have begun to address the sense of fragmentation, or 'disembodiment' often associated with this dualistic view. As Capra (1982); Gilligan, Rogers, and Tolman (1991); and Varela, Thompson, and Rosch (1993) remind us, in the West we have a tendency to interpret our experiences in terms of black or white. As Capra (1982, p. 35) states, 'It is important, and very difficult for us . . . to understand that these opposites do not belong to different categories but are extreme poles of a single whole.' It is not as if scientific understanding is not necessary, however we believe as Varela *et al.* suggest, 'In our present world science is so dominant that we give it the authority to explain even when it denies what is most immediate and direct — our every day experience' (p. 12).

Mead (1934) explores the problematic mind–body dichotomy inherent in classical theories of self. In particular, Mead criticized Watson's behaviorism for trying to impose an unacceptable structure on the self, and for delineating some single set of traits that constitute the basic substance of the self. Mead posited self as process and not as a definable, circumscribed entity, fixed and localized in time and space: 'The self is something which has a development; it is not initially there, at birth, but arises in the process of social experience and activity' (Mead, 1934, p. 135). We take two key points from Mead's work.

Firstly, Mead disputes competing theories that view the self as substantive rather than an ongoing process of experience. Mead's emphasis on process recognizes the basic temporality of experience, experience that is grounded in life itself. The self is in process rather than a static structure unrelated to time and space. More recently, Kerby (1991, p. 6) suggests a person is conceived of as an embodied subject: 'The self, as implied subject, appears to be inseparable from the narrative or life story it constructs for itself or otherwise inherits . . . it is from this story that a sense of self is generated.'

Secondly, Mead views self as a social being and suggests human beings create meaning in their world through the process of interaction with other selves. Kerby (1991, p. 34) tells us 'The self is a social and linguistic construct, a nexus of meaning rather than an unchanging entity.' Mead does not deny the factual existence of objects and events, but he maintains that the significance and meanings of those events and objects can and do change. For example, the fact that Karyn's grandmother immigrated to Canada does not change but the significance of, and meaning of, this event changes over time and according to the perspective of the person interpreting the event. 'Self can never be described without reference to those who surround it' (Taylor, 1989, p. 35). Like Mead and Taylor, we believe that a sense of self develops through transactions between the person and the world, through the personal, cultural and historical aspects of shared narratives. The whole receives its definition from the parts, and reciprocally, the parts can only be understood in reference to the whole. Different aspects of our relationships are interconnected moments that can be separated only artificially for purposes of analysis. To separate is to abstract.

Merleau-Ponty (1962, p. xiii) takes us beyond the modernist dualities of Watson to suggest that as human beings we are in the world but also of the world. 'We are through and through compounded of relationships with the world.' The relationship between mind and body, body and world returns us to life in the broadest possible way. These, as Mead (1934), Merleau-Ponty (1962), Taylor (1989), and Kerby (1991) suggest, identity formation is an ongoing process that involves the interpretation and reinterpretation of our experiences as we live through them — suggesting that focusing on transactive relationships rather than linear models might provide a deeper understanding of the multiple 'I's' of teacher identity. Like Taylor (1989), we imagine many 'sources of the self'.

Sources of the Self

Our understanding of teacher identity is informed by Dewey's (1938) notion that the longitudinal and lateral aspects of experience intercept and unite. This coincides with Mead's theory of self. Thus, teacher identity is continually being informed, formed, and reformed as individuals develop over time and through interaction with others. We now begin to articulate the relationships which shape self-identity by interweaving stories of our own and other people's experience. We illuminate historical, sociological, psychological and cultural influences which shape teacher identity and endeavor to understand factors which influence the continuous process of teacher identity. It is the simultaneousness of these aspects which leads to the multidimensional, multifaceted nature of teacher identity.

Atwood (1988) tells us:

> Time is not a line but a dimension, like the dimensions of space . . . You don't look back along time but down through it, like water. Sometimes this comes to the surface, sometimes that, sometimes nothing. Nothing goes away. (Atwood, 1988, p. 3)

The three narrative fragments below have surfaced for Karyn.

> I open the school door. It is massive, just as massive as the sinking feeling I always have when I get inside. *If* the walls could speak what would they say about the tone plastered upon them, neutral and sanitized, clean and quite respectable like me? (I am the student teacher, the impostor.)
>
> I never see my brother at school. At home we make potato bombs together. We share secret passwords and play, sometimes like contented kittens, sometimes like war mongers. But I never see my brother at school. He lines up on one side of the school and I on the other. (I am the student, child of 6.)
>
> I walk into the school office. I see Christopher. He is standing in the corner, head hung low, body crumpled against the wall . . . Time stands still, his eyes meet mine. I did not expect this 'look' to sweep in from yesterday on the hands of today. Not three feet away, stands our school mission statement, it begins: WE RESPECT THE CHILD. (I am the teacher, caught off guard.)

In reflecting back and forth through these fragments it is possible to make certain preconceptions, theories, and assumptions more explicit, thus opening the questions of how society, history and culture influences who we become as teachers. Gadamer (1991) expounds on this in his notion of effective-historical consciousness. Understanding refers to the moment when one comprehends or re-experiences the lived experience of self or other. Understanding and self-understanding frees one to fuller self-knowledge. 'Meaning is what understanding grasps in the essential reciprocal interaction of the whole and parts' (Palmer, 1969, p. 118).

Compliance to Stereotypical Images: A Given Role

The first fragment presented above portrays the feelings Karyn had as a student teacher. Returning to school as teacher brought her in direct contact with those 'sinking feelings', the ghosts of childhood agonies. Those childhood agonies were knocking on the door in some distant room but could barely be heard against the backdrop of child development models and theories she was being taught to absorb within the context of teacher education. Margaret shares a similar story of Susan, a preservice teacher:

> Susan entered her preservice education determined to help all children. Her focus on special needs students in particular was a reflection of her story of her younger brother's experience as a special needs student in elementary schools. One of Susan's preservice courses focused on assessment. As Susan learned all the theories which she initially imagined would enable her to help students like her brother, she began to feel a sense of discomfort. She could not make connections between the decontextualized theories which she was memorizing and any of her still very uncertain beliefs of how to interact with students. Her nemesis came the day she was required to go out to a school and do a reading assessment on a particular student. She had prepared carefully ahead of time in order to do the best job possible. However, she could make no connections between the objective, standardized test she was expected to administer and the child sitting in front of her. She described the actual situation to me as 'sitting with an alien'. (Olson, 1993, p. 131)

For Susan and for us, and for many other preservice, inservice and university teachers there is a tension between personal knowledge of children (our own childhood histories) and the many objectivist models in teacher education. Clandinin and Connelly (1992, p. 368) suggest that a predominant mode of teacher preparation grows out of a long tradition of the objective construction of knowledge that leads to distanced ways of knowing, which also limits the ability of the teacher to see oneself as a curriculum maker.

We believe that the story of becoming a teacher begins early. As Mead's theories suggest, the present has meaning only as it relates to the past (history) and future (purpose). Jalongo and Isenberg (1995, p. 36) illustrate how 'teachers integrate their reminiscences of childhood and their present and future actions' with a story, 'Kindergarten Rebel', told by Mark Connelly. Mark tells of being reprimanded by his kindergarten teacher for attempting to join the girls at the 'kitchen table where the females of the class learned to serve tea and cookies like proper young ladies' (p. 37). He knew he would be allowed out of the 'think box' if he could apologize convincingly enough. However, in this particular instance, when his teacher asked Mark if he had anything he wanted to tell her, he replied, 'Yes. I don't think that it is fair that boys aren't allowed to play in the kitchen.' He goes on to describe the situation that followed:

> Confident that I held the high moral ground, I awaited a stimulating debate. Instead, a look of rage swept across my teacher's face as she spat out, 'Young man, I thought that I told you to come back here and think about your poor behavior. Apparently, you did no thinking at all. You will spend the remaining hour of the morning right here, and I don't want to hear another word out of your mouth!' (p. 38).

Now a high school teacher, Mark concludes that 'looking back on it now, I realize what Mrs McWilliams gave to me during that hour in the "thinking box"

— an opportunity to contemplate my new role in life as a defender of gender equity' (p. 39). Mark's story exemplifies that we are social beings and that preservice teachers' actions are not strictly determined by present circumstances nor tightly constrained by the past. Rather they are creating their world while also being shaped by it.

One may, however, wonder how preservice teachers will be free to act within their chosen profession, especially when traditional models of teacher education seem to be based on objectivist traditions which tend to sever mind from body thereby forcing the eradication of bodily history or personal knowledge. Is it little wonder, then, that Susan felt like she was sitting with an alien? Was she not being forced to assume a role that was in many ways foreign to her. Perhaps this is because, as Britzman (1991) suggests, the stereotypical images of the profession compel preservice teachers to 'take on' an identity more than construct one . . . 'becoming a teacher may mean becoming someone you are not' (Britzman, 1991, p. 4). It seems to us that this assumed role entails knowing at a distance; to survive may mean to soak one's self in traditional stereotypical images that do little to encourage 'real' living relationships between human beings. Currently, teacher identity is shaped predominantly by an over-reliance on the technical theories of behaviorism and cognitivism. We now turn directly to some of these theories to examine their influence on teacher identity.

Psychological Theories: Creating an Unnatural Split Between Child and Adult Identity

One would be hard pressed to find a preservice or inservice teacher who can not recite Piaget's stage theories on child development. While such theories may provide useful developmental indicators, they do little to help us understand the holistic significance or meaning of a child's actions and how the child relates to the world. The over-reliance on developmental stage theories and our insidious penchant for prediction and control places us on a path that faces one direction, a direction that often ignores an organic relationship between child and adult. Kennedy (1986) speaks of the way in which so much education theory is 'adultomorphic' taking some adult end state as the norm toward which children should be socialized.[2] O'Neill (1989, p. 50) also suggests that cognitive approaches to child development fail to recognize a 'living cohesion', 'in which the embodied self experiences it self while belonging to this world and others, clinging to them for its content'. Of particular relevance to self identity and teacher identity (the two are inseparable except for purposes of analysis) is the fact that children have been storied socially, intellectually and culturally as separate despite the fact that we may know on 'a tacit level that there exists an immutable union between children and adults'. Van den Berg (1975) echoes this sentiment:

> The child today has become separated from every thing belonging to the adult's life. Nowadays, two separate states of human life can be

distinguished: the state of maturity, with all the very mature attributes belonging to it, birth, death, faith, and sexuality; and the state of immaturity, which lacks these attributes. (Van den Berg, 1975, p. 32)

While these theories reflect and are reflected in cultural and societal values and beliefs, ignoring the organic relationship between childhood and adulthood results in a compartmentalized self.[3] Aries (1972) sheds further light on how this situation has come into being. In particular he speaks about the societal shift in education when children were separated from adults, sent off to buildings to be educated *en masse*. Home and school became separate; families became separate. Karyn's story of lining up on the opposite side of the school building from her brother epitomizes this fragmentation. Individuals are not only separated according to particular characteristics (e.g., adult–child, male–female, biology–history), but these categories also have different levels of status. This hierarchical framework is particularly problematic in regard to identity because it renders the child inferior to the adult. The child is always found to be lacking. We believe the hierarchy inherent in stage theories of development create fragmentation both within ourselves and between ourselves and our students. An example of this hierarchical fragmentation from one's own past and one's students is shown in the following story told to Karyn:

> I went to the university library to copy a few articles. As I went through the turnstile to gain access to the library I noted just how unusually crowded the library was . . . It occurred to me that the library was probably packed because of final exams. This sudden thought produced an odd feeling in my gut. I wondered why I felt such an intense feeling bubble up inside. It was dead silent. No visiting, just people sitting all alone, cramming and stuffing themselves with the appropriate knowledge to spit out later. I could not help remembering being in the same position as those 'poor students!' I wanted to leave as quickly as possible. I grabbed the articles and set to my task at the copy machine. That familiar smell of the photocopy machine transported me back to the time when I was teaching . . . I was now standing in front of that machine as teacher. Strangely, I felt better. I would be the one giving the exam. (Cooper, in press)

As the child moves toward becoming an 'educated adult', the child is lost as the previous story shows. Many theories ask us to forget ourselves and yet to understand who we are we must pay attention to ourselves and others in and through our relationships. In attempting to replace the self-identity developed through the embodied history of the child with an imposed external reality, the pressure to conform may lead us to deny our sense of self-identity when we perceive ourselves as separate objects. When self becomes separate and objectified, the compartmentalized nature severs relationships. Is it little wonder then, that as 'teacher' Karyn was caught off-guard and uneasy by the look on Christopher's face as he stood near that empty mission statement. It was in Christopher's look that Karyn was reminded that our relationship with children affects us as we affect it. The hypocrisy of the dead mission statement epitomized the lack of lived connection between adult and child.

It was in Christopher's look that Karyn realized we have lost our way. Despite this unease, she too became part of the many theories and banal mission statements involving children that underpin our cultural stories. As Craig (1995, p. 24) tells us, it is situations like this which 'create the dilemmas that gnaw at my soul'. And yet how could it be any different when the story in traditional teacher education programs may be so akin to the childhood experience of school for many teachers in training (and we use this word advisedly) that they may not question the need for the story to be any different. And often, if they do there may be few places to question that the story should be otherwise.

Where Our Prescribed Role as Teacher Begins

Teacher identity is also embedded within the larger historical and cultural story of education. We now look at a brief history of education in North America in general and Canada in particular. Beginning in the mid-nineteenth century, Canadian schools were viewed as 'an important instrument of social cohesion — so necessary in an era of rapid change. It would bind the diverse social elements together with one set of values and political beliefs' (Titley and Miller, 1982, p. 58). When Canada became a nation in its own right in 1867, the schools became a crucial means for cementing a cohesive Canadian identity. Titley and Miller (1982) tell us:

> The new nation of Canada, a shaky amalgam of disparate entities unsure of its identity and future, looked to public education to forge a sense of unity and political loyalty. This was of particular concern in Ontario where the tactic employed was the 'Canadianization' of the curriculum. Yet the new English-Canadian nationalism did not undermine one of the original purposes of the school — the inculcation of the Victorian puritan ethic. Canadian texts were equally redolent of a vigilant moralizing as those they replaced. Social stability remained a central aim of education and the concept of Canadian nationality was wedded to this. (Titley and Miller, 1982, p. 58)

Teachers were selected and trained to conform with this vision. This history has had a profound effect on the identities of all teachers.[4] Currently, Canada's multiculturalism policies espouse 'pluralism, diversity, and variety, which, it is confidently maintained, are the essence of Canada's national identity' (Lupul, 1982, p. 211). Yet when this pluralism is focused at the level of individuals, 'the pluralism rooted in ethnicity and thus the pluralism of language is ignored in the hope that it will somehow go away' (Lupul, 1982, p. 212). Lost voice represents lost identity. The following story told to Margaret (Personal communication, 14 February, 1994) by one of her students is a telling example:

Carla approached me hesitantly, saying she would like to talk about the difficulties she was having in completing her practicum journal. She wanted to become a teacher to help others share in the advantages she felt she could bring back to the reservation where many of her people lived. Carla had been educated off the reserve in a white, middle class, English speaking environment where she had thrived. She wanted to share the things she had learned with Native students who lived on the reservation and whom she initially perceived as less fortunate than herself. She was tremendously excited about her practicum placement which was in a grade one Ojibwa immersion classroom. However, this experience brought terrifying questions of self-identity to the surface for Carla. It soon became apparent to her how fundamentally different the Native culture was from the culture in which she had been educated. She felt an overwhelming sense of loss when she realized that the grade one students were much more fluent in Ojibwa than she, who was taking a course in Ojibwa for the first time. How could she teach these children when she could not even speak the language? And if she could speak, whose voice would she use? Where was her sense of herself as an Ojibwa woman? Everything she had learned to value in society (and in herself) was brought into question as she realized she had lost the essential connections she needed with her Native culture if she were going to help educate these children. Who was she anyway?

There have also been other consequences for women in particular as teachers. When schools were opened to the general public in the late nineteenth century, the increased need for teachers led to the employment of women. As more women moved into teaching positions, men moved up in the educational hierarchy (Patterson, 1986; Urban, 1990), becoming administrators or teacher educators. Patterson (1986, p. 14) points out that 'growth of professional commitment and responsibility among teachers was retarded by the obvious depreciation of the role of teacher and by the society's failure to give women teachers equal place with their male counterparts'.

Grumet (1988) describes structures in classrooms and demands on teachers which perpetuate the established paternal authority where prediction and control silences personal voices. Le Guin refers to this dominant discourse as the 'father tongue'. She calls for a new discourse which involves also listening to the 'mother tongue' the language of poor men, women, and our children (Le Guin, 1989). Teachers who entered the profession found it nearly impossible to build and sustain the kinds of human relationships which would support the risk and trust necessary for learning to occur as classrooms became increasingly objective and impersonal. Instead, they were delivering their students to a patriarchy with its disdain for the private and the familiar. Grumet states: 'The ideal teacher was one who could control the children and be controlled by her superiors' (p. 43). It is little wonder then, that many feel like impostors when taking on the prescribed role of 'teacher' when this role seems to imply abandoning the child by perpetuating the notion that the child is a lesser being with no voice apart from the one we give it. In a setting where the private and the familiar are denied, or where the private and familiar feel out-of-place and awkward, neither teachers nor students will risk personal expression. Difficulties occur when multiplicity of meaning is suppressed in order to take on a prescribed role. For these reasons we believe it is essential to look a little closer at how and why teachers, particularly women, have been silenced over time.

Emerging from Patriarchy: A Silent Identity

Michelle Fine (1987, p. 172) documents the insidious push towards silence in low-income schools. In essence she shows us children learn to emulate passivity and silence through the teacher's (in most cases women) who have often been silenced themselves. In particular, her essay looks at how conversations in schools are often closed, while others are dichotomized. Fine states that 'a self-critical analysis of the fundamental ways in which we teach children to betray their own voices is crucial'. Belenky, Clinchy, Goldberg, and Tarule (1986), in linking self, voice, and mind, show us how integral voice is to the development of self-identity. It seems somewhat inevitable that voiceless children later go on to be voiceless adults (and teachers). Our system of education with its emphasis on control and the inevitable silence that results, is reproduced through our children who may themselves go on to be teachers. It seems likely that we will always expect our young to ascribe to certain values and beliefs that affect their sense of identity, however we feel it is important to be both aware and critical of just exactly what it is that we are asking our children and teachers to become. Failure to do so may result in the continuous perpetuation of a 'prescribed' and passive role, one that ultimately affects us all.

Revisiting the Text

In this essay we have looked at some of the cultural, psychological, sociological and historical aspects which influence our sense of self as teachers. In particular we have shown how such influences create tensions between systems and individuals. The real problem arises when the multiplicity of meaning is suppressed in order to take on a 'prescribed' role. This prescribed role often entails suppressing the personal voice in favour of an objective and distanced voice. In such cases, individuals lacking power to define the situation are left with little alternative other than to assume the prescribed role. In other words the dominant person or group does not need to take the role of the other, while the subordinate must do so or drop out of the system. If we ignore this situation, and the extent to which traditional models of education, educational theories, social codes, and traditions delimit who we are, we do little other than perpetuate out-dated views that cause a fundamental lack of connection and greater responsibility towards children.

For these reasons we believe we must become more aware of what happens when the multiplicity of selves, our many voices, are suppressed under a dominant discourse which has spanned centuries and take action within our institutions. We

Karyn Cooper and Margaret R. Olson

believe that by understanding selfhood as a process of social interaction we can explore the extent to which social norms both delimit and embrace who we are and what we may become through our action.

Notes

1 See Richard Rorty's (1989) *Philosophy and the Mirror of Nature* for a comprehensive understanding of objectivism and its assumptions and implications. It is also well worth noting that Susan Bordo's (1990) essay entitled 'Feminism, postmodernism, and gender-scepticism' in *Feminism/Postmodernism* reminds us that feminism 'initiated the cultural work of exposing and articulating the *gendered* nature of history, culture, and society' (p. 137).
2 A brief look at a class in child studies reveals that one of the upcoming films called *Breaking the Child in*, focuses on reinforcers, punishment and training sessions all based on socializing children into what many experts would regard as appropriate adult behavior.
3 Many of these theories seem to do little more than separate children from a greater relationship with the adult community. The perpetuation of such theories is understandable given that we seem to be a culture with a desire for control, efficiency and quick answers rather than one that strives to understand life as a web of relationships.
4 Egerton Ryerson's influence continued long after his death in 1882. In 1908 the author of the first history of Ontario education concluded: 'So complete is the system, so carefully is every contingency provided for, that the observer . . . is apt to feel that its completeness is perhaps its greatest defect.' Sixty years later the Hall-Dennis Report came to the same conclusion (Wilson, 1982, p. 88).

References

ARIES, P. (1972) *Centuries of Childhood*, BALDICK, R. (Transl), New York, Vintage Books.
ATWOOD, M. (1988) *Cat's Eye*, Toronto, McClelland and Stewart.
BELENKY, M., CLINCHY, B., GOLDBERG, N. and TARULE, J. (1986) *Women's Ways of Knowing: The Development of Self, Voice, and Mind*, New York, Basic Books.
BORDO, S. (1990) 'Feminism, postmodernism, and gender-scepticism', in NICHOLSON, L.J. (Ed) *Feminism/Postmodernism*, New York, Routledge, pp. 133–56.
BRITZMAN, D. (1991) *Practice Makes Practice: A Critical Study of Learning to Teach*, New York, Suny Press.
CAPRA, F. (1982) *The Turning Point: Science, Society, and the Rising Culture*, Toronto, Bantam.
CLANDININ, D.J. and CONNELLY, F.M. (1992) 'Teacher as curriculum maker', in JACKSON, P.W. (Ed) *Handbook of Research on Curriculum*, New York, Macmillan, pp. 363–401.
COOPER, K. (in press) 'On returning to school: Adults' lived experiences', *The Journal of Educational Thought*.
CRAIG, C. (1995) 'A story of Tim's coming to know sacred stories in school', in CLANDININ, D.J. and CONNELLY, F.M., *Teachers' Professional Knowledge Landscapes*, New York, Teachers College Press, pp. 88–101.
DEWEY, J. (1938) *Experience and Education*, New York, Macmillan.
FINE, M. (1987) 'Silencing in public schools', *Language Arts*, **64**, 2, pp. 157–74.

GADAMER, H.G. (1991) *Truth and Method*, New York, Crossroad Publishing Corp.

GILLIGAN, C., ROGERS, A.G. and TOLMAN, D. (Eds) (1991) *Women and Girls in Psychotherapy: Reframing Resistance*, Binghamton, NY, Harrington Park Press.

GRUMET, M. (1988) *Bitter Milk: Women and Teaching*, Amherst, University of Massachusetts Press.

JALONGO, M.R. and ISENBERG, J.P. (1995) *Teachers' Stories: From Personal Narrative to Professional Insight*, San Francisco, Jossey-Bass.

JOHNSON, M. (1987) *The Mind in the Body*, Chicago, The University of Chicago Press.

KENNEDY, D. (1986) 'Young children's thinking: An interpretation from phenomenology', Unpublished doctoral dissertation, University of Kentucky.

KERBY, A. (1991) *Narrative and the Self*, Bloomington, Indiana University Press.

LE GUIN, U. (1989) *Dancing at the Edge of the World*, New York, Harper and Row.

LUPUL, M.R. (1982) 'Multiculturalism and Canadian national identity: The Alberta experience', in TITLEY, E.B. and MILLER, P.J. (Eds) *Education in Canada: An Interpretation*, Calgary, AB, Detselig Enterprises, pp. 209–18.

MEAD, G. (1934) *Mind, Self and Society*, Chicago, University of Chicago Press.

MERLEAU-PONTY, M. (1962) *Phenomenology of Perception*, SMITH, C. (Transl), London, Routledge and Kegan Paul.

O'NEILL, J. (1989) *The Communicative Body: Studies in Communicative Philosophy, Politics, and Sociology*, Evanston, Northwestern University Press.

OLSON, M. (1993) 'Narrative authority in (teacher) education', Unpublished doctoral dissertation, University of Alberta. Edmonton, Alberta.

PALMER, R. (1969) *Hermeneutics: Interpretation Theory in Schleiermacher, Dilthey, Heidegger and Gadamer*, Evanston, Northwestern Press.

PATTERSON, R.S. (1986) 'Voices from the past: The personal and professional struggle of rural school teachers', in JONES, D.C., SHEEHAN, N.M. and WILSON, J.D. (Eds) *Schools in the West: Essays in Canadian Educational History*, Calgary, AB, Detselig Enterprises.

RORTY, R. (1979) *Philosophy and the Mirror of Nature*, Princeton, Princeton University Press.

TAYLOR, C. (1989) *Sources of the Self*, Cambridge, Harvard University Press.

TITLEY, E.B. and MILLER, P.J. (1982) 'Education in Ontario in the nineteenth century', in TITLEY, E.B. and MILLER, P.J. (Eds) *Education in Canada: An Interpretation*, Calgary, AB, Detselig Enterprises, pp. 57–9.

URBAN, W.J. (1990) 'Historical studies of teacher education', in HOUSTON, W.R. (Ed) *Handbook of Research on Teacher Education*, New York, Macmillan, pp. 59–71.

VAN DEN BERG, J. (1975) *The Changing Nature of Man*, New York, Delta Publishing.

VARELA, F., THOMPSON, E. and ROSCH, E. (1993) *The Embodied Mind*, Cambridge, The MIT Press.

WILSON, J.D. (1982) 'The Ryerson years in Canada west', In TITLEY, E.B. and MILLER, P.J. (Eds) *Education in Canada: An Interpretation*, Calgary, AB, Detselig Enterprises, pp. 61–91.

8 Teaching in Inclusive Classroom Settings: The Use of Journals and Concept Mapping Techniques

Janice M. Martin and Michael Kompf

Abstract

The inclusion of exceptional students in the mainstream of education presents many challenges, the greatest of which may relate to behaviorally difficult/disordered students. A process to assist teachers in this regard was investigated. Concept mapping techniques were used to determine teacher concepts of effective teaching practice and to evaluate changes in that conceptualization. Through a process of journalling emphasizing reflection and goal setting teachers appeared able to modify teaching practice to better accommodate student needs. Teachers were partners as well as leaders in the practice of education. They further determined relinquishing control of the goings on in the classroom and gave more ownership and responsibility to students. This was a reversal of the findings from the preliminary concept map. The need for reflective practice techniques was claimed to be beneficial to teachers of the inclusive classroom. Concept mapping was a invaluable tool in this process.

Introduction

The current trend during this decade has been the merger of special and regular education streams resulting in a movement called inclusion. Definitions for inclusion range from partial integration and partial inclusion, to full integration. The confusing discussion of definitions underscores the uncertainty of approach as well as 'best practice' with respect to inclusion. For our purposes, inclusion is defined as the practice of fully including exceptional students in the regular education setting. The challenges of inclusion are dealt with primarily by the regular education teacher. Special education teachers have become resource teachers whose responsibilities may be expanded to serve the special educational needs of a region rather than a single school. Should a school be fortunate enough to have a special education resource teacher, this teacher must provide resource services to the entire school. Thus the services which can be provided are rather limited with respect to individual teacher and/or student. The regular education teachers are left on their own to face any challenges which may become overwhelming with behaviorally difficult students. Without appropriate supports, resources, knowledge and skills available, the exclusion of the behaviorally difficult/disordered student from the classroom may result. These students can often be found warming the bench by the principal's office or sitting on the floor outside a closed classroom door. How can these teachers be assisted in becoming more willing and able to deal effectively so that exclusion is not a teaching strategy? The answer may lie within each individual teacher and their conceptualization of effective teaching practice, which if examined, may indicate need. If the teacher is able to identify these needs, then changes may facilitate inclusive educational practice.

Background

The improvement of educational opportunities for children and youth is fraught with challenges that seem insurmountable. Inclusion initiatives have caused an uproar in educational research and practice communities with strong division of opinion as to the merits in educational practice. With respect to the behaviorally disordered, the division becomes extreme. Violence free schools/safe schools initiatives have a detrimental effect for the now-included behaviorally disordered student. Economic factors force cutbacks in resources and services, with negative results. It thus rests with the regular classroom teacher to act as a positive change agent for this at-risk student population. While regular educators do not have the benefit of specific training in the context of the regular education classroom, alternative methods having the teacher: focus on themselves; include the use of concept mapping, journalling and interviews as a strategy for reflective practice can benefit all students. An understanding of knowledge assimilation and construction forms the basis for understanding how these powerful heuristics serve teachers.

Knowledge is constructed (Novak and Gowin, 1984, p. 4). As a person experiences an event, he or she assimilates information into his or her existing concept structure and reorganizes the affected domain. This involves reconstruction of concepts in addition to reorganization of concept structures, much like finding a missing piece to a puzzle that was thought to be complete. The additional piece requires a shifting and rearrangement of others. If changes are minor, the change is trivial. If changes are dramatic and carry the need for reordering and remapping of the concepts and conceptual change, then the impact is deemed to be radical. Knowledge then is not some found commodity like oil or gold, although Novak and Gowin (1984) point out that discovery plays a part in providing the experience from which knowledge is constructed. Knowledge is conceptualized in the mind where different concepts are assimilated and added into prior existing stores of concepts (like the puzzle piece). Language is the symbolic representation of the understanding of the constructed concepts.

New knowledge is assimilated into existing knowledge (the constructivist view of knowledge acquisition). As such, progressive differentiation occurs when new concepts are linked non-arbitrarily to existing cognitive structures (Novak, 1990, p. 10). 'Integrative reconciliation occurs when sets of concepts are seen in new relationships' (Novak, 1990, p. 10). There are two levels of concept structures, superordinate and subordinate concepts that are organized into a hierarchical construction. This structure of concepts is not permanent, it undergoes constant change as new knowledge is assimilated and 'constructed' into the existing hierarchy. When a superordinate concept is assimilated, there occurs significant integrative reconciliation of subordinate concept structures along with further concept differentiation. In essence, a ripple effect is created which results in a change in perception. It is this potential for change in perception that suggests a powerful heuristic for teacher education. 'If new experiences provide a basis for meaningful learning, new concepts will be added to an individual's concept map and/or new relationships will be evident between previous concepts. Over time, concept relationships may take on new hierarchical organization' (Novak, 1990, p. 10). According to Novak (1990) superordinate learning occurs only infrequently and only as the result of meaningful learning. Most learning occurs at the subsumption level with resultant progressive differentiation. To make meaning from new experiences is a uniquely human ability that Novak (1990) refers to as 'human constructivism'. Meaningful learning occurs when there is a radical change in the hierarchical organization of existing concepts through the assimilation of new ones.

The need for time is echoed by Purkey (1992). Concepts are described as being 'remarkably conservative' and tending to resist change. He states 'From a phenomenal viewpoint, to ask a person to change is to ask that person to be someone else' (Purkey, 1992, p. 20). Change is not impossible, it takes time and must be viewed as non-threatening. As new ideas 'filter into the perceptual world of the perceiving person, old ideas fade away' (p. 21). What Purkey is describing here is that prior knowledge, concepts, are undergoing a process of progressive differentiation as new concepts are assimilated and new meaning is thus constructed. It is a continuous process of assimilation and change. Much of the change as described is seen as trivial constructivism, that is, the modification and hierarchical reorganization of existing knowledge due to the assimilation of new concepts. Radical constructivism occurs, as stated, only infrequently, and only as the result of meaningful learning that corrects misperception and therefore misconception of previously held perceived truths. Such radical reconstruction will see a dramatic reorganization of the hierarchical arrangement of concepts as well as the linkages between them and further, actual changes in the concepts held as true.

If knowledge is constructed by each individual through their perceptions and expressed conceptually, then a diagram or map of how individuals perceive the portion of the world that is being studied can be devised. In the field of education, the mapping of a teacher's conceptualization of teaching practice can form a powerful tool for teacher education. Existing knowledge construction can be mapped and examined, deficits, omissions and errors can be noted, and, through the provision of meaningful learning opportunities, can be more positively constructed.

Teacher Perception and Attitude

If education is the 'laboratory' as Dewey (cited in Novak, 1989, p. 230) has suggested, then the teacher can be viewed as the scientist functioning within the laboratory of the classroom. How the teachers perceive their function and their students is critical for success. In a study of teacher attitude with respect to the mainstreaming of learning disabled students, Larrivee and Cook (1979) conclude that 'teacher perception of degree of success in dealing with the special needs child is the single most important variable' (p. 321). With respect to the behaviorally disordered student, teacher attitudes and confidence levels are considerably less than positive (Antonak, 1980) resulting in a less than positive educational experience for the behaviorally disordered student, whose population has the highest referral rates for alternative placement than any other, and whose population is least desirable in the regular education setting than any other exceptionality (save the severely and profoundly impaired) (Antonak, 1980). This can be attributed to teacher misconceptualizations of the disability. Campbell, Dobson and Bost (1985) state that 'educators' perceptions of the seriousness of behavior problems may be based, in part, on the judgment of whether the student has the capacity to 'know better' (p. 302). When teachers perceived that students were capable of controlling inappropriate behavior 'a 6:1 ratio was found between the frequency of authoritarian types of recommended treatments to the frequency of non-authoritarian types of recommended treatments' (p. 302). In short, where the student was perceived by the teacher to be capable, punishment was the treatment of choice in spite of indications 'that punishment is generally ineffective and may even lead to further behavioral problems' (Meacham and Wiesen cited by Campbell, Dobson and Bost, 1985, p. 302). Students with emotional or behavioral disorders are often considered by school personnel to choose deliberately to exhibit a pattern of social deviance that is highly aversive to others. That is, these children and youth are thought of as capable of behaving in more appropriate ways but as actively deciding not to do so (Kauffman *et al.*, 1991, p. 306).

Further to this, problems are erroneously thought to be more suitably addressed through procedures designed simply to control, contain, and punish their misbehavior under the assumption that they simply must be forced to behave appropriately (Weinberg and Weinberg, 1990 cited in Kauffman *et al.*, 1991, p. 306). Teacher attitude matters in the success of students, academically and socially (Cooper and Good, 1983; Horne, 1985; Larrivee and Cook, 1979; and, Larrivee and Horne, 1991) and supports findings that teacher attitudes, expectation and self efficacy are largely negative with respect to the behaviorally disordered student. To make a positive change then, it will be necessary to enhance teacher attitude, increase self efficacy, and reconceptualize the disability through meaningful learning opportunities.

Concept Mapping

Concept mapping is a process whereby a graphic representation is created of the various concepts and linkages of knowledge and understanding. Linkages between the concepts reveal pathways of individual rationalization and understanding. A visual 'road map' (Novak and Gowin, 1984, p. 15) demonstrates how concepts and meanings are connected and interconnected in a hierarchical schematic. Concept mapping can be carried out in non-structured manner (where there is a free recall of concepts and/or a brainstorming of concepts organized into a map about a general topic) or in a structured method involving 'a fixed list of concepts from which to draw upon' (Winitzky *et al.*, 1994, p. 126). Maps can be scored and/or compared in a variety of ways ranging from simple comparisons to a detailed examination of structural complexity.

Concept mapping is versatile and can be used as an assessment and evaluative device documenting the current level of understanding and subsequent growth. It can be effectively used as a learning tool for the teaching of others and self instruction. Beyerbach uses concept mapping for student assessment with the following conclusion; 'Perhaps the best argument for the use of concept maps in assessing students' representation of structural knowledge is that students were able to see a visual representation of the changes in their thinking from pre to post' (1988, p. 346). Her findings 'from both the quantitative and qualitative analysis indicated students' maps became more differentiated, organized, and evidenced the development of a shared technical vocabulary' (Beyerbach, 1986, p. 2). Beyerbach also found that 'the qualitative analysis of the maps was the richest source of information about content and organization of students' thinking' (p. 11). SenGupta (1993) used concept mapping techniques as part of a mixed-method research design as the method by itself is a blend of qualitative and quantitative elements. Both elements play significant roles and are both required to make the process meaningful (SenGupta, 1993, p. 5). Roegge *et al.*, found that concept mapping 'proved to be an effective tool for getting the stakeholder groups to conceptualize Tech Prep' [technical preparation programs] (1993, p. 13). Dana (1993) studied preservice elementary teachers in a social studies methods course. Concept mapping was taught as pedagogical tool to be used by the teachers in their teaching of the subject and to determine how teachers make sense of teaching. These teachers had to reflect on their beliefs regarding knowledge to complete the final concept mapping exercise.

Prospective teachers realize that knowledge about the teaching and learning of elementary school social studies exists inside their own heads as they reflect on, and make sense of, their experiences and describe this realization as empowering. Having this personal vision represented visually through a concept map gives prospective teachers confidence in their ability to teach (Dana, 1993, p. 10).

Reflection

In many studies, teacher reflection was part of the process through which teachers can identify and thus capture meaningful learning experiences. The practice of reflection refers to intentionally examining a specific event and/or experience, evaluating the components of the event/experience, and using the conclusions drawn in future planning to enhance teaching and learning. It recognizes that teachers have much professional knowledge and skill but need to intentionally take the time to read the textbook of their minds to gain benefit. Teachers need to be taught how to open this textbook within and access the knowledge therein in order to refine, reconstruct, reorganize and reorder existing concepts through assimilation and meaningful learning. In short, teachers will be engaged in the activity of constructing knowledge and will have become the 'human constructionists' that Joseph Novak has described (1990). It is the intentionality of the act of reflection that makes it part of professional practice.

Reflective practice is described as occurring on three levels which are; the technical, the practical, and the critical in ascending order of importance and influence. Regardless of model used, researchers have expressed difficulty in the encouragement of teachers to 'attain the "higher" levels of reflection' (Zeichner, 1993, p. 14) required for meaningful learning. The higher levels are defined as critical reflection levels. This may be due in large part by the logistical organization of the school operations. Zeichner calls for the reorganization of schooling to facilitate a culture of inquiry and reflection. Reflective practices can be viewed as 'the enabling constructs that permit "that reconstruction or reorganization of experience which adds to meaning of experience and which increases ability to direct the course of subsequent experience"' (Dewey, 1916, p. 76 cited by Novak, 1989, p. 239). In other words, teachers need effective methods of 'getting smarter about important things' (Novak, 1989, p. 239).

Cognitive Rehearsal (Debriefing)

Debriefing is the process by which a subject shares his or her recollection and interpretation of an experience with another. It stems from the recognition that people involved in complex situations cannot recall in detail without distortion all that they have experienced unless given the opportunity to share and review their accounts with others. Such a process was effectively employed for use with spies and astronauts after the completion of a mission (Raths, 1987, p. 25). Debriefing allows the subject to reflect on the learning experience and to make sense of what has been experienced.

Debriefing gives students relatively free rein to organize, compare, classify, evaluate, summarize, or analyze an experience. The product of the debriefing process is an articulated sense of 'meaning' (Raths, 1987, p. 27). While Raths describes the use of the debriefing strategy with elementary students, it follows that the findings would hold for their teachers as well. The process of recalling and sharing is referred to as 'cognitive rehearsal' (Raths, 1987, p. 27) and serves to enhance meaningful learning. Cognitive rehearsal can be identified as a positive adjunct to reflective practice.

Improving Teacher Practice in the Inclusive Classroom: Research Study

Teachers bring into their classrooms various perceptions, biases, expectations and a conceptual representation of their teaching practice. Teachers have a negative bias towards the behaviorally disordered student in the context of the regular education classroom which can be seen to be related to teacher self efficacy as well as a conceptual misperception of the disorder. Unless these two key aspects are radically reconstructed, many behaviorally disordered students will find that the legislative and economic forces driving school boards and districts to an inclusive model of educational service delivery, will serve to facilitate their exclusion from an equitable educational opportunity, or at worst, an educational opportunity. Concept mapping and reflective practice along with cognitive rehearsal are identified as powerful heuristics that may well serve this purpose.

Purpose

The purpose of the research study was to determine if concept mapping, reflective practice and cognitive rehearsal through teacher interviewing would effect positive change in the conceptual understanding of effective teaching practice as it pertains to the inclusive classroom with particular emphasis on the behaviorally exceptional student. The research questions were:

1 Given an effective heuristic, will regular education teachers alter and/or change their conceptualization of effective teaching practice in the inclusive classroom setting;
2 Will such change (if any) be of a trivial or radical nature; and
3 What effect will such change (if any) have on the self efficacy of the teachers in the study.

Participants

Five teachers (two female and three male teachers — experience ranging from two to twenty-five years) from one urban school (k-8) volunteered to participate in the study. The teachers (volunteers) represented a cross section and taught kindergarten, grade three, grade four, grade seven and grade eight.

Methods

An initial meeting gave participants an overview of the study presented as five components: 1) a preliminary group concept mapping exercise; 2) individual teacher journalling; 3) individual teacher interviewing; 4) a concluding group concept mapping exercise; and, 5) follow up reporting back to the teachers as a group.

1   Concept mapping — The group met concept mapping. After understanding, the group brainstormed for concepts and decided to create one collaborative concept map representative of the group.

2   Journalling — Teachers were instructed in the process of reflective journalling based on the work of David Hunt (1992) and the Kolb Experiential Cycle (Hunt, 1992, p. 11) and were instructed to identify a positive experience involving an at risk behaviorally difficult student (not necessarily formally identified and labeled as such). Next they had to visualize and recall the incident and make jot notes of everything (especially their feelings) that they could recall. The order was deemed unimportant. The third step was to identify the possible reasons for the positive experience. The final step was to develop a short action plan that would facilitate possible replication of the positive experience. The teachers were also instructed to identify a negative experience with the same type of student. They were to analyze the experience in much the same fashion as they did the positive experience with the notable difference that the action planning would facilitate the avoidance of replication of the negative experience. Finally, the teachers were requested to identify metaphorically how the experience (positive or negative) made them feel.

3   Interviewing (cognitive rehearsal) — The teachers were interviewed on a frequent and regular basis during the research period. Essentially the teachers expressed their feelings about the journalling exercise and how they perceived it affecting their thinking and their practice. The researcher became more the observer/reporter making copious notations of the teachers' verbal explorations of their experiences.

4   Concept mapping — The group met together to share experiences and to produce a concluding concept map in much the same fashion as the preliminary map.

5   Follow up reporting — The research group met about a week after the completion of the research study to have a follow up to the research study and the findings that were identified.

Results and Discussion

A qualitative analysis of the data (both concept maps, the actual teacher journal entries if they were given, as well as the interview notes) was conducted with the following results.

Preliminary Concept Map

This first/preliminary concept map illustrates the teachers' perceived conceptualization of effective teaching practice in the inclusive classroom. It is very structured and predictable in organization. Effective teaching was conceptualized into two superordinate concepts; program and practice. Program was guided by resources, documents, curriculum guidelines, and learning outcomes (subordinate concepts). Program was cross linked to practice through academic expectations and students. The superordinate concept of practice contained the subordinate concepts of students, expectations, skills, methods and training. Students contained the subordinates of regular and exceptional; expectations contained the subordinates academic and behavior; skills contained the subordinates professional ability, personal attributes and communication; and methods and training contained the subordinates new directions and specific to exceptional needs students. Other than the cross linkages previously cited there were no additional cross links to connect program with practice. Additional linkages were noted within the subordinate area of communication. A further superordinate was identified as teacher response. It was determined that the superordinate teacher response represented the teachers' self efficacy, a concept that in the research was cited as critical to success in effective practice. The teachers conceptualized effective teaching as a function of program and practice. Program was viewed as a very large and teacher directed superordinate, separate from practice and teacher response. Under practice they viewed themselves as needing to have 'control'. It is very much a top–down approach, teacher directed and controlled. Teacher response indicates that regardless of program and practice, they conceptualized their response to teaching in the inclusive classroom as frustrating, exhausting, stressful, occasionally rewarding, time consuming, challenging and ineffective. The number of negative responses would indicate that teacher self efficacy was deemed to be low.

Journalling and Interviews

Journalling had an immediate and dramatic effect on the teachers' perceptions of their practice and their students. At first the journals were concise and to the point. The first noted impact on student behavior was the effect of the environment (temperature, time of day) on the performance of the students. Very quickly they focused on the cause and effect aspect of not only the environment, but teacher needs, student needs, class needs as well as recognition of the limitations of the situation. Teachers' needs were expressed as the teacher attempting to accomplish a particular task. For example; a teacher expressed frustration with a student's behavior as it interfered with him handing out work to other students as they were leaving the room. Student needs were identified and incorporated into the daily planning. A teacher who had perceived a student as being intentionally confrontational and non-compliant was able to identify that the boy was attempting to exercise some control, given that the youth was an abandoned refugee from a war torn state, the teacher recognized the need and was able to constructively plan to incorporate the boy's need for some control with the teacher's need to have the student comply. In planning to meet the students' needs, teachers were able to achieve success by intentionally trying new approaches and noting their effectiveness, then refining and/or redesigning them or looking for new ones. A young boy in kindergarten suffering from Tourette's Syndrome realized that his planned release time was actually a reward for focusing. Support was appropriately provided and the student 'did not look on it as a punishment but as something necessary and appropriate' (teacher journal entry). There were negative moments but even the negative interactions provided the teachers with more information to work with in their planning. 'Suggest that [student] change his activity after about 10–15 min. That seems to be the average for him on a good day. Touch base with him frequently to get a feel for the level of concentration and moods' (teacher journal entry). The teacher in this situation has actively planned to attempt to prevent the recurrence of the undesirable behavior. While this teacher 'felt like a soldier in an endless war', the teacher also on the same day with the same student, was able to experience a 'positive resulting in future planning, get [student] participating — maybe helping organizing or something early in the game and continue his active role' (teacher journal entry). The teacher characterized her feelings as 'I felt like another piece of the puzzle had been found'. Another teacher in working with an attention deficit hyperactivity disordered grade three student found that the child's behavior was easier to deal with when the class and the teacher were actively engaged. It appears that this occurrence had something to do with: the environment; tone of voice; and non-confrontational approach which tried to redirect his or her attention to get him or her to focus on something positive, put things as a request, not as a demand — gave him or her choices (teacher journal entry). The interviewing with the teachers revealed much more detail with the teachers often commenting that they would 'have to add that to my journal' or 'I'll have to try that [strategy] tomorrow'. The researcher was very much in the role of recorder as the teachers explored their experiences. What was observable was the teacher 'disengaging' from the emotional aspect of student behavior. They were attempting to work with the student and not simply reacting to the behavior. The teachers began to see the student, the person, existed beyond the behavior. This enabled the teachers to empower the students, to take risks so that the students were more a part of the process rather than the recipient of the program. A particularly positive episode helped the kindergarten teacher realize the effects of such empowerment. Two of her very disabled youngsters, one wheelchair bound and unable to speak or communicate with the use of any assistive devices whatsoever, was outside at playtime with her class, sitting in a wagon. Another child, a boy suffering from Batten's Disease and also unable to communicate, was attempting to get her to play train with him using a second wagon. The female student was unable to because of her condition and also was unable to communicate this. Rather than intervening and helping as was the usual reaction of the teacher and the assistant, the teacher tried letting the students work it out.

Finally, after we encouraged and allowed his attempts to continue (he was very persistent) he got into the wagon with her. The interaction was wonderful to watch. There was touching and sounds (because neither can speak), smiles and laughter (journal entry). In the interview with the teacher, the teacher said she 'felt like light' and wanted to get into the wagon with them. This was a major breakthrough for the boy as he had not interacted or initiated anything like this all year. The teacher was excited and almost moved to tears about the initiative shown. She planned to set up further opportunities to help the students interact more. There were many examples of positive interactions as well as negative but in each and every situation the teacher used the information gleaned for understanding and future planning. They seemed to have acquired a professional distance that allowed them to better see the students beyond the behavior, as well as to see the effects of their methods. They could then plan for positive change. One teacher summed up the group's sense in stating that 'I feel like a scientist.'

Final Concept Map

The final concept map was dramatically different from the first map in both structure and organization as well as in concepts identified as being crucial to effective teaching in the inclusive classroom. The key elements are not practice and program but the interaction between teacher and students. The concepts of documents and guidelines and curriculum have been replaced with student input and student outcomes based on abilities and special needs. The cross-linkages are numerous and complex and are related to issues of communication. In the preliminary map the top–down conceptualization reflected a perceived need for control that was the sole domain of the teacher. In the post map the issue of control was a very significant one in that the teachers reversed their position and now saw that to be effective, they had to relinquish that control in order to involve the students in the program as well as in the practice. They reported that they felt 'uncomfortable' with this but stated that the risk was a necessary one to achieve some sense of personal empowerment. They recognized the students' role as well as that of the parent as being very important. Teaching was conceptualized as a 'working with' and highly 'interactive' relationship. Effective teaching practice was identified as existing in the interconnection and relationships between the teachers, the students, parents, support staff and resources. It is a network of team players with much consultation, collaboration and negotiation involved.

While much of what the teachers identified through the research study was positive, there were some negatives noted as well. Teachers expressed that they were 'overwhelmed' by the sheer enormity of the task of inclusion of exceptional students, particularly behaviorally difficult ones, in the regular class. They believed that academic expectations were lower as more of their time was spent dealing with management issues. They identified their teacher response as being frustrated, downtrodden, angry, depressed as well as overwhelming. What is notable is that they also identified being proud, uplifted, relieved, successful, peaceful and worthwhile as well as empowered. There was anxiety expressed with respect to 'relinquishing control' because 'teachers like to be in the driver's seat and it's hard to give that up' (teacher observation). The teacher response at the conclusion of the study was much more positive than that at the outset. The teachers were more confident and felt more directed, less helpless and more assured of their abilities than before. In summation, the teachers' self efficacy was vastly enhanced through their participation in the research study.

The research study findings would suggest that teachers will change their conceptualization of effective teaching practice in the inclusive classroom if they are given an effective heuristic to do so. The findings of this study strongly suggest that such a heuristic exists in concept mapping and reflection through the use of journals and interviews. The nature of the change is deemed to be radical as changes involved assimilation of new concepts, redefining existing concepts, and adding many more cross links between the various concepts. This necessitated the dramatic change in the structure and organization of concepts as evidenced by the post map.

Conclusion and Future Directions

The results of the research study indicate that the methodology of concept mapping with reflection through journalling and interview may well prove to be a powerful teacher education tool. The dramatic changes in the teachers' conceptualization would indicate the necessity of sharing the experience with other teachers of inclusive classrooms in order for them to experience the benefits of improved practice as well as enhanced self efficacy. One issue which cannot be ignored is the teachers' continued sense of frustration and of being overwhelmed with the demands of teaching exceptional students within the regular class setting. While this is an issue which may well serve to increase incidence of teacher burnout, it is also an issue that will require recognition and remediation from administrative levels. Regardless of this concern, the current study addressed possible ways and means of assisting teachers, improving practice and increasing meaningful learning for teachers as well as students. What was found supports that intent. This holds significant promise for those behaviorally difficult/disordered students who find themselves included in the regular education classroom with few resources available to them or to the teachers facing the challenge of working with them. Further, the findings suggest that teachers, rather than holding to the traditional 'teacher at the front' role, actually hold a leadership position in the class. Leadership in the sense that leadership is used in the businesses and corporations of the country. Each class can be viewed as a small business with the teacher being the chairperson of the board. From this perspective, teachers would benefit greatly from inservices related to the leadership functions of running a business, of team building, professional networking, collaboration and the like, more so than curriculum content of the 'make and take' variety. In summation, if teachers are expected to produce the leaders of tomorrow, then they need the leaders of today to model that leadership role in the classroom. Leadership, not teachership skills is what is required. The concept map at the conclusion of the research study appears to support such a position.

While this study was limited in its scope there exists enough evidence to warrant further study to determine if findings were unique to the site location and/or the personalities involved. Of interest would be to determine the longevity of the changes noted in conceptualization of effective teaching practice. Future research directions should attempt to address these issues.

Janice M. Martin and Michael Kompf

References

ANTONAK, R.F. (1980) 'A hierarchy of attitudes toward exceptionality', *The Journal of Special Education*, **14**, 2, pp. 231–40.

BEYERBACH, B.A. (1986) *Concept Mapping in Assessing Prospective Teachers' Concept Development*, ERIC Document 291 800.

BEYERBACH, B.A. (1988) 'Developing a technical vocabulary on teacher planning: Preservice teachers' concepts maps', *Teaching and Teacher Education*, **3**, 4, pp. 339–47.

CAMPBELL, N.J., DOBSON, J.E. and BOST, J.M. (1985) 'Educator perceptions of behaviour problems of mainstreamed students: Exceptional children', **51**, 4, pp. 298–303.

COOPER, H.M. and GOOD, T.L. (1983) *Pygmalion Grows Up*, New York, NY, Longman.

DANA, N.F. (1993) 'Elementary school preservice teachers' conceptions of social studies teaching and learning: 24 report on concept mapping', Paper presented at the Annual Meeting of the National Council for the Social Studies, Nashville, Tennessee.

HORNE, M.D. (1985) *Attitudes toward Handicapped Students: Professional, Peer, and Parent Reactions*, Hillsdale, NJ, Erlbaum.

HUNT, D.E. (1987) *Beginning with Ourselves*, Toronto, ON, OISE Press.

HUNT, D.E. (1992) *The Renewal of Personal Energy*, Toronto, ON, OISE Press.

JONES, M.G. and VESILIND, E. (1994) 'Changes in the structure of pedagogical knowledge of middle school preservice teachers', Paper presented at the American Educational Research Association, New Orleans, Louisiana.

KAGAN, D.M. (1990) 'Ways of evaluating teacher cognition: Inferences concerning the goldilocks principle, *Review of Educational Research*, **60**, 3, pp. 419–69.

KAUFFMAN, J.M., LLOYD, J.W., COOK, L., CULLINAN, D., EPSTEIN, M.H., FORNESS, S.R., HALLAHAN, D., NELSON, C., POLSGROVE, L., SABORNIE, E.J., STRAIN, P.S. and WALKER, H.M. (1991) 'Problems and promises in special education and related services for children and youth with emotional or behavioral disorders', *Behavioral Disorders*, **16**, 4, pp. 299–313.

LAKOFF, G. and JOHNSON, M. (1980) *Metaphors We Live by*, Chicago, ILL, The University of Chicago Press.

LARRIVEE, B. and COOK, L. (1979) 'Mainstreaming: A study of the variables affecting teacher attitude', *The Journal of Special Education*, **13**, 3, pp. 315–24.

LARRIVEE, B. and HORNE, M.D. (1991) 'Social status: A comparison of mainstreamed students with peers of different ability levels', *The Journal of Special Education*, **25**, 1, pp. 90–101.

NOVAK, J.M. (1989) 'Advancing constructive education: A framework for teacher education advances', *in Personal Construct Psychology*, **1**, pp. 225–47.

NOVAK, J.D. (1990) 'Human constructivism: Explication of psychological and epistemological phenomena in meaning making', Paper presented at the 4th North American Conference on Personal Construct Psychology, San Antonio, Texas.

NOVAK, J.D. and GOWIN, D.B. (1984) *Learning How to Learn*, New York, Cambridge University Press.

POWELL, R.R. (1991) 'The development of pedagogical schemata in alternative preservice teachers', Paper presented at the American Educational Research Association. Chicago, Illinois.

PURKEY, W.W. (1992) 'Avoiding erosion in the foundations of invitational education: The seven deadly sins of self-concept theory', in NOVAK J.M. (Ed) *Advancing Invitational Thinking*, San Francisco, CA, Caddo Gap Press, (pp. 15–25).

RATHS, J. (1987) 'Enhancing understanding through debriefing', *Educational Leadership*, pp. 24–7.

ROEGGE, C.A., WENTLING, T.L., LEACH, J.A. and BROWN, D.C. (1993) 'Using concept mapping techniques to compare stakeholder groups' perceptions of tech prep', Paper presented at the American Educational Research Association, Atlanta, Georgia.

ROSENTHAL, R. and JACOBSON, L. (1968) *Pygmalion in the Classroom: Teacher Expectation and Pupils' Intellectual Development*, New York, NY, Holt, Rinehart and Winston.

SENGUPTA, S. (1993) 'Mixed-method design for practical purposes: Combination of concept mapping, questionnaire and interviews', Paper presented at the Annual Conference of the American Evaluation Association, Dallas, Texas.

WINITZKY, N., KAUCHAK, D. and KELLY, M. (1994) 'Measuring teachers' structural knowledge', *Teaching and Teacher Education*, **10**, 2, pp. 125–39.

ZEICHNER, K.M. (1993a) 'Alternative paradigms of teacher education', *Behaviouristic Teacher Education*, **34**, 3, pp. 3–9.

ZEICHNER, K.M. (1993b) 'Research on teacher thinking and different views of reflective practice in teaching and teacher education', Paper presented at the 6th International Conference of the International Study Association on Teacher Thinking, Goteborg, Sweden.

9 Thinking about Stress: The Student Teacher's Viewpoint

Maureen Pope and Ka Wa Yeung

Introduction

The number of studies on teacher thinking continues to expand. However, the vast proportion of these concentrate on issues such as teacher thinking as it may affect classroom practice, curriculum design and implications for teachers' professional development. Elbaz (1990) drew attention to the fact that most studies concentrated on the thinking of the 'extraordinary' teacher and that there is a need to consider teachers in a wide range of settings. Pope (1993) suggested that, if research on teacher thinking was to remain a progressive endeavour, new areas need to be investigated. Whilst research on student teacher thinking is not a new research area within ISATT, it nevertheless represents an area that warrants further attention. Students in training are already working in schools and developing their personal knowledge and thinking about the craft of teaching. Their experiences during training will have impact on their thinking when they enter the profession. In our view, it is important that teacher educators are sensitive to student teachers' views and that personal tutors and student counsellors should be aware of student thinking with regard to aspects of experience in college or within schools that may be particularly stressful.

This chapter will focus on student teachers' thinking with respect to their individual experience of stress during training. Whilst a certain degree of stress can be a motivational factor for performance improvement and development, too much stress in training may also cause undesirable effects on student teachers' 'well being', such as frustration, depression, deterioration in work performance and interpersonal relationships. If student teachers are too overwhelmed by stress in training they may opt to leave the profession. Many teacher educators and researchers are therefore concerned about student teacher stress.

Research has shown that there can be a high incidence of stress experienced by student teachers during training (Abernathy, Manera and Wright, 1985; Kaunitz, Spokane, Lissitz and Strein, 1986). In Abernathy *et al.*'s study thirteen stress factors were sorted into four categories of stress level using Q sort design. It was found that the four greatest stress producing factors were 'classroom discipline, unmotivated pupils, lecturing to noisy apathetic and uninterested pupils, and time management for preparation and marking assignments and paperwork'. Kaunitz *et al.*'s study used a multidimensional scaling analysis (MDS) of student teacher stress. A total of ten stressful situations were incorporated into a questionnaire and student teachers were asked to judge the degree of similarity between all possible comparisons of stressful situations. A further seven semantic-differential scales were brainstormed by researchers to measure the feelings, thoughts and emotions that these situations could evoke. There was little relationship between the semantic-differential scales and dimensions obtained from the questionnaire. Buitink and Kemme (1986) used teacher anxiety scales and the Texas-Leiden scale to study changes in anxiety levels of student teachers during the course of training.

A review of student teachers and teachers' stress research (Yeung, 1992) confirmed Blase's (1986) suggestion that research into student teacher and teacher stress has primarily relied on quantitative methods using highly structured instruments. Participants' responses were excessively controlled and did not reflect the subjects' perception of given phenomena. Most of the instruments used to measure teacher stress were developed from stress inventories based on theoretical ideas developed from studies outside the area of education.

It is often difficult to compare results of studies since definitions of stress vary between studies and also terms such as 'student teacher anxiety' are often used alongside the term 'student stress'. However stress or anxiety may be defined in research studies, teacher educators are concerned to identify ways of recognising student teacher stress during training and consider different ways in which it may be possible to reduce the negative effects of high stress (Calhoun, 1986).

The present study is an attempt to understand student teachers' thinking with respect to their experience of stress during training. By adopting a more qualitative approach we hope to gain insight into the student teachers' views and provide a framework that could be useful for the students, teacher educators and counsellors.

Personal Construct Psychology places as high a premium on research which allows insight and understanding of the views of participants within the study. This was highlighted by Pope and Denicolo (1993, p. 164) when attention was drawn to the role of *Verstehen* within Personal Construct Psychology research. More recently, Schwandt (1994), in highlighting common points between constructivism and interpretativism noted that:

> Proponents of these persuasions share the goal of understanding the complex world of lived experience from the point of view of those that live it. This goal is variously spoken of as an abiding concern for the life world, for the emic point of view, for understanding meaning, for grasping the actor definition of the situation, for *Verstehen*. (p. 118)

Utilizing a Personal Construct Psychology perspective and using the Repertory Grid technique and interviews, we have attempted to avoid some of the problems inherent in previous research in the field of student teacher stress. We were concerned to identify how stress is perceived by the student teachers themselves without the constraints of prestructured questionnaires and stress inventories. Personal Construct Psychology has been used in a number of studies within teacher training research, e.g., Ben-Peretz (1984), McQualter (1985), Diamond (1991) and Kompf (1993).

Method

The study was conducted in three phases. During the first phase of the study, student teachers took part in open ended interviews and in Phase 2 a further group of student teachers completed Repertory Grid interviews. In the final phase student counsellors in universities in England which offered teacher training were asked to complete questionnaires.

Phase 1

Sixteen student teachers from one university, eleven on the BEd course and five on the PGCE course, were interviewed. The student teachers were informed that the study was aimed at finding out how they thought about stress and aspects of their course that were more or less stressful. The students were invited to describe openly and freely what they had done during their terms at the university and to identify specific course activities. It is recognised that a course within any particular teacher training institution will have its unique context. We were concerned to allow the students the opportunity to define course activities that they perceived as meaningful and also to encourage them to define their own meaning of stress.

At the end of each interview course activities that had been identified were then considered further, each activity being rated according to three levels of perceived stress, (i) 'for low stress', (ii) 'for medium stress', and (iii) 'for high stress'. On completion of the sixteen interviews, a list of course activities was chosen that were commonly mentioned by both BEd and PGCE students and which were distributed across the three stress levels, in order to facilitate the generation of bipolar constructs during the elicitation of the Repertory Grid. Seventeen elements were chosen which represent the 'universe of discourse' (Kelly, 1955). Below is the element list chosen for the Repertory Grid:

1   lectures
2   teaching practice file
3   subject specialism
4   visits by tutors
5   teaching practice self evaluation
6   curricular areas — related studies
7   practical work/performance
8   lessons plans
9   exams
10 teaching practice
11 seminars
12 projects
13 National Curriculum
14 school visits
15 essays/assignments
16 education and professional studies (EPS)
17 classroom teaching

Phase 2

A volunteer sample of twenty-one students was obtained within the same university. The students covered the four years of BEd study, PGCE students and four groups of subject specialisms. The twenty-one students completed Repertory Grids. The elements for the grid were the seventeen course activities elicited in Phase 1. These elements were the course activities that were experienced by student teachers during their training, and served as contextual situations for eliciting stress constructs for the study. In addition to the supplied elements, each student was free to add further elements if he or she wished to. Below are some of the additional elements supplied by BEd students:

- tutorials
- living in hall
- teaching practice preparation
- teaching practice — decisions by college
- college transport
- record keeping
- dissertation
- music competition
- music committee
- performance to audience
- schemes of work
- practical display work

Additional elements supplied by PGCE students:

- interviews for jobs
- daily travel to school
- practical work in school

The elements 1–17 were ordered in a sequence that alternated the expected levels of stress based on student perceptions in Phase 1 of the study. As well as adding elements interviewees were also free to discard elements if they felt it was appropriate. In fact, no students availed themselves of the option to discard an element.

The triadic elicitation method was used at the beginning of the interview. Students were asked to identify ways in which three of the elements could be differentiated so that two of the elements were perceived as similar to one another and in contrast to the other. Towards the end of the interview the full context approach was used so that students were free to offer any combinations of elements in contrast to others without the constraints of particular triads. (For fuller details on grid administration see Pope and Keen, 1981; Pope and Denicolo, 1993.)

The first seventeen elements were the same for all participants and therefore the grids could be compared using the SOCIO program within the REPGRID package which is an integrated suite of programs for the AppleMac (Shaw and Gaines, 1986). Each grid was also analysed individually using the FOCUS program within the REPGRID package. The FOCUS program uses a two way cluster analysis technique to reorder systematically the rows of constructs and columns of elements to produce a FOCUS grid showing the least variation between adjacent constructs and adjacent elements.

A supplied construct, 'a lot of stress' versus 'a little stress', was used. By comparing the relationship between the supplied construct and other personally elicited constructs, we were able to identify which pole of the construct represented the high stress pole. The ratings of each element on the high stress end of each construct dimension was calculated and Table 9.1 shows the element stress rank order for BEd students and Table 9.2 the element stress rank order for PGCE

Table 9.1: Elements stress rank order (BEd)

Elements	Rank
E2 Teaching practice file	1
E10 Teaching practice	2
E4 Visits by tutors	3
E17 Classroom teaching	4
E5 TP self evaluations	5
E14 School visits	6.5
E15 Essays/assignments	6.5
E9 Examinations	8
E8 Lesson plans	9
E7 Practical work/performance	10
E13 National Curriculum	11
E12 Projects	12
E6 Curriculum areas/related subjects	13
E3 Subject specialism	14
E11 Seminars	15
E16 Education and professional studies	16
E1 Lectures	17

Table 9.2: Elements stress rank order (PGCE)

Elements	Rank
E10 Teaching practice	1
E4 Visits by tutors	2
E2 Teaching practice file	3
E17 Classroom teaching	4
E8 Lessons plans	5
E15 Essays/assignments	6
E5 TP Self evaluations	7
E7 Practical work/performance	8
E14 School visits	9
E3 Subject specialism	10
E9 Examinations	11
E16 Education and professional studies	12
E11 Seminars	14
E12 Projects	14
E13 National Curriculum	14
E1 Lectures	16.5
E6 Curriculum areas/related studies	16.5

students. In identifying the rank order, only the seventeen elements supplied were considered for ranking.

It will be seen from Tables 9.1 and 9.2 above that the elements 'teaching practice, visits by tutors, teaching practice files and classroom teaching' are seen as aspects of the course that both the BEd and PGCE students found most stressful. Course related elements such as 'seminars, projects, lectures, education and professional studies, and curriculum areas/related studies' are seen to be less stressful.

Space precludes the presentation of many of the individual grids; however, two are presented in Figures 9.1 and 9.2.

Figure 9.1 is the FOCUS grid from a third year BEd student. The supplied construct pole 'a lot of stress' is clustered with 'interesting, threatening because of evaluation, need to succeed, a lot of work, expect intellectual understanding'. The elements 'visits by tutors, teaching practice, classroom teaching, TP file and TP self evaluation' rate particularly highly on these constructs.

Figure 9.2 is the FOCUS grid for one of the PGCE students. For this student 'visits by tutors, practical works/performance, teaching practice and TP file' are high stress elements. This student links high stress with constructs such as 'being on show, being judged by others, expectations from college, not functioning when the tutor is watching'.

The individual grids were further analysed using the SOCIO program and it was possible to identify the mode constructs, i.e., those constructs most commonly used by the participants in the study. A content analysis of all constructs as they were applied to the elements was also carried out and a number of categories emerged.

> Evaluation stress — This dimension referred to student teachers' constructs that reflected feelings of being 'assessed', 'examined' and 'evaluated'. This was the largest category in the BEd students' construing (23.1 percent) and the second largest category amongst PGCE students (24.7 percent).
>
> Workload stress — This stress included reference to 'workload pressure and the exhaustion involved in completing tasks'. This was the most frequent response amongst PGCE students (26.2 percent) and the second highest category amongst BEd students (20 percent).
>
> Expectation/uncertainty stress — Many students indicated that they felt stressful when they were 'uncertain of what was required of them and unsure of what tutors expected'. This was particularly noticeable in the grids of BEd students (14 percent) as opposed to 7.1 percent of PGCE students' constructs being identified in this category.
>
> Figures 9.1 and 9.2 have examples of these constructs and further examples of constructs that were classified under these three dimensions can be seen in the Appendix 9.1.
>
> Efficacy stress — This includes constructs referring to 'fear of failure and the lack of confidence and competence in coping with work' (BEd students 12.6 percent, PGCE students 8.7 percent).

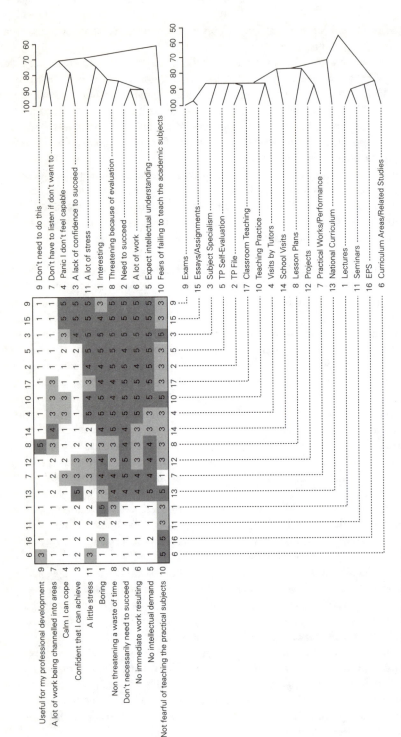

Figure 9.1: The grid of CC (BEd Year 3)

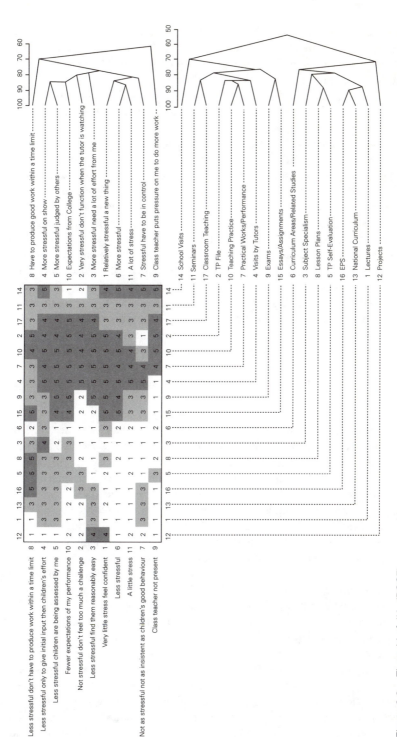

Figure 9.2: The grid of JHu (PGCE)

Course meaningfulness — This type of stress occurred when student teachers felt that they were 'wasting their time, were bored and irritated' during their course of study at the university (BEd students 7.9 percent, PGCE students 2.3 percent).

It would appear that BEd students found their course less meaningful than the PGCE students. However, we are mindful of the small sample of students in the present study.

Importance stress — This construct dimension refers to feelings of stress which occurred when a course activity was considered to be particularly important, often when the activity is seen as 'important for career prospects' (BEd students 7.7 percent, PGCE students 8.7 percent).

Class control and student learning — Constructs classified under this dimension referred to stress that some student teachers feel when they need to accept 'responsibility for students' learning and control of classroom discipline'. This concern was more marked in the interviews and grids of the PGCE students, 10.7 percent of their constructs being classified under this category, reflecting the third highest stress indicator. Although 6.7 percent of the BEd students' constructs were classified under this heading, such constructs ranked 7th out of the nine construct areas identified.

Tutor stress — This refers to constructs where the students indicated that they were stressed when their 'tutors were unsupportive or unduly critical' (BEd 3.9 percent, PGCE 8.3 percent). PGCE students seem to find their tutors less supportive and this was also commented on during interviews with the students.

The categories identified above are the major themes that were identified in the construing of stress when students considered various course activities. The categorization was our attempt to identify common themes and the intensity of use of such constructs as applied to the element set. Interviews with each student and the individual grids represent a rich diversity and teacher educators and counsellors would be advised to use individual grids as a basis for any further consultation. As with all classifications, it proved difficult to collapse all data into neat themes, therefore students' high stress constructs, such as 'finding it hard and slow to use the computer or stressful because of competition' were left unclassified.

During Phase 2 of the study, the students welcomed the opportunity to talk about their course activities and discuss which aspects of the course they found particularly stressful. It was clear that 'teaching practice' was the major source of stress to student teachers and activities relating to teaching practice, including 'preparation of schemes of work, writing lesson plans, classroom teaching, visits by tutors and writing self evaluations' were seen as demanding, and many of the students viewed them as stressful. The tutors' support during teaching practice was seen as important. Students felt upset and demoralized when tutors' criticisms were not given in a constructive manner. Several students talked most forcibly about the neglect they felt whilst being evaluated in the schools and felt apprehension at being examined on their competence as a teacher within the classroom. Students often felt uncertain about what was expected of them and would have welcomed more advice from college tutors and mentors in schools. 'Heavy workload' was a problem for many students, although this seemed to be most evident amongst PGCE students. 'Classroom discipline and responsibility for children's behaviour' were also sources of stress. These findings concur with those found by Veenman (1984) and Abernathy *et al.* (1985).

Given that the student teachers recognised teaching practice to be highly evaluative and an aspect of the course they found particularly stressful, the guidance role of tutors in college and in schools is vitally important and when this is not carried out effectively, students may become overwhelmed, demoralized, unable to cope and if support is lacking they may leave a course prematurely. The profession may lose potentially good recruits.

Earlier in this paper we suggested that tools used by personal tutors and counsellors were inadequate, since they were often stress inventories unrelated to the context in which students will find themselves during training. One outcome of Phase 2 of this research was a listing of constructs that students used when describing feelings of stress when considering their course. These were grouped under the major categories identified above. These may prove a useful checklist for personal tutors when they wish to gain insight into the way in which students experience stress during training. We were mindful of the small sample in Phase 2 and were interested to find out from student counsellors the degree to which the students' statements reflected their experience when student teachers present themselves for counselling.

Phase 3

Questionnaires were sent to the directors of counselling services of the sixty-two universities in England offering both BEd and PGCE courses leading to qualified teacher status. A covering letter was sent to the counsellors with brief information regarding Phase 2 of the project and asking the counsellors to indicate the extent to which the students' statements under the categories identified reflected their experiences. Counsellors were asked to indicate whether statements were frequently made by student teachers, sometimes heard during counselling sessions, or whether a particular statement was never heard. To date, thirty counsellors have replied (48 percent). Of these, four felt that they saw student teachers so infrequently that they did not feel it sensible to complete the questionnaire. Appendix 9.1 gives the results of this survey.

It can be seen from Appendix 9.1 that the statements under 'evaluation stress' are reflected in the counsellors' experience, particularly 'being watched while teaching' and 'apprehensive about being judged'. Items under the 'workload stress' were also recognised by counsellors, particularly 'stressful, the amount of work to be prepared for school' and 'having to produce good work within time limits' and 'a lot of stress due to assignments and deadlines'. However, the statement 'boring and tiring, takes up too much time' was a statement that twelve out of the twenty-six counsellors said they had never experienced.

Under 'expectation/uncertainty stress' there was agreement on some of the statements. However, statements such as being concerned with 'meeting the objectives of National Curriculum, being scared, kept in the dark' were not identified.

Whilst not identified very frequently, statements such as 'apprehension, not knowing what to expect' and 'worried that I will not reach a satisfactory standard' are recognized by the student counsellors.

Under 'efficacy stress' statements such as 'worried, lacking in confidence and experience' are particularly noted by counsellors. Most of the statements under efficacy stress have been experienced by the counsellors, whereas under 'course meaningfulness' statements such as 'boring and mundane' and 'boring, unhelpful' were not common. Statements with respect to 'tutor stress' have been noted, albeit not frequently. 'Importance stress' is recognised although only 'panic, certain things are important to get through the course' had been identified by some counsellors as a frequent statement.

'Class control and children learning stress' is clearly a category recognised by counsellors. Statements such as 'unsure if I can control children' and 'having to respond to demands and discipline' are particularly noticed.

It is apparent from the survey of counsellors' experience that, whilst there are differences amongst the counsellors in terms of their experience of particular statements, most of the statements are recognised by the majority of counsellors.

Counsellors were told that the statements presented to them were 'the most frequent comments made by students in our sample'. They were asked to 'add any statement that students have made to you that have not been included'. Space was provided for this. Relatively few counsellors added further statements. However below are some offered by counsellors:

- there is a huge difference between what the college requires and has taught and what the class teacher wants me to teach;
- stress is enormous when the class teacher appears antagonistic or competitive (this is increasing in partnership situations);
- stress from covert competition between students;
- adverse personal situations (e.g., divorce/illness);
- having to be aware of, and respond to, children on several levels — learning, behaviour, emotional well being;
- stress in relationship to school staff's demands;
- personal problems relating to relationships, home sickness, sexuality, post-rape;
- course induced stress factors tend to emerge as secondary issues;
- reconciling their own philosophy of education and that of the class teacher/school; and
- discrimination, i.e., race/class from tutors and peers.

Given past criticism of the use of general stress inventories we asked counsellors to give details of any stress inventories they were using. No counsellor used inventories although some mentioned the use of 'evaluation sheets' using best/most valuable, worst/least valuable sentence completion questions. This is used as a basis for open group discussion of issues with 'ample opportunity for individual follow up sessions'. The stress on individual sessions was clear. As one counsellor put it:

> I don't use stress inventories: particularly not with students. They are not 'individual enough' I keep one evening a week 5–9 pm open to see students on teaching practice and/or work placement, which is a well used time.

It would appear that British counsellors, unlike their American counterparts, are not using stress inventories for student counselling.

Counsellors also made reference to the stress caused by changes in the delivery of teacher training. Students often find it difficult to see a counsellor if this is required. As one counsellor put it:

> the new PGCE school pattern based system is causing a great deal of stress for students (and staff!) — since most of their time is off-site, they find it difficult getting to see counsellors. Reference to 'stressed staff'. PGCE students in particular have shown aware that they empathise with course tutors who are 'over worked' and stressed themselves. 'They' (the tutors) are very busy. It is difficult to get opportunities to talk to them.

Conclusion

This study has highlighted the way a number of student teachers think about stress and particular aspects of the course that may cause problems. The constructs used by the students are, in the main, recognised by the counsellors that replied to the questionnaire. Given the frequent reference to the need for tutor support, particularly during teaching practice, and the comments of counsellors with respect to additional stress that may be related to changing patterns in the delivery of teacher training in the UK, renewed attempts must be made to find ways to help student teachers articulate their thinking regarding stress within college and during teaching practice. A modified version of Appendix 9.1 omitting ratings could be used as a basis for discussion amongst college tutors and mentors in schools as an indication of some of the ways in which students might be thinking about their experience. Whilst the student counsellor has extensive experience of dealing with student stress, college and school tutors may have more limited awareness of the issues involved. If the government pursues the current direction, i.e., to switch most, if not all, responsibility for training from higher education to schools, more effort will be needed to ensure that the professional tutor and subject mentor in schools and the college link tutor and subject tutor become more conscious of the role they may need to play in helping student teachers overcome the types of stress indicated in this study.

A good place to start is with the students' own ways of thinking about stress in relation to their particular course context.

Appendix 9.1: Aspects of Course That Students Found Stressful

Please tick the appropriate statement which reflects your experience

	Frequently	Sometimes	Never
Evaluation Stress			
Don't like self evaluation, having to write good points about myself	2	16	8
Worry about my weak points exposed	9	15	2
Being watched while teaching	11	13	2
Nervous standing in front of the class	9	15	2
Threatening because of being evaluated	9	13	4
Stressful to give something that might not match up	6	13	7
Stressful when required to show how you feel	3	15	8
Stressful given a short amount of time to prove yourself	8	16	2
Very stressful, don't function when tutor is watching	5	19	2
Worry about not being seen as a competent teacher	8	18	—
Apprehensive about being assessed and judged	12	12	2
Work Load Stress			
Stressful, need to find out a lot of information	5	18	3
Being on your own, all the pressures are on you	6	16	4
Stressful, the amount of work to be prepared for school	15	10	1
High workload stressful, very tiring to complete it	13	12	1
Boring and tiring, takes up too much time	2	12	12
Very stressful having to devise a complex plan for teaching	5	20	1
Having to produce good work within time limit	6	20	—
Class teacher puts pressure on me to do more work	5	17	4
A lot of stress due to assignments and deadlines	14	11	1
Expectation / Uncertainty Stress			
Didn't know what I was expected to do, frustrated	5	15	6
Feelings of uncertainty	7	19	—
Apprehension, not knowing what to expect	5	19	2
Meeting objectives of National Curriculum	1	15	10
Don't know what is expected, worried	4	19	3
Course expects intellectual understanding	—	16	10
Scared, kept in the dark	2	11	13
Every day is different	2	16	8
Worried that I will not reach a satisfactory standard	8	17	1
Worrying, required by law	—	17	9

	Frequently	Sometimes	Never
Efficacy Stress			
Anxious to get these right	9	17	—
Worried, lacking in confidence and experience	21	5	—
Panic, I don't feel capable	8	15	3
Feelings of failing to teach the academic subjects	3	17	6
Uncertainty about my capabilities	8	18	—
Apprehensive that I might not be of a suitable standard	9	16	1
If you fail, could affect your job and life	9	14	3
Scared of failing	8	17	1
Course Meaningfulness			
Don't really enjoy	5	18	3
Boring and mundane	2	14	10
Boring, unhelpful	2	13	11
Tedious, something to be done but not always relevant	2	16	8
Irritating, a waste of time	1	16	9
Chores, not so keen to do	—	20	6
Stressful to conform to their ideas	3	20	3
Does not make me more capable	2	17	7
Tutor Stress			
Very stressful, I was criticized all the time	4	18	4
Tutor was unsupportive	5	19	2
The tutor was incompetent and did not get support	7	13	6
Being criticized by self and tutor	4	20	2
Worried about being criticized	5	19	2
Looked at by tutor, upsetting, demoralized	6	17	3
When criticized, demoralizing, resentful	5	20	1
Have to do what the tutor wants, force fed	2	16	8
Made more stress by visits from tutors	6	19	1
Importance Stress			
Important and useful causing stress	—	18	8
Judge when things are important, more urgent	—	22	4
Some things are important, these tell if I'll make a good teacher	2	20	4
These I have to remember, and put into practice	2	20	4
Panic [certain things are important to get through the course]	6	16	4
Class Control and Children Learning Stress			
Have to keep class order, occasional panic	10	16	—
Unsure if I can control children	14	11	1
Apprehension, classroom not well organised	10	13	3

	Frequently	Sometimes	Never
Stressful classes causing particular concern	10	14	2
Being responsible for my class	6	18	2
Worried about children misbehaving	8	15	3
Need to ensure adequate learning for children	4	20	2
High stress, not wanting to give children a bad experience	5	16	5
Having to respond to demands and discipline	12	13	1
Stressful, children are demanding and challenging	10	14	2
Stressful, responsibility for children learning	6	18	2

References

ABERNATHY, S., MANERA, E. and WRIGHT, R.E. (1985) 'What stresses student teachers most?', *Clearing House*, **58**, 8, pp. 361–62.

BEN-PERETZ, M. (1984) 'Kelly's theory of personal constructs as a paradigm for investigating teacher thinking', in HALKES, R. and OLSEN, J.K. (Eds) *Teacher Thinking: A New Perspective on Persisting Problems in Education*, Lisse, Swets and Zeitlinger, pp. 103–12.

BLASE, J.J. (1986) 'A qualitative analysis of sources of teacher stress: Consequences for performance', *American Educational Research Journal*, **23**, pp. 13–40.

BUITINK, J. and KEMME, S. (1986) 'Changes in student teacher thinking', *European Journal of Teacher Education*, **9**, 1, pp. 75–84.

CALHOUN, S.E. (1986) 'Are our future teachers prepared for the stress that lies ahead?', *Clearing House*, **60**, 4, pp. 178–79.

DIAMOND, C.T.P. (1991) *Teacher Education as Transformation*, Milton Keynes, Open University Press.

ELBAZ, F. (1990) 'Knowledge and discourse: Evolution of research on teacher thinking', in DAY, C., POPE, M. and DENICOLO, P. (Eds) *Insights into Teacher Thinking and Practice*, London, Falmer Press, pp. 15–42.

KAUNITZ, N., SPOKANE, A.R., LISSITZ, R.W. and STREIN, W.O. (1986) 'Stress in student teachers: A multi dimensional scaling analysis of elicited stressful situations', *Teacher and Teacher Education*, **2**, 2, pp. 169–80.

KELLY, G.A. (1955) *The Psychology of Personal Constructs*, (vols 1 & 2), New York, W.W. Norton.

KOMPF, M. (1993) 'Construing teachers' personal development: Reflecting on landmark events using career mapping', in DAY, C., CALDERHEAD, J. and DENICOLO, P. (Eds) *Research on Teacher Thinking: Understanding Professional Development*, London, Falmer Press, pp. 166–76.

MCQUALTER, J.W. (1985) 'Becoming a teacher: Preservice teacher education using personal construct theory', *Journal of Education for Teaching*, **11**, 2, pp. 177–86.

POPE, M.L. (1993) 'Anticipating teacher thinking', in DAY, C., CALDERHEAD, J. and DENICOLO, P. (Eds) *Research on Teacher Thinking: Understanding Professional Development*, London, Falmer Press, pp. 19–33.

POPE, M.L. and DENICOLO, P. (1993) 'The art and science of constructivist research in teacher thinking', *Teacher and Teacher Education*, **9**, 5 and 6, pp. 529–44.

POPE, M.L. and KEEN, T.R. (1981) *Personal Construct Psychology and Education*, London, Academic Press.

SCHWANDT, T.A. (1994) 'Constructivist, interpretavist approaches to human inquiry', in DENZIN, N. and LINCOLN, Y.S. (Eds) *Handbook of Qualitative Research*, London, Sage, pp. 118–37.

SHAW, M.L.G. and GAINES, B.R. (1986) 'Interactive elicitation of knowledge from experts', *Future Computer Systems*, **1**, 2, Maruzen Co Ltd and Oxford University Press.

VEENMAN, S. (1984) 'Perceived problems of beginning teachers', *Review of Educational Research*, **54**, 2, pp. 143–78.

YEUNG, K.W. (1992) 'The use of Repertory Grid technique to study student teacher stress', Unpublished MA thesis, The University of Reading, UK.

10   From Performer to School Music Teacher: A Problem of Identity

Joan Tucker

Abstract

Based on a case study of a Jamaican music teacher's thinking and curriculum practice, this chapter focuses on teacher identity by examining professional goals and negative perceptions of the teaching career. It highlights the difficulties faced in developing a professional identity within a society that values performers, but lacks a clear conception of music in education and the role that music educators should play.

Introduction

In Jamaica where there are limited job opportunities and relative ease of entry to a teachers' college, school leavers are apt to consider teaching a career option. Teachers' colleges are often entered by persons with varying levels of commitment to teaching, as well as those who may never enter the profession, but merely use their teaching qualifications as a stepping stone to more lucrative jobs in the commercial sector.

Reasons for choosing a career in teaching are many and varied. One reason may be the interest in, or attachment to, a particular subject and the desire to pass it on to others (Lyons, 1981; Sikes, 1985). With respect to teachers of the arts, attachment or devotion to a subject is likely to be one of the primary reasons for choosing to teach. The development of artistic sensibilities requires the early commencement of an education, which may begin when a child is 6 or 7 and last for approximately eleven years prior to professional education. It is because of devotion to their art form that the often off-putting rigors of those eleven years of training are entertained and dedication to learning sustained, despite the competing interests of the adolescent years.

It was devotion to visual art that made Carey Bennet's (1985) teachers more concerned with the personally fulfilling aspects of art teaching than with gaining promotion in their schools. But there are many teachers of the arts who may have entered the teaching profession because of devotion to their art only to find that practicing an art form is very different to teaching it.

This may well apply to music teachers, whose preprofessional education focuses largely on the development of instrumental competence. To young musicians embarking on a teaching career, a three-year professional program may constitute a brief intervention in already formed and ongoing musical lives — lives that center on musical performance. If the program fails to broaden their experiences of music, and also fails to address the aims of music in education and a range of activities that serve those aims, in the years to come those teachers are likely to operate from the narrow perspective of the instrumentalist. In the long run, although there may be sustained devotion to music, there may be less devotion to music as a school subject.

In this chapter, I examine the thinking and classroom practices of a teacher whose devotion to music surpasses his interest in teaching. After twelve years in the profession, he continues to experience difficulty in making the transition from instrumental performer to class music teacher. Briefly, I look at the teacher's early career goals and his musical and preservice education. I then examine his approach to the curriculum and the way in which institutional values sustain the teacher's latent identity as a performer. I next discuss the teacher's negative perceptions of his career and the strategies that he employs to deal with his circumstances. Throughout the paper I point to problems that exist in the education system in Jamaica with respect to music in schools and the education of music teachers. Overall, in presenting this paper my intention is to initiate discussion on what is a relatively unexplored area.

The Research

This paper is based on data collected in an ethnographic study on teacher thinking and curriculum practice in music. The research was conducted in a secondary school in Kingston, Jamaica. The main data sources were interviews, the teacher's journal and the field notes of lessons delivered over an academic year. Triangulation of data was employed to increase internal validity.

On entering the field, my focus was on the music program offered during the year of the research and the philosophical perspectives that informed it. However, the teacher, who was a male in his mid-30s and the main participant, made constant reference to past events of both a personal and professional nature. Although I sought to 'frame' those school events that occurred during the year of the research, and direct attention only to them, it became apparent that by ignoring the past I would stand to lose information that could contextualize and give greater depth to the data I initially sought. The value of incorporating personal biography with situational analysis (Beynon, 1985; Goodson, 1981) became evident and led to the inclusion of life history interviews. These interviews in which 'the respondent is stimulated by the researcher to look back reflectively on the personal career' (Kelchtermans, 1994, p. 101) facilitated the collection of data on the teacher's preservice education and his early career goals. I use that data here to show that, for this teacher, the past and the present are linked by unchanging interests and commitments. In this paper the teacher is referred to as Joe Spence and the school in which the research was conducted as Hall Secondary.

Brief Overview of Joe Spence's Musical and Professional Education

Joe displayed musical talent at an early age but he lacked proper tuition. Piano lessons with his village teacher were lively and enjoyable but unstructured. He became musically literate through personal initiative; and his instrumental accomplishments brought him early recognition in his village community, where he played the organ in church every Sunday and contributed in various ways to the cultural life of the community. Joe's desire was to become a performer. In his late teens he decided to enter a teachers' college. He had no vocational commitment to teaching but he had outgrown his village teacher and entering the college offered him free education and an opportunity to have piano lessons with a reputable teacher.

Joe showed promise of becoming a fine pianist whose competence in performing western art music was displayed by his passing many of the overseas examinations of the Royal Schools of Music, England. But Joe was unable to tackle the more demanding repertory of the concert artist because of injuries he had sustained from an accident in his youth when he had broken both arms. Joe was not deterred. His interest in performing continued and he broadened his range of instrumental competencies by learning to play other instruments.

The three years spent at teachers' college helped Joe to improve his performing skills, but in retrospect he sees the college as having offered little in professional education. He had no understanding of the many ways in which music could be experienced by students of mixed abilities.

The teaching model to which Joe had been exposed prior to his preservice education was that of a 'musical education' (Paynter, 1977) in which focus is on the development of the formal musical skills of the professional musician. Pretraining influences are believed to have a major impact on the socialization of a teacher. And one viewpoint (Lortie, 1975) is that the many hours that teachers spend on pupils — 'the apprenticeship of observation' — contribute significantly to a teacher's conception of teaching.

Joe's pretraining experiences left him with the belief that music teaching, be it in school or elsewhere, is always aimed at the development of high levels of instrumental skill. Those misconceptions were reinforced by the teachers' college curriculum which focused narrowly on the development of instrumental skill. When Joe graduated from college his main interest was still in musical performance, and as a competent instrumentalist with little knowledge of teaching he embarked on his teaching career. He taught for twelve years in rural and urban schools before joining the staff of Hall Secondary where he now heads the music department.

The Reinforcing Effects of Institutional Values

Modeled on the British system of education, Jamaican schools are committed to offering music classes within the school day for all students (class music). Ideally, these classes should provide meaningful educational encounters in which a child's innate responses to musical sound are nurtured through the experiential modes of listening, composing and performing. Like Britain, it is also customary for some schools to provide extracurricular instrumental lessons/rehearsals which may be attended by volunteers and/or those students perceived to merit additional opportunities to develop musical skills. These extracurricular activities can be fruitfully used to enrich the musical experiences of all students and to lay the foundations for careers in music. But in many Jamaican schools extracurricular activities are aimed only at the training of performers by methods that lack educational benefits. Additionally, these activities often foster musical elitism and misconceptions of how musical growth is achieved.

As head of the music department at Hall Secondary and the only full-time music teacher, Joe is responsible for all of the department's work. Like other teachers who think of themselves as musicians rather than teachers, Joe has views of the curriculum that are 'predicated on the standards and practices of the Western "serious" tradition' (Swanwick, 1988, p. 9). He therefore assesses student aptitude and ability by the performance standards of that tradition. Finding students generally incapable of achieving those standards he concludes that students lack the motivation and discipline needed to participate in musical activities of quality and depth. Reflective of these beliefs, Joe's curriculum for class music provides a superficial exposure to music. In extracurricular rehearsals, where he trains a small and carefully selected groups of 'talented' students to perform in public events, Joe engages in work that has greater accord with his interest in professional performance.

These practices result from Joe's predilection for performance and from institutional values. Schools value the public approbation that they gain from performing groups. Hall Secondary respects Joe because of his abilities in the sphere of musical performance and his ability to recreate the 'world' of musical performance within the school community. The fact that Joe concentrates his energies only on a minority is not a concern. As Charles Plummeridge (1991) has observed:

> . . . the school teacher will acquire high status if he is regarded by school colleagues more as a professional musician, and one way in which he can achieve this status is through conducting performances of the school orchestra or school choir. (Plummeridge, 1991, p. 113)

Similar to the way in which Joe's preservice education accorded with his pretraining musical education and had the likely effect of reinforcing Joe's interest in professional performance, by its narrow concentration on musical performance Hall Secondary also reinforces Joe's latent identity as performer/professional musician.

But in previous jobs Joe also encountered a similar approach to music and it is his experience that schools have generally concentrated on the training of small performing groups. Because of this, Joe has not been challenged to broaden his understanding of music as a school subject and thereby adopt a greater variety of teaching roles. He has been allowed to remain within the narrow ambit of his personal preferences.

It has been argued that institutional values are strong determinants of teachers' perspectives toward teaching (Fenstermacher, 1980). Joe's perspective toward teaching owe as much to the characteristics of the institutions in which he has taught and continues to teach as to his predisposition to performance and his preservice education. The extent to which Joe gains satisfaction from teaching and how he copes with classroom life are matters to which I will now attend.

Joe's Perceptions of His Career

Theories have been advanced on the various phases and stages of a teacher's career (e.g., Huberman, 1988; Measor, 1985; Sikes, 1985). Joe's career falls within the fifth of Measor's six stages of a teacher's career. At the fifth stage, 'mid career moves and promotion' are prominent features (Measor, 1985). But as Joe readily admits to being an embittered and frustrated teacher he does not contemplate promotion and he has no career goals. He perceives teaching as having many disincentives, and prominent among them is the absence of adequate financial remuneration. The increase in familial responsibilities that he and other teachers experience at this age (Sikes, 1985) leads him to be concerned with the monetary rewards of teaching. Joe's recent promotion to senior teacher has caused him to question the worth of moving up in the system, because the increase in duties that have accompanied his promotion far outweighs the monetary increase. He has a general disinterest in promotion, a response that shows accord with the disinterest in vertical mobility displayed by Bennet's (1985) art teachers. This may suggest the existence of certain commonalities in the way that teachers of the arts view their careers in schools. But Joe's attitudes to his career also highlight the demotivating effects of Jamaica's education system on teachers.

Joe has wide-ranging concerns about teaching. In his classroom, his sensitivity about the existing differences between his musical interests and those of his students result in him being constantly on the defensive about how he and his curriculum offerings are regarded:

> Teachers are not looked up to! Its the DJs that are influencing people. Things are changing fast. I think my students see me as old-fashioned. They gravitate to the popular musicians. That is what is affecting my choir rehearsals. DJ is the in-thing!

Joe is also troubled about the relatively low status that teachers have in society because of their salaries and the duties that they are required to carry out. He is particularly concerned about certain pastoral duties carried out by Jamaican teachers within and outside of classes. He points to the authority role that he believes teachers should have in their classrooms and contrasts it to the role that teachers play in attending to what he calls 'trivial tasks'. These concerns would suggest that he experiences the type of role conflict that was found to occur when teachers performed undesirable duties (the Real I), rather than duties perceived to be compatible with their career (the Ideal I). And although research focused mainly on the different types of duties performed within classrooms, those findings illuminate the data here which do not differ substantially.

Joe's concerns about status go beyond life in school to a teacher's position in society for he perceives Jamaican society as being hostile to its teachers, which in his estimation has resulted in a general decline in teacher status:

> This society has lost respect for its teachers. What did we gain from the strike last year? Nothing much. The society is against us teachers. When you sum it up, the whole situation is discouraging to teachers.

A recent dispute on teachers' salaries highlighted Jamaica's changing attitudes to its teachers, who in the past, had gained unconditional respect from all sectors of the society. Webb (1985) records similar changes in American society where teachers have been known to display concern about how their salaries reflect a teacher's dwindling status. It is also not unknown for teachers to feel persecuted and attacked (Ranjard, 1984). In some instances those feelings may be justified but they may also be held in balance with more positive perceptions of the teaching career.

But Joe has no positive perceptions of his career. Financial problems interact with his concerns on status and concerns about a possible loss of authority in his classroom. They all combine to result in despondence and the absence of job satisfaction:

> I can do so much and no more. Teaching has so many problems without solutions . . . if you don't feel that you are contributing your sense of worth is debased. I have made so many compromises, eventually I feel that I can't make any more. The situation is frustrating and overwhelming. Sometimes I feel cut up, cut up and torn into several little pieces. I would like to do something worthwhile!

Joe's reference to having made many compromises points to the process of accommodation and adaptation that teachers generally undergo in the early years of teaching as they are socialized into the occupational culture of the career. It is evident that for Joe the process of accommodation and adaptation has been a particularly painful and long-lasting one. Understandably so because Joe's entry into teaching did not result from a sense of vocation but evolved out of his desire to have a musical education.

Although many of Joe's concerns about the teaching career are shared by other teachers and have been documented in the professional literature, nevertheless, there are several factors particular to this study that can be advanced to explain his discontent. Among these are the deficiencies of Joe's professional education, the absence of opportunities in Jamaica for ongoing staff development [particularly for music teachers], the low status that the subject has in the curriculum, and above all, Joe's preference for personal performance rather than class music teaching. But it is to the likely effects of teaching a subject low on the subject hierarchy that attention will be directed now.

Music is a 'practical' subject. And 'practical' subjects have been consistently disadvantaged in a system where abstract knowledge has high status, and 'practical' or 'non-academic' subjects are perceived to provide less educational benefits. Although school administrators value the positive impact that choirs and other ensembles have on the cultural life of the school community, music as a subject in the curriculum has little status in many countries.

Indicative of its low status in Jamaican schools, music is among a small group of subjects allotted the least time on the school's timetable. In schools there is a general scarcity of teaching materials for all subjects, the distribution of which underscores the marginalization of music. At Hall Secondary, for example, the school's administrators openly admit that due to budgetary constraints 'music is often the one [subject] that gets left out'. Music is further disadvantaged by the absence of a Ministry of Education syllabus and public examinations — provisions that are made for other subjects.

It is likely, therefore, that Joe perceives his sense of worth in relation to the subject's low status in the curriculum, the former becoming a reflection of the latter. The dialectic relationship between a teacher's sense of self, personal identity and the subject he or she teaches has been emphasized in other studies for example (Sikes *et al.*, 1985, Woods, 1984). Teaching a marginalized subject and constantly fighting for resources must have a significant impact on a teacher's career experiences and ultimately a teacher's identity.

Ways of Coping

Much of Joe's classroom behavior appears to grow out of his frustration and disinterest in school life. And in his actions there is evidence that he has adopted certain strategies to cope with his circumstances. For a while Joe continues to fulfill his duties to provide musical items for the school's special events through extracurricular rehearsals, in classes where he encounters the students of mixed abilities, music teaching is given low priority and Joe attends to a wider range of concerns and perceived needs.

From his perspective, the socialization of Hall's working-class students is of primary importance. Joe argues that the students are immoral and display undesirable social behaviors. Socializing these working-class students into the middle-class codes of school becomes a priority. Joe focuses attention on speech, hygiene, appropriate dress, care of furniture and equipment. Cleaning recorders becomes a time-consuming ritual in which thirty minutes of each lesson is expended on the task. This results in a sizable reduction to the time spent in teaching and learning music. In all lessons 'preparation' becomes a ritualistic activity in which students learn to respect the social order of Joe's classroom.

Joe's avoidance of teaching is shown by the infrequency and nature of his interventions. In classes he appears to have mentally retired to a distant position from which he merely goes through the routines needed to execute elementary tasks. His teaching style is that of a courteous instructor who directs activity without the appraisal or critical comment necessary and common to music teaching. Classroom activities center on repetitious drills, and the 'misbehavior' that often results provides Joe with further justification to abandon music teaching and to concentrate on control. The result is that after three years students show little evidence of having attended music classes.

Woods (1977) speaks of the strong 'continuance commitment' among teachers even in the face of growing pressures. In looking at Joe's career one sees evidence of continuance commitment by his length of service. Joe has been teaching for twelve years and despite his negative perceptions of his career he remains in teaching. But his investment in teaching has not been without rewards. Having come from a humble background, entering the teaching profession has brought him respect in his community. Therefore, there are assets and drawbacks. It is in an attempt to address the drawbacks that Joe uses the strategies outlined above as a means of adapting to his circumstances.

Drawing on Waller's observation of strategies used in classrooms, Woods (1977) has identified eight survival strategies that teachers use in circumstances where there are numerous pressures and problems and accommodation prevails over teaching. The classroom practices and actions described above are compatible with three of these survival strategies — socialization, absence or removal, ritual and routine. Five others — fraternization, occupational therapy, morale — boosting, domination and negotiation are also used by Joe. He may have gradually adopted these strategies over the years but they have now become a replacement for teaching.

The overall outcome is that Joe's engagement in teaching is minimal and he shows little concern with competence and efficiency at the work place — except in organizing special events for the school community. Instead, he displays considerable interest in his out-of-school musical commitments, and his ongoing goal is to strengthen his musical profile as performer and conductor. Therefore, where he does not seek professional development in, or discourse on, music teaching, he seeks both in the field of vocal and instrumental performance. Joe's out-of-school musical activities provide him with rewards not gained in school. His church choir can undertake a more sophisticated and musically satisfying repertoire than the school choir. And he believes that the members of his church choir are more cooperative and responsive than Hall's students. So like Bennet's (1985) art teachers, Joe engages in activities outside of school that provide the satisfaction needed from his subject, satisfaction that teaching alone does not provide. The data in Bennet's (1985) research suggests that:

> amongst art teachers 'career' is understood in broader terms than simply
> the teaching job, and that career needs and satisfactions are met through

involvement in activities outside teaching, not simply as an extension of the teaching career, but, in some cases, as a concurrent career. Art teachers, along with teachers in certain other subjects (such as Music and English) are in the special position of being able to pursue their subject interest whilst in teaching. (Bennet, 1985, p. 131)

But where Bennet's art teachers may hold their teaching careers in balance with their concurrent careers, Joe does not. And although this may be a problem specific to Joe it raises the question of whether there may be tensions not easily resolved for those who both practice music in society and teach it in schools. For where there are similarities between being a practicing artist and being an art teacher, there are perhaps less similarities between being musically active as a performer and being a teacher of music in school.

Visual art, be it practiced in school or society, is primarily concerned with an individual's creation of original aesthetic objects. Music as practiced in society is primarily concerned with musical performance. And even for those musicians who both compose and perform [like pop and jazz musicians] it is the musical product as performed and experienced in concert to which attention is directed.

In contrast, music in school should not only be concerned with performance. Attention should be placed on the many activities in listening, composing and performing that provide learners of different needs and interests with direct experiences of music. Music in school should place more value on constant engagement in worthwhile musical activity than on periodic displays of musical excellence in concerts. Therefore, there are likely to be differences between the thinking of a practicing musician and that of a school music teacher which may result from different dispositions and needs. And while, as Bennet (1985) suggests, teachers of music, art and English may accrue certain advantages from being able to pursue their subject interest while teaching, they may also find themselves in similar circumstances to Joe, where there are tensions between the different careers that their subject offers, and the different uses of the subject that those careers dictate.

There is undeniably a need for artist/teachers to be actively engaged in their art form as practicing artists. Apart from the personal satisfaction that this provides and the ongoing development of craft skills, their teaching will benefit from the constant awareness of the psychological and emotional rewards of artistic involvement. But in the final analysis, it is whether involvement as a practicing artist can be held in balance with loyalty to, and interest in, their teaching careers. And, most importantly, whether they see themselves as teachers or like Joe flounder around in despondency unable to find a workable identity.

Conclusion

Jamaican society lays strong emphasis on musical performance. And the process of enculturation that began in Jamaican society approximately three decades ago, after the country gained its independence from Britain, has done much to foster musical performance by highlighting Jamaican music of all genres. Within this cultural context there is need for schools and teachers' colleges to identify the distinctive features of music in education, and to establish how it differs from, or is similar to, the practice of music in society.

In a society that has spawned a thriving music industry which has gained world-wide recognition, music in education will have many benefits to derive from the musical culture of society. But as the training of secondary school music teachers (subject specialists) has been undertaken in Jamaica only in the last three decades, attention must be paid to building a tradition of teacher training through programs that not only draw on the cultural mores of the society, but also address the educational benefits that music as a school subject can provide.

A subject's culture is defined and developed not only by the knowledge embodied in that subject but also by the roles that its teachers play. Music as taught in Jamaican schools does not convey to budding musicians clear messages on the many roles that a music teacher should play — only one of which is that of professional musician. Weaknesses in the content and delivery of music programs in teacher education also result in further ambiguities on the nature and purpose of music in school. These are problems that have to be addressed, without which music will continue to lie outside of the mainstream of the schools' curriculum and may continue to be taught by persons whose interests lie only in music, not in music teaching.

References

ABRAHAM, A. (1985) in ESTEVE, J. (1989) 'Teacher burnout and teacher stress', in COLE, M. and WALKER, S. (Eds) *Teaching and Stress*, Milton Keynes, Philadelphia, Open University Press.

BENNET, C. (1985) 'Paints, pots or promotion: Art teachers' attitudes toward their careers', in BALL, S.J. and GOODSON, I.F. (Eds) *Teachers' Lives and Careers*, London, Falmer Press.

BEYNON, J. (1985) 'Institutional change and career histories in a comprehensive school', in BALL, S.J. and GOODSON, I.F. (Eds) *Teachers' Lives and Careers*, London, Falmer Press.

FENSTERMACHER (1980) cited in ZEICHNER, K.M., TABACHNICK, B.R. and DESMERE, K. (1987) in CALDERHEAD, J. (Ed) *Exploring Teachers' Thinking*, Cassell Educational Limited.

GOODSON, I. (1981) 'Life histories and the study of schooling', *Interchange*, **11**, 4/1980–81.

HUBERMAN, M. (1988) 'Teachers' careers and school improvement', *Journal of Curriculum Studies*, **20**, 2, pp. 119–32.

KELCHTERMANS, G. (1994) 'Biographical methods in the study of teachers' professional development', in CARLGREN, I., HANDAL, G. and SVEINUNG, V. (Eds) *Teachers' Minds and Actions: Research on Teachers' Thinking and Practice*, Falmer Press, London, Washington, DC.

LORTIE, D. (1975) *School Teacher: A Sociological Study*, Chicago, University of Chicago Press.

LYONS, G. (1981) *Teacher Careers and Career Perceptions*, Slough, NFER.

MEASOR, L. (1985) 'Critical incidents in the classroom: Identities, choices and careers', in BALL, S.J. and GOODSON, I.F. (Eds) *Teachers' Lives and Careers*, London, Falmer Press.

PAYNTER, J. (1977) 'The role of creativity in the school music curriculum', in BURNETT, M. (Ed) *Music Education Review*, **1**, London, Chappell.

PLUMMERIDGE, C. (1991) *Music Education in Theory and Practice*, London, Falmer Press.

RANJARD, P. (1984) cited in ESTEVE, J. (1989) 'Teacher burnout and teacher stress', in COLE, M. and WALKER, S. (Eds) *Teaching and Stress*, Milton Keynes, Philadelphia, Open University Press.

SIKES, P.J. (1985) 'The life cycle of the teacher', in BALL, S.J. and GOODSON, I.F. (Eds) *Teachers' Lives and Careers*, London, Falmer Press.

SIKES, P., MEASOR, L. and WOODS, P. (1985) *Teacher Careers: Crises and Continuities*, Lewes, Falmer Press.

SWANWICK, J. (1988) *Music, Mind and Education*, London and New York, Routledge.

WEBB, R.B. (1985) 'Teacher status panic: Moving up the down escalator', in BALL, S.J. and GOODSON, I.F. (Eds) *Teachers' Lives and Careers*, London, Falmer Press.

WOODS, P. (1977) 'Teaching for survival', in WOODS, P. and HAMMERSLEY, M. (Eds) *School Experience*, New York, St Martin's Press.

WOODS, P. (1984) 'Teacher, self and curriculum', in GOODSON, I.F. and BALL, S.J. (Eds) *Defining the Curriculum*, London, Falmer Press.

Part III

Teachers' Knowledge: Overview

R. Terrance Boak

Clark and Peterson's (1986) chapter 'Teachers' thought processes' in the 3rd *Handbook of Research on Teaching* illustrates that research on teacher thinking and teacher knowledge had a short tradition and the sum of its findings up to 1986 do not offer much insight. Boak (1995) commented on Clark and Peterson:

> Studies of teacher knowledge from the 'teacher thinking' literature usually focuses on particular aspects of thinking related to particular constructs of teaching (for example, preactive and interactive teaching) or components of teaching, such as teacher planning and decision-making. This literature indirectly informs the process of school reform, in instances when implementation targets an aspect of teaching, such as planning, which is part of that literature. But the general conclusions about teacher thinking and teacher knowledge within this literature are weak and commonsensical. For example, these include: 'thinking plays an important part of teaching . . . Teachers do plan in a rich variety of ways . . . Teachers do have thoughts and make decisions frequently . . . Teachers do have theories and belief systems that influence their perceptions, plans, and actions'. (Boak, 1995, p. 7)

On the other hand Shulman (1987) built a foundation for teaching reform on 'an idea of teaching that emphasizes comprehension and reasoning, transformation and reflection' (p. 1) thus advancing and changing the direction of research on teachers' knowledge. He introduced categories of the knowledge base including: content, general pedagogical, curriculum, pedagogical content, knowledge of learners and their characteristics, of educational contexts and educational ends, purposes and values and their philosophical and historical grounds.

Elbaz defined teachers' knowledge 'in its own terms rather than in terms derived from theory' (cited in Clandinin, 1986, p. 18), as emerged from interviews in which a teacher reflected on her teaching. Other researchers (Clandinin, 1986; Connelly and Clandinin, 1988; 1990; Beattie, 1995) worked with Elbaz's concept of practical knowledge, extending and refining her original concepts. Connelly and Clandinin (1988) define 'personal practical knowledge' as 'a moral, affective and aesthetic way of knowing life's educational situations' (p. 59) extending concepts of knowledge to 'professional knowledge landscapes' in order to explore how teachers' knowledge 'shapes, and is shaped by, their professional knowledge context' (Clandinin and Connelly, 1995, p. 3) and to appreciate the complexity of professional knowledge as evidenced within teachers' practice. The newness of the research and the complexity of the area merit consulting reviews of the teacher knowledge literature (e.g., Clark and Peterson, 1986; Shulman, 1987; Carter, 1990; 1993; Fenstermacher, 1994).

The papers contained in this section are diverse views on teachers' knowledge and how that knowledge informs both practice and theory. Jean Clandinin and F. Michael Connelly tell three stories about the professional knowledge landscape understood as the knowledge context within which teachers work, intellectually and morally, through two configurations: 'in' and 'out' of the classroom knowledge.

Out of the classroom knowledge is comprised of implementation strategies, research findings, plans, policy statements and improvement schemes contrasting with the classroom; an action-based practical place. The teacher's way of being in the classroom is storied; expressed through narrative. A teacher's stories are referred to as the expression of his or her personal practical knowledge in practice. 'School stories' are those narratives shared by the people in a school. Symbols can be the key to unlocking school stories and gaining a special understanding of them and therefore acquire the tools to change the stories and consequently the school culture. The authors wonder if, by living new stories in their in-classroom place in the landscape, they could shape the landscape. Their work on understanding the landscape gives a way to see and navigate the complex landscapes they live in and has implications for those trying to navigate teacher education and school reform. Their work makes it clear to us that teachers are not autonomous agents working in contextless spaces.

The cooperating teacher develops student's practical theories and abilities to reflect critically. With the learning/cognition approach the student participates in a community, at first peripheral like an apprenticeship but increasing gradually in complexity and engagement. Students come to know the knowledge in the performance and are thus both absorbing and absorbed into a culture. Although there are limits for participation in the community, the student has access to a range of experiences through members of the community and their experiences.

The guided practice approach reveals that a student cannot be taught what he or she needs to know, but can be coached. The student must see on his or her own behalf the relation between means, methods and results. The teacher needs to use the structures/systems within the community to make situations transparent so that the student and others can see.

Chris Day and Mark Hadfield attempt to identify the key influences at institutional, political and cultural levels on teachers' construction of their curricula. They hypothesize that whether or not teachers begin to question their classroom routines depends on attitude, role conception and environmental variables. By adopting the stance of a 'critical friend' in second order action research, they were able to videotape teachers discussing problems they wanted to look at. As teachers spoke, the ideas that the professional knowledge of teachers is embedded in their own interpretations of experience and that they deconstruct and reconstruct their contexts and themselves were reinforced.

They conclude that teachers need reflection to understand and act on their understanding of what they do, needing assistance however, for locating themselves within their own image of their roles. In other words, intervention is a necessary catalyst to move teachers from implicit to explicit models of thinking. Biographical projections of teachers are as crucial as context to the investigation. The need for growth is seen in developing ideas on how the past might be linked to the future by identifying teachers' present dominant images.

Susan Brown, Marcella Kysilka and Maureen Warner view the learner as maker of his or her own knowledge. Perspectives and opinions of other learners can enrich process and deepen knowledge. A constructivist teacher's role in the classroom is one of fellow investigator which the authors deem appropriate to demonstrate appreciation of multicultural perspectives in class.

Six descriptors for constructivist teachers are given in addition to the idea that constructivist teachers must encourage students to engage in reflective thinking. They reason that, if students construct their own knowledge, they must have time to consolidate it, and expand upon it. Because this learner-centered approach honors the individual and provides for his or her interests and needs it is well suited to multicultural content.

C.T. Patrick Diamond, C.A. Mullen and Mary Beattie tell a shared story of how educational research can be re-imagined as an improvisatory and also framed form of art based on a model they create called IICO (Intuition, Imagination, Collaboration and Orchestration). They believe a reconstruction of professional knowledge takes place when image and imagination are linked, and heightened when understood and pursued as art. They position themselves against traditional research and wish to escape the constricting single point perspective. Diamond uses self-narratives to draw his attention to the formal taken-for-granted constructions through which he has been accustomed to view research. Mullen uses marginalized narratives to reveal the less apparent sides of mainstream academic knowledge and describes teacher education and research as a merry-go-round of paradigmatic and institutional restrictions. Finally, Beattie learns the necessity of both solitary and shared creative activity to further knowledge. Meaning is further developed and transformed when individuals engage in responsive sets of exchanges with each other to a main point of renewal and refocusing of attention by entertaining alternative versions of theory and practice — location through dislocation.

Elisabeth Ahlstrand and colleagues provide a detailed look at the Swedish educational system and its roots and traces its development to show the development in stages of teachers' knowledge. They identify two ways of conceiving a teacher's professional knowledge; formal (handed down) and experiential. Student teachers' assumed filters (paradigms) decided how that student will accept/reject different messages expressed by researchers. An intervention towards personal development helps reveal variations in teachers' identities, knowledge and knowledge development.

Ivor Goodson focuses on the 'new genre' of teachers' knowledge, stories and narratives. He sees the development of a 'new genre' as a response to a crisis of representation where the teachers' voices have been muffled by the researchers' voices. He outlines the argument for listening to teachers and summarizes the growing movement and points to the relationship between stories and their social context and deciding that they should not only be *narrated* but *located*. Because language is ambiguous, the danger of stories marginalizing the people to whom they appear to give voice cannot be overlooked. Goodson sees the content of the new genre embraced by researchers but the context aspect urgently needing development. The virtues of stories are that they make our experiences concrete and they provide insights into the socially constructed nature of our experiences. Goodson echoes as other researchers have the concern that sanctifying storytelling will not serve the community well if we are simply substituting one paradigmatic domination for another without challenging domination itself. We need to ask why we are telling the stories in the first place.

All of the papers contained in this section are educative. They advance our understanding of teachers' knowledge and also contribute to our personal practice/theory dialectic and thus play an important role in revitalizing and advancing our knowledge. I believe that the papers contained in this section have met the challenge that Fenstermacher (1994) spoke of:

> The challenge for teacher knowledge research is not simply one of showing us that teachers think, believe, or have opinions but they know. And even more important, that they know they know (Fenstermacher, 1994, p. 51).

References

BEATTIE, M. (1995) *Constructing Professional Knowledge in Teaching: A Narrative of Change and Development*, New York, Teachers College Press.

BOAK, C. (1995) 'Knowledge and inquiry within teaching', Unpublished paper, Ontario Institute for Studies in Education, Toronto, ON.

CARTER, K. (1990) 'Teachers' knowledge and learning to teach', in HOUSTON, W. (Ed) *Handbook of Research on Teacher Education*, New York, Macmillan, pp. 291–310.

CARTER, K. (1993) 'The place of story in the study of teaching and teacher education', *Educational Researcher*, **22**, 1, pp. 5–18.

CLANDININ, D.J. (1986). *Classroom Practice: Teacher Images in Action*, Philadelphia, PA, Falmer Press.

CLANDININ, D.J. and CONNELLY, F.M. (1995) *Teachers' Professional Knowledge Landscapes*, New York, Teachers College Press.

CLARK, C. and PETERSON, P. (1986) 'Teachers' thought processes', in WITTROCK, M. *Handbook of Research on Teaching* (3rd ed.), New York, Macmillan, pp. 255–96.

CONNELLY, F.M. and CLANDININ, D.J. (1988) *Teachers as Curriculum Planners: Narratives of Experience*, Toronto, ON, OISE Press.

CONNELLY, F.M. and CLANDININ, D.J. (1990) 'Stories of experience and narrative inquiry', *Educational Researcher*, **19**, 5, pp. 2–14.

ELBAZ, F. (1980) 'The teacher's practical knowledge: A case study', Unpublished doctoral dissertation, Ontario Institute for Studies in Education, University of Toronto Graduate Department of Education, Toronto, ON.

FENSTERMACHER, G. (1994) 'The knower and the known: The nature of knowledge in research on teaching', in DARLING-HAMMOND, L. (Ed) *Review of Research in Education*, Washington, DC, AERA, **20**, pp. 3–56.

SHULMAN, L. (1987) 'Knowledge and teaching: Foundations of the new reform', *Harvard Educational Review*, **57**, 1, pp. 1–22.

11 A Storied Landscape as a Context for Teacher Knowledge[1]

D. Jean Clandinin and F. Michael Connelly

Introduction[2]

In this paper we continue our research into the question of how the embodied, narrative, relational, knowledge teachers carry autobiographically and by virtue of their formal education shapes, and is shaped by, their professional knowledge context (Clandinin, 1986; Connelly and Clandinin, 1988; Clandinin and Connelly, 1995a). This question has been in the background of our work for many years. Beginning with our early studies where we concentrated on teachers' personal practical knowledge, we understood the intellectual risk of the work which might, for some, encourage too partial a view of teachers' knowledge. We were constantly reminded that teachers do not work in isolation, nor do they work in environments solely of their own choosing. Our work in the last few years has focused on these professional knowledge contexts for teachers' personal practical knowledge.

In order to provide an imaginative context for you, we begin with a story, a research text created from our early field texts at Bay Street School, our school research site from some fifteen years ago.

In our first walk through Bay Street School with Phil Bingham, the newly appointed principal, we noticed the bench outside the main school office. It was a plain brown bench with no back. From our view it fitted into the woodwork of the school and was hardly noticeable as a piece of furniture. As we walked by, Phil, noticing a child sitting on the bench, stopped, spoke to him briefly and the child went down the hall. We assumed he went back to class.

At that moment, on our first day as researchers in the school, the bench and Phil's exchange with the child seemed of little note. So much was happening in the school. Phil described the physical changes: new lighting, new paint, freshly painted lockers, displays of children's work and so on. Phil did not comment on the bench nor on his exchange with the child. As we continued to spend weeks and months in the school, however, we did begin to pay attention to the bench and to what happened to children who sat on it. And we did talk with Phil about it.

It turns out that the bench was called the punishment bench by the staff and students at Bay Street School. At the time of Phil's arrival at Bay Street, the school practice was that children were sent out of their classrooms and down to sit on the

137

punishment bench to wait to be dealt with by the principal or assistant principal. The bench was situated in a very public place so that anyone walking into the school or walking down the main hallway of the school could see who was sitting on it. The school story about the bench meant everyone understood what it meant to be seated on it. It meant you were a student in trouble, and you were waiting, in this highly visible place on the out-of-classroom place on the landscape, for your punishment to be meted out by the principal or his designate, the assistant principal. The story for children, teachers and administrators had been lived out many times. 'Go and sit on the bench' was the common directive to children whose teachers were frustrated and unable to engage in more productive ways with them. After each recess and noon break the bench was full to overflowing with children sent in for misbehavior by teachers on outdoor and hallway supervision.

It was this school story that was being lived out when Phil arrived in the school. The bench was a symbol for the lived out story. A child seated on the bench meant a living out of the story was in progress. When no one was on the bench it meant everything was under control. No one but children ever sat on the bench.

Phil knew the school story of the bench and he knew what it symbolized in the school. He knew that sending a child there was an acknowledgment that something was not working between a teacher and a child and that the teacher wanted administrator intervention in punishing the child. The plot line was one that positioned children as objects to be acted on by teachers.

It was not a school story that Phil wanted lived out in Bay Street School. It conflicted with the plot line of the stories he thought children and teachers were to live out together. In Phil's story of school, teachers were to be in relationship with children. His story of school was lived and told, in part, around a personal philosophy which he often summarized in a series of points. We had seen him list these points and talk about his philosophy on several occasions such as professional development days and so on. The points he made as he spoke of his philosophy were:

1 the importance of other people;
2 and communication;
3 within a loving relationship or atmosphere;
4 with individuals holding a workable concept of self;
5 and having the freedom to function;
6 with creativity. (Notes to file, 19 February 1982)

This personal philosophy lived and told by Phil as principal created a story of school, a story with a storyline of relationships and community among children, teachers, administrators and parents. Sending children out of a classroom to sit in a public place as characters in a school story of misbehavior and punishment did not fit with his story of school.

Phil recognized this and began to work to change the school story for which the punishment bench served as a symbol. When students were sent to the bench Phil talked with them quickly, often in full view of any passerby. This is what we had observed that very first day we were researchers in the school. He did not mete out punishment for those on the bench but sent the children quickly back to their classrooms. He began to sit on the bench and encouraged others, us, teachers, children, to join him. We often were encouraged to sit with him as he chatted with us and greeted staff, students and visitors to the school. Gradually teachers stopped sending children to the bench as the school story changed about relationships with children. Gradually the bench no longer was a symbol of the school story of misbehavior and punishment and became a useful piece of furniture to sit on in the front hallway.

The bench has stayed with us as a telling feature of the professional knowledge landscape. Coming to understand how the bench acted as a symbol for teachers, children, parents and adminstrators of a school story has made us aware of other school stories and helps us understand more about teachers' professional knowledge landscape. Understanding more about the storied nature of the professional knowledge landscape helps us understand more about teacher knowledge.

Before revisiting this story and telling other stories, we set a context for this Bay Street story within our other professional knowledge work.

A Brief Recap: Researching the Professional Knowledge Landscape

We have begun to conceptualize the knowledge context within which teachers work in terms of a professional knowledge landscape (Clandinin and Connelly, 1995a). Conceptualizing the professional knowledge context as a landscape is particularly well-suited to our purpose. It allows us to talk about space, place and time. Furthermore, it has a sense of expansiveness and the possibility of being filled with diverse people, things and events in different relationships. Because we see the professional knowledge landscape as composed of relationships among people, places and things, we see it as both an intellectual and moral landscape.

We characterized the landscape in which teachers live and work as comprised of two fundamentally different places: one behind the classroom door with students and the other in professional, communal places with others. While it seemed quite obvious that teachers spend part of their time in classrooms and part of their time in other communal places, we had not paid close attention to the relationship between how teachers live in their classrooms and how teachers live in those other places nor had we looked at the epistemological nature of those two places. We began to see the dilemmas teachers experienced as they crossed the boundaries between these two places many times each day and we began to see they were two epistemologically different places on the landscape.

The place on the landscape outside of classrooms is a place filled with knowledge funneled into the school system for the purpose of altering teachers' and children's classroom lives. Teachers talk about this knowledge all the time. We all make reference to this knowledge in comments such as 'What's coming down the pipe?' In such metaphorical expressions, teachers express their knowledge of their out-of-classroom place as a place littered with imposed prescriptions. It is a place filled with other people's visions of what is right for children. Researchers, policy makers, senior administrators and others, using various implementation strategies, push research findings, policy statements, plans, improvement schemes and so on down what we have called, in other work, the conduit onto this out-of-classroom place on the landscape.

The conduit for us is a metaphor that characterizes the deeply embedded notion of thoery-driven practice in North American education. The universality and taken-for-grantedness of the supremacy of theory over practice gives it the quality of a sacred story (Crites, 1971). Crites makes the point that sacred stories are so pervasive they remain mostly unnoticed and when named are hard to define. He writes 'these stories seem to be elusive expressions of stories that cannot be fully and directly told, because they live, so to speak, in the arms and legs and bellies of the celebrants. These stories lie too deep in the consciousness of the people to be directly told' (p. 294). The relationship of theory to practice in North American education has this quality and for that reason we say that the professional knowledge landscape is embedded in a sacred story of theory-driven practice. The metaphor of a conduit allows us to name this sacred story and to give a sense of how it functions in relating theory to practice (Clandinin and Connelly, 1992).

Classrooms are a special place on the professional knowledge landscape. Classrooms are, in Schwab's (1971) terms, practical places. They are places of action where teachers teach and where curriculum is made, at least the curriculum that matters as far as students are concerned. The in-classroom place on the landscape is, in our view, epistemologically different than the out-of-classroom place. In our view, the practices of teaching and curriculum making that fill the in-classroom place are expressions of teachers' knowledge, knowledge which we see as narrative knowledge. In our view of teachers' knowledge, teachers know their lives in terms of stories, that is, their way of being in the classroom is storied. In other places we have pointed out how dramatically different teachers' narrative knowledge expressed in practice on the in-classroom place is from the knowledge context on the out-of-classroom place.

The in-classroom place tends to be a private place in the sense that teachers and students work behind closed doors. This privacy of the classroom plays an important epistemological function. It is a safe place, generally free from scrutiny, where teachers are free to live stories of practice. These lived stories are essentially secret ones.

As teachers move from the in-classroom to the out-of-classroom place, they tell us they learn to live and tell cover stories, stories constructed around story plot lines which fit the expectations of the out-of-classroom place. As we studied the landscape and thought more about the cover stories teachers learned to live and tell, we began to identify the plot outlines of other kinds of stories. We began to ask what kinds of stories filled the out-of-classroom place on the professional knowledge landscape.

This led us to begin to understand the stories of school that were lived out and shaped the landscape (Clandinin and Connelly, 1995a). For example, in our revisit to the field texts of our Bay Street work, we were mindful of the story of school lived and told when we first arrived at Bay Street School. The story of school was told around a plot line of low achievement, of racial problems, of a school that needed to be 'cleaned up'. It was these stories of Bay Street School that prompted the appointment of Phil Bingham, the principal. The school board's senior administrators wanted a new story of Bay Street School.

But as we studied the broad outlines of the story of school at Bay Street and the stories of school lived out at other schools in which we work, we realized there were still other kinds of stories that shaped the professional knowledge landscape. There were, of course, teacher stories, that is, the expression of teachers' personal practical knowledge in practice. Teacher stories were most apparent on the in-classroom place on the landscape. Earlier we characterized them as mostly secret stories. Teacher stories were also lived and told on the out-of-classroom place. Some of these were cover stories, particularly important when teacher stories conflicted with the story of school that school principals or senior administrators wanted lived and told.

But we realized there was yet another kind of story, stories we named school stories, that is, stories of school events and practices, stories shared by those people in the schools. Some were of recent events. Others seemed more enduring, lived but not told. Initially we had not attended to these stories as we went about our research work but when we named these as school stories, we began to be mindful of their powerful shaping influences. We began to be observant of how school events and practices were storied. With this in mind, we return to our opening story.

Revisiting the Story of 'the Bench' As a School Story

In the story with which we began this paper, we had our first insight into the shaping power of a school story. To recap, when Phil was brought to Bay Street, the story of school was of a racially troubled school with low achievement. Phil was brought in to 'clean up' the school, to restory the story of school. Embedded within the story of school lived and told prior to Phil's arrival was a school story of discipline. When a child misbehaved, a teacher would punish the child. When a teacher's punishment or discipline did not influence the child's behavior, the child was sent down to the bench outside the principal's office for his or her intervention. It was this school story that was being lived out at Bay Street School when we first walked down the hall with Phil. Phil was already aware of that school story and was working to change it. We became awake to the plot outlines of this school story when we observed what happened at the bench. As we watched, we saw the bench as a symbol of that particular school story.

We were, we think, not the only ones who recognized the bench as a powerful symbol of the story, although we may have been the only ones who named it as such. Phil, too, realized that it was a symbol for the school story.

Our interest in symbols was triggered by our interest in what we could learn about school stories and, hence, about the nature of the professional knowledge context in which teachers lived and worked. If we could identify symbols, perhaps we could learn more about school stories. For example, we realized that the bench was a symbol for a school story of discipline at Bay Street. It was a symbol for a school story Phil wanted to change. Eventually we saw how Phil changed the school story as the bench faded into the woodwork and was no longer a symbol of anything.

In current work, we are involved on the professional knowledge landscape of other schools trying to learn about school stories and what objects, events or people seem to symbolize the stories. Our thinking is that if we can understand these school stories, we will be able to understand more about how the storied landscape shapes teacher knowledge and how teachers' knowledge shapes the landscape.

In project discussions among people who work in the University of Alberta part of this research, that is, Cheryl Craig, Annie Davies, Janice Huber, Chuck Rose, Karen Whelan and Jean Clandinin, we began to talk about our schools in an attempt to identify the plot outlines of school stories.

At this point we are all living within schools, some of us as researcher-teachers and others as teacher-researchers. To try to identify school stories on our professional knowledge landscapes, we began to tell stories about our schools to each other. Our stories were of diverse practices such as team teaching and new formats for school conferences; of people such as new administrators; of places such as redecorated staffrooms (Clandinin, *et al.*, 1995).

As we responded to each other's accounts, several things happened. We were, of course, interested in each other's stories but we also resonated with each other's accounts. Sometimes we knew the school in question, the people in question and sometimes we recognized similar situations in our own experiences. For example, Cheryl Craig told a story about a team teaching relationship that was storied on the out-of-classroom place on the landscape as working well. Cheryl described the teachers as having opened the dividing curtain which separated their two classroom spaces. In many Canadian schools built in the last thirty years, schools tend to be open with dividing curtains or barriers which can be opened or closed dependent upon teachers' instructional requirements. Annie Davies responded to Cheryl's story by telling of a team teaching relationship within which she had worked in which the story of success which the participants had told on the out-of-classroom place was not the lived story (Davies, 1996). The story told of success was what we call a cover story. In Annie's story, the dividing curtain was also open to give sense of successful team teaching. Chuck Rose, a school principal, spoke of touring visitors through his schools. When the story of school that was told in one of his schools was one in which collegiality and cooperation figured strongly and where school stories of team teaching supported that story of school, he took visitors to areas where the dividing curtain between classroom spaces was pulled open. The open curtain, he knew, was for himself and for visitors, a symbol that the story of team teaching was a successful one.

We all nodded in agreement that this was a symbol that told others that a school story of successful team teaching was being lived out. A curtain drawn closed between the two areas was a symbol that a successful team teaching story was not being lived out. We also knew that sometimes the story that team teachers told was a cover story. Annie Davies in her research on team teaching is helping us to understand this in new ways.

This telling of stories and responding to stories helped us to make sense of what we were calling school stories. We began to explore these school stories to see what we could learn about teachers' professional knowledge landscapes. We retell two of them here.

Staying after School: Changing a School Story

Janice Huber, a year one/two teacher-researcher, is part of the professional knowledge landscape project (Connelly and Clandinin, in preparation). She has participated in our conversations. She told the following story which we retell here.

In Janice's classroom, children are encouraged to participate in a support circle where class members come together to talk about their concerns. Children come to the circle to talk of issues that concern them, of playground incidences, of events they want to story. As Janice described these sessions, they were rich sessions, full of stories and response as children learned how to live in a classroom community. As the school year progressed, some children began to ask to stay after school to extend the possibility of a smaller support circle with Janice and other children to whom they wanted to tell their stories and to hear response. Children who wanted to gather together to talk about an issue with Janice and their peers put their names on the whiteboard and Janice then knew there would be a meeting after school. At the end of each day, with children gathered around her on the carpet, Janice handed out notices, reminded children of various responsibilities such as papers to be taken home and so on. She also glanced at the board and asked if the children who had written their names down were staying for a support circle discussion. For Janice and the children, writing their names on the board was an important reminder of children's active participation in the kind of community being lived out in their classroom.

One day, when I was visiting in the classroom, a distraught mother appeared to collect her son. She said to Janice in an upset way that she did not want her son's name on the board so he would be 'kept' after school any longer. Her son, she said, was not to blame for the playground problems. Another child was the troublemaker. Janice, confused, began to explain that her son had initiated his participation in the after-school sessions. He had asked to stay to share his accounts and to try to find a way to work through the difficulties.

Revisiting 'Names on the Board' as a Symbol of a School Story

As we talked about this event we began to understand how having a child's name on the blackboard was a symbol of a school story being lived out on the in-classroom place on the landscape. The child's mother had interpreted the symbol as pointing to the most taken-for-granted meaning of the school story. The plot line of the 'usual' school story was that a child misbehaved, a teacher wrote his or her name on the board, the child was kept after school for punishment. The child's name on the board was a symbol that the story was in the process of being lived out. It is such a commonplace story that the mother, new to the school, knew the plotline.

The distraught mother interpreted the symbol of names on the board and saw the school story of blame and punishment for her child being lived out. Janice and the children were unmindful of how their use of names on the board and time with the teacher after school could be read in that commonplace way. They were also unmindful that others would be interpreting the symbol as pointing to a common school story. For Janice and the children the symbol was embedded in one story, a story of community responsibility. For the distraught mother the symbol was embedded in another story, a story of misbehavior by a child and punishment by a teacher. The symbol could be read from within different plot lines.

That there were at least two stories that the symbol of names on the board and staying after school could point to was interesting. To Janice and the children, authors of the school story in their classroom, having your name on the board was a symbol for one story. To the child's mother and possibly to other outsiders to the school story in the classroom, having your name on the board was a symbol for another story.

We were reminded of the dividing curtain that was open or shut between team teachers. We knew from Annie Davies's and Cheryl Craig's research that teachers who were living an unsuccessful team teaching story would sometimes leave the curtain open as part of their cover story of successful team teaching. The symbol of an open curtain would point outsiders to the cover story of success. By leaving the curtain open, it was a symbol for many on the out-of-classroom place of a successful school story of team teaching.

We began to speculate on what happens when a teacher tries to restory a symbol, as Janice and the children had. While Janice and the children had done so without consideration of what writing names on the board for time after school symbolized, were there other instances of restorying a symbol?

Could we see symbols which pointed to different school stories being lived out? Could school stories be changed if the symbols remained visible? We began to talk of school conferences which were part of Karen Whelan's and my stories.

School Conferences: Changing a School Story

The parent-teacher reporting conference is a common event on the professional knowledge landscape in many North American schools. Several times each school year, parents come into schools to meet with teachers. These conference meeting times form an important cycle in the school year. Teachers know a rhythm of the school year around this cycle.

There is a school story about parent–teacher conferences. The school story usually is built around a plotline that has teachers with knowledge of a child's academic, social, emotional and physical achievement reporting to parents. Parents are assumed not to have such knowledge of the child. The conference usually centers around some kind of written report card or document in which a child's achievement is summed up by the teacher or teachers. The document is provided and the conference held. The preparation of the document by teachers and the reporting to parents is part of the reporting cycle in schools. This is the plot outline of the most common school story. The conference itself is a symbol of teacher expert knowledge about a child being given to the child's parents. The intricacies of this school story with its symbol of parent conferences was one with which all of us in our project group were familiar. And, as we shared stories, we realized that in many of our research schools, teachers were trying to live and tell a new school story of working with parents and children to discuss progress.

I told the following story of a school staff attempting to compose a new school story of working with parents and children.

At Bisset School the story of school is one of community, of parents, teachers, children, other school personnel, and others who live in the school, working together. The story of school was first told by the principal as she opened this new school. Teachers who came to the school were selected if they told teacher stories which were congruent with this story of school.

As the staff began to work together, they mindfully began to compose, live and tell school stories which supported the plotline of the story of school. They paid close attention to evaluation and reporting, perhaps knowing that how the school stories of evaluation and reporting were lived and told were particularly powerful shaping influences on the storied professional knowledge landscape.

There are still conferences at Bisset School. However, at Bisset School, conferences are a time for parents, a teacher and a child to meet to discuss a child's achievements. Each child develops a portfolio in consultation with his or her parents and his or her teachers including in the portfolio samples of various aspects of his or her work. The conference is a time for the child to share the portfolio with teachers and parents. The school story in which these conferences are embedded is a story in which all voices are heard in conversation and reflection. The school story which the staff at Bisset live and tell is a markedly different one than the usual one. The staff know this and they work hard at living this restoried story. The conferences are still there but the school story is changed.

We know only how most teachers tell the restoried story of evaluation and reporting. We know only that most teachers see the symbol of conferences as pointing to that school story of working together. What is unknown is if some participants, teachers, children, parents new to the school, read the symbol of conferences as pointing to the more familiar school story. Do they come to the conferences and live out the familiar story of teacher as expert knower, parent as receiver of knowledge and child as voiceless object being reported on?

As we reflected on these school stories of change we began to wonder about how teachers and principals restory their professional knowledge landscapes. We wondered if by living new stories on their in-classroom place on the landscape they could shape the landscape? If by living new stories on the out-of-classroom place on the landscape could they shape the landscape?

When some school stories are so taken-for-granted, can the stories which symbols point to be restoried? As we shared these research questions, we began to wonder if school stories could be changed if the same people, practices, places, events that were symbols in more taken-for-granted stories were left in place and new stories told and lived around them?

Revisiting the Stories

In the story of Janice's classroom, we saw how Janice and the children began to live and tell a new school story in which the symbol of names on the board and after school meetings were expressions of classroom community. The symbol of names written on the board pointed to that school story shared among them. But that symbol was most commonly embedded within another school story. At least one parent knew the usual story and raised her concerns. Janice and the children set out to live a school story in their classroom that inadvertently drew on practices that were common symbols of another story. The situation was different for the teachers at Bisset School. They composed and began to live a new school story of working together, of valuing all voices in conversations among children, parents and teachers. Together they agreed that there would still be school conferences but in their restoried story, conferences would be a symbol of a school story with a plotline of collaboration among children, parents and teachers.

As we reflected on Janice's account and on the account of Bisset School, we realized that in both instances the symbols were ones that are familiar in many schools, that is, children's names written on the board and conferences. We wondered if we could live new school stories if we kept familiar symbols which usually pointed us to familiar stories. Could new school stories be lived and told which used familiar practices, practices which usually symbolized the old stories?

We saw something different at Bay Street School. There we saw how the new principal, Phil Bingham, did not like the school story for which the bench served as symbol. That school story was in conflict with the story of school which he had been brought to Bay Street to live and tell. As he began to change the story of school at Bay Street, he also began to change the school story of the bench. Eventually the bench no longer served as a symbol of anything. It became only a useful piece of furniture. The school story of discipline changed. The bench no longer played a part.

Contextualizing Teachers' Personal Practical Knowledge within the Professional Knowledge Landscape

We began this paper by asking how teachers' personal practical knowledge shaped, and was shaped by, their professional knowledge contexts. We have begun to answer this question by conceptualizing their contexts as a professional knowledge landscape which we understand narratively. We began by positing a landscape with in- and out-of-classroom places which are morally and epistemologically different places. The landscape, situated at the interface of theory and practice in teachers' lives, can be understood as filled with different kinds of stories: secret, sacred and cover stories. But the landscape is also filled with stories of schools, school stories, stories of teachers and teacher stories. These stories are all intricately interwoven.

As we tried to understand the landscape and its interconnections with teachers' knowledge, we tried to understand school stories and the ways that certain events, people, places and things were storied as school stories. We realized that some things served as symbols which pointed us, as teacher-researchers and researcher-teachers, to these stories. As we told the stories, we recognized the symbols and began to see the complexity.

Symbols could point to different school stories as Janice, the children and parents learned. Symbols could be highlighted and discussed like the conferences at Bisset School in a mindful attempt to change the underlying school story. Or symbols could vanish from the landscape as the bench as a symbol did at Bay Street School.

As we thought about the ways the landscape shapes teachers' knowledge, we realized how powerful these school stories are. Janice, in the safety of her in-classroom place on the landscape has to consider how she will restory her practices so she can continue to try to live a story of community in her classroom. The staff at Bisset School need to be always attentive to how teachers, parents, and children will return to the comfort of a familiar story line.

As we continue our study of the professional knowledge landscape, we see that the work gives, as Jonas Soltis notes, 'teachers, teacher educators, and educational researchers a way to see into and meaningfully navigate the complex professional landscapes they live in' (Soltis, 1995).

The work has, we think, significant implications for those of us who are trying to meaningfully navigate teacher education and school reform. As we work with teacher education students and teachers, we need to work together in order to educate all of us to be mindful of our own stories, that is, to our personal practical knowledge, but also to be mindful of the storied nature of the personal and professional knowledge landscapes in which we live and work. The work on understanding the landscape makes clear to us that teachers are not autonomous agents working in contextless spaces. Rather teachers and teacher education students live on complex storied landscapes in which the expressions of their knowledge are shaped by the landscape. As Janice learned, and helped us see more clearly, even in the safety of her in-classroom place on the landscape, the expression of her storied knowledge in practice was restoried as a parent storied one of Janice's practices into the plot-line of a story Janice and the children had not authored. Our work in teacher education needs, then, to consider the ways in which we can all stay awake to the on-going shifting complexities of the storied professional knowledge landscapes which we inhabit.

For us, for Phil Bingham and for the staff at Bisset School, another matter to be navigated is school reform. In this paper, we tried to make clear that what on one level seemed a simple matter of living and telling a new story of school, as in Janice's classroom and at Bay Street and Bisset Schools, became a complex matter of sorting out the multiple meanings of school stories. As reformers work to change practices, they need to understand complex, interconnected, historical storied nature of the schools' knowledge contexts in which they work. We think the work on the professional knowledge landscape is a place from which to begin to understand the complexity of school reform.

Notes

1 Parts of this paper are drawn from Clandinin and Connelly's (1995) book *Teacher's Professional Knowledge Landscapes*. This paper draws on research supported by the Social Sciences and Humanities Research Council of Canada.
2 This paper is drawn from Jean Clandinin's keynote address for the Teacher's Knowledge portion of the ISATT 1995 gathering.

References

CLANDININ, D.J. (1986) *Classroom Practices: Teacher Images in Action*, London, Falmer Press.

CLANDININ, D.J. and CONNELLY, F. M. (1992) 'Teachers as curriculum makers', in JACKSON, P. (Ed) *Handbook of Research on Curriculum*, American Educational Research Association, New York, Macmillan, pp. 363–401.

CLANDININ, D.J. and CONNELLY, F.M. (1995a) *Teachers' Professional Knowledge Landscapes*, New York, Teachers' College Press.

CLANDININ, D.J. and CONNELLY, F.M. (1995b) 'Teacher stories/school stories/stories of schools', Paper presented at the annual meeting of Qualitative Research Conference, University of Georgia, Athens.

CLANDININ, D.J., DEVISE, A., CRAIG, C., HUBER, J., ROSE, C. and WHELAN, K. (1995) 'Symbols on the landscape', Paper presented at the annual meeting of International Teacher Research Conference, University of California, Davis.

CONNELLY, F.M. and CLANDININ, D.J. (1988) *Teachers as Curriculum Planners: Narratives of Experience*, New York, Teachers College Press.

CONNELLY, F.M. and CLANDININ, D.J. (in preparation) *Teachers Professional Knowledge Landscapes: Shaping Teacher Identities*.

CRITES, S. (1971) 'The narrative quality of experience', *Journal of the American Academy of Religion*, **39**, 3, pp. 291–311.

DAVIES, A. (1996) 'Team teaching relationships: Teachers' stories and stories of school on the professional knowledge landscape', Unpublished doctoral dissertation, University of Alberta.

SCHWAB, J.J. (1971) 'The practical: Arts of eclectic', *School Review*, **79**, 4, pp. 493–542.

SOLTIS, J. (1995) 'Foreword', in CLANDININ, D.J. and CONNELLY, F.M. *Teachers Professional Knowledge Landscapes*, New York, Teachers College Press.

12 Metaphors for Movement: Accounts of Professional Development

Christopher Day and Mark Hadfield

Introduction

The purpose of the broader project of this research is to conduct a classroom based comparative analysis of teachers' construction of their curriculum and classroom decision-making in UK and Hong Kong primary schools. This paper discusses the methodological development of the pilot project in England and the present analysis of the UK findings based on our work with five teachers in four primary schools.

Developing a Comparative Methodology

Any form of comparative analysis needs to accommodate the diverse institutional, cultural and political contexts in which these groups of teachers operate. A phenomenological approach was adopted since this enabled a common comparative focus upon the structure of teachers' personal theories — more specifically the 'dilemmas' or contradictions that teachers face within their own professional contexts. Our work with three of the five teachers is presented in this paper.

We hypothesized that

1 In Hong Kong and England teachers' learning about teaching is through a mixture of formal training, personal experiences, reading materials, advice from other teachers, and the transference of ideas and understandings from their personal lives and biographies. This has resulted in the content of their professional theories and the 'architecture of their professional selves' (Pinar, 1988) becoming discontinuous and fragmented. Aspects of their professional theories would, therefore, exist in very differing forms of knowledge which were not necessarily integrated by the structure of their personal or professional theories.

2 It should be possible, then, to identify discrepancies, contradictions and dilemmas both within individual teachers personal and professional theories and between those held by Hong Kong and English teachers.

We regarded 'dilemmas' as a value free term in the sense that they can act as both an opportunity for, and a restriction on, professional development. They can be a spur to professional growth when the identification of a contradiction reveals explicitly to teachers new insights into the nature of their professional knowledge (Hadfield and Hayes, 1993). In his account of the 'history of ideas' Foucault (1974) discusses the various functions which contradictions or 'oppositions' can have in the development of an idea over time. We would argue that there is a relationship between the role served by oppositions, or contradictions which cause dilemmas in teacher learning and development and the genealogy of the teachers professional theory through their personal biography.

Teachers may well start to learn in only certain limited ways. In such single loop learning teaching may, therefore, become an instrument of control rather than development (Argyris and Schön, 1976). Whilst there is much work through narrative, storying, critical incident, and action research in particular which is aimed at assisting teachers in identifying dilemmas or discrepancies within and between practice and theory, there have been few studies which examine the metaprocesses in which teacher and researcher engage and through which they learn. This study aimed to identify these more clearly. Three 'phases' of development were identified — actual, transitional and ideal — which add to our knowledge of teacher thinking. The dominant influence of particular phases varied among the teachers. In doing this, the research also addressed issues of researcher influence.

There were two methodological problems in pursuing this approach,

1   How to get teachers to articulate and examine the origins of these dilemmas.
2   How to prompt critical reflection on dilemmas without overlaying the researchers' theoretical perspective or language onto the teachers' accounts.

This kind of research with teachers may be seen as:

> An embodiment of democratic principles in research, allowing participants to influence, if not determine, the conditions of their own lives and work, and collaboratively to develop critiques of social conditions which sustain dependence, inequality or exploitation in any research enterprise in particular, or in social life in general. (Kemmis, 1993, p. 179)

The aim of the research was to assist teachers in the processes of reflective thinking which had to do with

> a critical examination of . . . beliefs and actions in the world understood as historical and social assumptions and choices. Teachers were encouraged to examine their beliefs and teaching practices in ways that considered more than the technical aspects of teaching. The aim was to think critically about oneself, one's assumptions, and one's teaching choices and actions . . . (Johnston, 1994)

The two major literature reviews on teachers' knowledge cast decision-making as an organizing construct (Clark and Peterson, 1986; Shavelson and Stern, 1981). However, this represents a 'process-product' view. The distinction between preactive and interactive decisions cast the business of teaching as a segmented cognitive, rational activity rather than holistic (Freeman, 1994, p. 81). Thanks largely to the work of narrative (Connelly and Clandinin, 1980; Elbaz, 1983) and biographical researchers (Goodson, 1991; Butt and Raymond, 1987) and those who have pointed to the complexities of the practice of teaching and its moral purposes (Sockett, 1993; Goodlad, 1991) the focus more recently has been on the teacher as a whole person. The researcher has become collaborator assisting teachers in making sense of their world (Carter, 1993) and working to improve it through reflection in, on and about the action (Schön, 1983; Day, 1981; Elliott, 1991; Zeichner, 1994). Rather than requiring only technical expertise, both research and teaching have become recognized as needing the integration of knowledge, technique and human relating skills (Day, 1991).

This movement away from attempts to prescribe formulae which might, by their adoption, improve teaching (and research), is paralleled also by increasing criticism of the 'stage' models of teacher development. Berliner's (1988) five stage model of teacher development, based closely on that developed by Dreyfus and Dreyfus (1986) which suggests a 'novice–advanced beginner–competent–proficient–expert' continuum was elaborated by Kagan (1992). In her review of preservice and beginning teachers she found that within novice and beginning teachers there were a number of phases each of which had prerequisites which, if not met, prevented development. Grossman's (cited in Kwo) work provided further evidence to refute the sequential, linear stage theories of development, pointing out that, 'having developed classroom routines that work, teachers will not necessarily begin to question those routines' (Kwo, 1994, p. 219).

Whether they do is dependent upon attitude, role conceptions and environmental variables. The first concerns factors such as 'commitment'. This will relate to personal and professional biographies, stories, histories; the second will relate to their view of teaching as instrumental or developmental (Keiny, 1994, p. 233); and the third relates to the ecology of teaching — the extent to which the culture or system provides opportunities for teacher learning and development.

Research suggests that learning opportunities for teachers are limited (Johnson, 1990; Hansen and Corcoran, 1989). Yet these may significantly affect teacher commitment (Rosenholtz, 1989; Louis, 1991). A Rand study of staff development in America showed that teacher commitment, 'had the most consistently positive relationship to all the project outcomes. The most powerful teacher attribute . . . was a teacher's sense of efficacy — a belief that the teacher can help even the most difficult or unmotivated students' (McLaughlin and Marsh, 1990, pp. 213–33).

Yet Lanier and Little, for example, identified that the classroom environment may provide a disincentive to teacher development. Studies have shown that when teachers are provided with practical support, affective encouragement, and time out of class their capacity to reflect increases (Bullough, 1989; Tabachnick and Zeichner, 1984; Day, 1981). However, the extent of this reflection and its ability to influence change is less easily predictable since it will depend upon the nature of the support, the profile of the teacher, their particular phase of development and beliefs (Clark and Peterson, 1986; Janesick, 1982; Johnson, 1994).

Actual, Transitional and Ideal Images: Reflecting on Dilemmas

To overcome these problems we adopted the general stance of the 'critical friend' in 'partisan' second order action research. During the early stages of action research (Day, 1981, 1985) we are concerned with helping teachers to identify and reflect on their professional theories. Habermas's notion of the 'critical theorem' describes a role for the 'therapist'. His discussion of Freudian psychoanalysis touches on a number of key concerns for the action research facilitator seeking to support others in thinking about their work without undermining their reflections, and its products, by overlaying their own theoretical frameworks and concerns (see also Day, 1991).

In action research the combination of rational reconstruction and self reflection sets up a dialectic which ensures that the client's perspective, however limited initially, is not swamped by the 'therapists' interventions. The process relies upon the critical friend and teacher-researcher constructing what Habermas calls a 'meta-hermeneutic'. The role of the metahermeneutic within a critical theorem is to provide overarching explanatory metaphors which provide the backdrop to the more specific critical challenges within the reflective dialogue between critical friend and the teacher-researcher. It is similar to the 'reflection about action' posited by Gore and Zeichner (1991). These metahermeneutics are the key to establishing the necessary reflexive understanding between the two as they are used by both to establish a common understanding of the holistic interpretation of self. It is a form of action research in which the teacher-researcher is discussing his or her research whilst, simultaneously, the critical friend is constructing challenges within this, designed to pose new problems which themselves will cause the teacher to move beyond the 'actual' or 'transitional' towards the 'ideal' (or perhaps to modify his or her ideal). We attempted to achieve this by asking the teachers to describe how they understood their classroom at present and how they would wish it to develop, their actual and ideal image, and how they saw themselves currently achieving this ideal, their transitional image. Once this was constructed then we had an interpretive framework through which we could understand and probe the dilemmas that they had started to articulate.

Reflecting on Dilemmas

If we accept that teachers experience a fragmented professional self then some form of temporary synthesis is required in the process of articulating these dilemmas and searching for their origins. Our metaphor for the form of reflection involved in this task was to treat it as involving a process of multiple translations between the variety of forms of knowledge in their professional theories (Shulman, 1986, 1987; Eraut, 1994). The question was how to support teachers in this translation. To assist in creating the metahermeneutic we adapted a technique frequently used in accounts of research on teachers' thinking, that of stimulated recall. In this piece of research we wanted to use a video based approach not to cause them to reflect on a specific area of their work e.g., their decision-making, but as a prompt to discussing their professional development, to help them clarify their images of the holistic 'actuality' of their classroom and to help shape their ideal images. Stimulated recall in this research was as much a projective as it was a reflective task.

An Initial Analysis of the Teachers' Dilemmas

Our discussions with the teachers were structured by the fact that the teachers had generally identified a dilemma or problem they wanted to look at, as this was part of the contract under which we worked with them. We began by prompting them to articulate the relationship between what we were viewing and this dilemma, the kind of resolutions they were seeking and the ways in which they thought they could achieve these. Video is particularly evocative in terms of reflection as translation. Because it is such a rich source it picks up on a range of different elements of practice allowing for the exploration of both the minutiae and the broad sweep of their practice. At this point in the research we have worked in four schools with five teachers over twelve months.

Harriet

Harriet has been teaching for over twenty years. Initially she trained as a junior/ secondary school teacher and has in her career taught in both phases. She has moved between education authorities, school districts, has taught in a number of schools and has taken a career break to raise a family. On returning to teaching she went through a period of supply (substitute) teaching before she found herself a position in her present school. She has recently completed a Masters in Education course and was at the time of the research looking for a deputy headship.

In her present school she described herself as 'something of a rebel' in terms of not wanting to follow the 'way things were done'. Although joint planning was being pushed heavily by the head teacher, and a rotating programme of topics had been established to ensure coverage of the National Curriculum she wanted 'to do her own thing' whenever possible. She mainly taught the oldest children in the school, age 10–11 years, and had created an image of her self, 'as something of a disciplinarian'. She described how initially children were 'scared' to come to her class because of the image she portrayed. She also pointed out that they soon realized that she was not such a disciplinarian. In keeping with her iconoclastic image her classroom contained desks which were laid out in rows, rather than the more normal groups of tables found in the rest of the school.

Initially it was difficult to comprehend her reasons for involvement in the research. At first she said she had no clear problem that she wanted to focus on and that she had got involved because she had done some classroom research as part of her Masters programme and, 'liked to help out' researchers. Lacking a clear image of what aspect of her 'actuality' she wanted to look at we decided to focus on the class 'topic' (project) work. This was based around a series of visits to a nearby village as her class was carrying out a comparison between life there and that in their own town.

The classroom sessions were a follow-up to the field visit to the village and were based around a set of twenty questions that the children had produced themselves. The children were having to answer all twenty questions individually. The questions ranged in difficulty, and many of them had not found out the answers on the field visit. The children were, therefore, working on the same general task but were all at different points on it. The replaying of the video prompted the following comment by Harriet.

> Normally people are running after me, trailing behind me, 'Can I start it here?' 'Do I do it like this?' 'Do I do it like that?' It does go in cycles. It'll go quiet for a while then it'll get busy again.

We were being drawn towards a classical discussion of the teacher's role as being primarily 'information processing' — the image was of an harassed teacher having short, fragmented interactions with pupils which involved on-the-spot decision-making. Instead of focusing on her accomplishments within this session we asked her how representative it was. Was is the kind of session she liked to teach? In effect we began to relate this session to her actual and ideal images. It was at this point that she began to discuss, initially jokingly, how she hated this kind of session. It was 'not structured enough', it was too much like the kind of group sessions she disliked. She found group work 'difficult to manage', and the children could be 'fussy' and seemed to lack confidence. She was persisting, though, because she felt that this type of session should increase the children's involvement in their work,

> I often wonder why I can't get the children really involved in what they are doing. I've asked them to think of the questions, I've taken them out, they've got everything they need. I've given them the freedom to do it the way they want yet half the class will work really well while the others see it as an opportunity to muck around and do less work than they do normally. I've never conquered this and it's always bothered me.

She began to describe her dilemma in broad terms as one between the use of techniques to increase pupils ownership of their work and the difficulties this created in terms of her role as disciplinarian, in particular her control of the classroom.

> We keep complaining that the children are not independent enough, but everybody blames it on everybody else, the lower school on the infants. Perhaps there is something wrong in what we are doing in school.

Her first reaction to exploring this dilemma was negative and based around a number of perceived practical problems. She was worried that changing her teaching so late in the school year would unfairly raise the children's expectations over how much freedom they could have because soon they would be going to secondary school where, she perceived, it would be a much more controlled environment.

What happened next was surprising. Between this discussion and the next Harriet had already began to experiment with different types of introductions to her sessions, stressing to the pupils the need to take more responsibility for their work. Later on in our work she began to change her organization of sessions so that she spent more time with individual children. What had occurred to prompt this change? Further discussions articulating her dilemma revealed a powerful transitional educator image based on her MEd experiences. This enabled her, as an experienced teacher-researcher to make changes and reflect on them. Yet she still had no clear image of her ideal, only a negative image of what she did not want to happen. A positive ideal only became clear during the last video session.

We filmed the afternoon topic session which was given over to completing the art work related to the topic. What was intriguing about this session was that in contrast with others the pupils were working independently in groups and as the teacher herself said

> It's a twiddling the thumbs session. I just go around giving advice making comments. I just walk around discussing what's going on. I felt a bit redundant actually. I didn't know what to do with myself.

As researchers we could not understand why there was such a difference in her role, until Harriet explained that because of the physical layout of the school children had been working since they had been in the school in art areas which were slightly detached from the main classrooms. In doing so they had learnt how to work independently, at least in their art work:

> They do art like this throughout the school, not within the classroom. Most areas have a wet area where the teacher will set them up and go away. They've got to get on their own. They're used to working by themselves. Nothing bothers them very much. They've got used to doing it, but only in art.

We asked whether this session was closer to her ideal than the earlier topic sessions and she asserted that it was. Why, if such an obvious practical ideal image was available to her had she not discussed it before? Three significant themes appeared to have limited her professional development:

The first and most significant involved her image of herself as a disciplinarian. She now began to talk about her fear of losing control of a class, something which had haunted her from early in her career and which had followed her through her various career moves.

> As you can see the class is set out in a very formal way, which you don't normally see in this school. Because I have found it easier to keep discipline with it laid out in this formal manner . . . I've thought a lot about it. I had real problems in one of the secondary schools and was really glad to get out of there and that made me aware of not wanting to be in that kind of situation again. Supply (substitute teaching) could be difficult as well. Moving from class to class made it difficult to form a relationship with pupils.

The impact of this concern on her practice was to limit or suppress her desire to experiment with the organization of the classroom. She had become trapped within her construction of herself as a disciplinarian. As her career progressed it had been more difficult for her to discuss this issue with her contemporaries. The ability to maintain class discipline was not only a key teaching competence it was also highly prized within her experienced culture of teaching.

The second issue was that she felt unclear about her role in these more independent sessions. She had developed the skill of dealing with being 'on demand' every thirty seconds but what was she to do when children appeared to be working well? What was her role?

> I wanted them to make decisions about what they wanted to do . . . In many ways I feel I should be going to the children, talking to them, talk about the work . . . but I feel I'm interrupting them. They are so concerned with what they are doing they don't really need you . . . I had told them to make the decision. If I came across to them and said you can't do this you can't do that I'm taking that away from them. I found that difficult. Should I go and say this isn't working do something else or should I let them carry on?

Notions of independence and ownership sat uneasily with other aspects of her professional theory, particularly the role she had created for herself as a disciplinarian. The video sessions and the discussions that followed them had started to draw these elements together at a number of levels from the broad ideological sweep to the minutiae of the decisions in her classroom of whether to intervene or not.

The final issue concerned her uncertainty about the teaching expectations of the National Curriculum. Since its implementation much more emphasis has been placed on the time management of the curriculum, and this had concentrated her thinking on issues such as balancing the needs of different subject areas, the length of activities, and the proportion of time to be spent on each subject area. These technical changes were creating a broader ideological shift in terms of what aspects of planning were seen to be significant in the task of teaching. There appeared to Harriet to be a general shift in the culture away from giving primacy to teachers' originality and ownership of the curriculum to their ability to technically control its delivery and ensure a uniformity of experience for pupils. Moving towards greater pupil independence was therefore a challenge to the new orthodoxy.

We can see the origins of her dilemma between increasing the children's participation with their work and her maintaining classroom discipline. In the actuality she describes we can see a mixture of long term biographical, very immediate institutional, and more subtle cultural influences on her construction of her and her curriculum. The transitional image reveals a general commitment to 'trying things out' but she is hampered in this specific area because of her previous experiences and concerns over how she would appear to colleagues. In her ideal she had eventually to settle on a highly practical and contextualized image of what she wished to develop. This, though, was still a limited ideal which would have to develop in the light of her initial attempts at change. In her movement between these different influences and images we can see Harriet having to perform a number of acts of translation between very different forms of understanding of her practice and her context.

Belinda

In many ways Belinda's career phase mirrored that of Harriet. She had been teaching for twenty-two years and was presently looking for deputy headships. She had been working in the infant department of her school for the last eight years. Her involvement in the research was prompted by a new headteacher who was supporting her applications for new posts and encouraging her to take up opportunities for professional development. Belinda wanted to look at 'multiculturalism'.

> **Belinda** What I was thinking of I don't think I'm multiculturally based . . . it's a white orientated/dominated school. I wondered about a more multicultural overview or something . . . I think I need a multicultural overview or something.
> **Researcher** What kind of things would you like to do but are worried about?
> **Belinda** I don't know what I want. I want to know if I am giving them an overall view of other cultures.

She was teaching a topic on 'France' and our initial discussions centred on whether this offered her an opportunity to explore multiculturalism in the way she wanted to. This discussion revealed that one of her key dilemmas was how to explore cultural differences with reception and first year infant children (aged 4–5 yrs) without stereotyping another culture, and how to work from the children's existing perspectives,

> It's basically so that they've got an awareness of other cultures other than the narrow bit that they're in, but taking it from what they know in the first place. Taking it from them . . . I felt like I'm doing it like in the way of a comparison and I'm not sure that that is the right way to go about it.

Everything we've done I'm comparing 'This is what we do, this is what they do.' I'm wondering whether I'm giving them the impression that all French people do this and all English people don't. They do that? I'm differentiating between 'ours' and 'theirs' and getting it across and therefore making comparisons.

We used the video as a means of revisiting her pupils' conversations during activities which contained a multicultural element. She was still unsure of their level of conceptual sophistication in this area. Replaying the video tapes prompted her to challenge her view of the 'actuality' of her classroom and provided her with at least a partial transitional idea of what she wanted to achieve.

The videos were of two teaching sessions which involved a group eight reception and year one children sitting around a table carrying out a writing task. There had already been a class discussion of the task and in both cases they were looking at how climate, in reference to the south of France, affected what people wore and the houses they lived in. The children then sat down to create a small booklet describing various forms of clothing and types of houses. In both instances three black children, two of whom had recently come from Jamaica, played a seminal role in the discussions captured on video. On the first occasion the children started to talk about their shared cultural identity

Child one   Danielle doesn't come from Jamaica.
Child two   Yes we come from Jamaica.
Child one   And Northampton.
Child two   Danielle doesn't come from anywhere.
Child three Yes I do, I come from Nottingham.

(Discussion of the video)

Belinda That would have been the point for me to have been there. I needed to be there at that point. That's them thinking that they've got a cultural background. They were saying that she doesn't have a background. She only comes from here. Isn't that funny that I turned up at the wrong time? I came in and said, 'Tidy up'.

What happened in the next video session was to challenge her view that it was simply due to chance that the children stopped talking about these issues just as she arrived. In this video, as Belinda approached the table the children started to ask her advice about their writing tasks. Only after she went did they resume their conversation. What struck Belinda on watching these videos was that not only was she never there when these conversations took place but that she was effectively excluded from them because the children saw her as a source only of technical advice about their writing. The videos showed that once the whole group introduction had finished Belinda started to turn the task into a technical writing one. On watching this extract Belinda created an 'actual' image of herself as a technician, a 'secretary' who helped the children with the basics. She began to reflect on how this was affecting the quality of her conversations with her pupils and her ability to permeate equal opportunities work.

> That what's just come over me watching this. Now it's become an English lesson, it's turned into a writing task. I'm now doing finger spacing, 'What does it begin with?', I literally am doing the English work with them now . . . It's always in the background what the parents want of you, the basics. The headteacher said the basics down here are really good and to keep on with this . . . I'm becoming a secretary to their work. 'How do you spell this word? How do you spell that?'

Her 'ideal' concerning the permeation of equal opportunities began to get clearer. Initially she had stated that she wanted to work from the children's 'natural' perspective and build on this, but the way she was designing her activities, and the way she organized her room meant that she was not around to pick upon their perspectives. She now began to ponder whether she needed to look at how to permeate multiculturalism much more deeply into the 'basics', to try and make the activities through which she taught these skills much more open. In the current situation she was working partially from the children's perspective but principally from within her construction of the curriculum.

The 'actual' images created in this case were dominant. Overall there was no strong sense of how she learnt as a teacher, no strong transitional image of her own professional construction. The transitional images that were starting to be articulated were about the steps forward she would like to make in order to develop her ideal approach to multiculturalism in the classroom.

Sarah

Sarah was in the seventh year of her career. She had taken a year out from teaching and this was her first post since returning. Eighteen months previously she had been appointed as a mathematics coordinator. She now found herself teaching a class of year four children (8–9-year-olds) and the issue she wanted to examine was differentiation in the mathematics curriculum. This was chosen because it was one of the areas which the school in impending OFSTED inspection would have to account for, and because in her recent appraisal this was an area raised by her head teacher. She wanted to work on this area also because of her role as mathematics coordinator so that she could pass on what she learned to her colleagues.

On viewing the video material Sarah began to discuss a lost 'ideal' now apparently unobtainable to her because of the National Curriculum. This lost ideal was now being reshaped by the 'advantages' she had found within her new actuality.

> We're now working more or less in totally separate subject areas with hardly any topic work. This is the second year we've done this. I like it

in one way because you are very focused, you've got specific lesson times for certain areas. You think 'Right what have I got to do now?' . . . On the other hand from a child's view of the world they're seeing everything in fragmented sections and that isn't what we want them to do. I think now we could go back to topic areas because we've got used to planning in such detail.

A key aspect of her 'actuality' that did become clearer as we discussed the video material was that she felt under public scrutiny. She was in a new school, which heightened her feeling of having to 'prove' herself to her colleagues. The National Curriculum was making her feel more accountable for what she taught and how long, and she was also under more direct observation.

Much of my planning is making sure we cover it (the National Curriculum) . . . it's fear; it's statutory legislation that's come in we're legally obliged to do. We have no choice. We can't strike against it . . . Our school's very National Curriculum led. We're very focused on OFSTED. The deputy head wants to meet OFSTED's notion of 'quality'. She feels her job description and the legislation mean she has to perform these things. I think it's terrible. It's not very child centred . . . Teachers have naturally picked up on this. They've formed this view which is more and more based on OFSTED. 'Headteachers are on our back. People are looking at our books when we are not there.'

In this context what the video replays revealed to her in terms of her dilemma was not that she was caught between how she wanted to teach and how she felt others were requiring her to teach but how this was affecting her learning about her own practice, her transitional image.

Our discussion on this area arose out of one video session in which she'd been attempting a new activity about measurement. She had designed the lesson so that it required the children to talk about their work and to move through a number of problem solving stages. In the midst of the activity she recognized that she had set too wide a task and that although a significant minority were demonstrating higher level mathematics skills and even those 'failing' were still making key discoveries, a large number of the children were having difficulty. To help the children she began to feedback the insights gained by other members of the class. She simplified the task for some of the children with difficulties, starting to draw out the main teaching points. She had 'set' the children according to ability so now she positioned herself on the lower ability table for the second half of the session and drew children on this table into the discussions she was having with those who had successfully completed key parts of the task.

Initially as we went through the session on video she was highly critical and she talked of all the mistakes she'd made. It was only when we started to discuss what she had learnt from the session that the issue of experimenting in the classroom was raised. We discussed how trying things out and failing was a part of developing new ideas and developing yourself. At this point Sarah began to reflect on how the dominant idea of ensuring that all the children were covering everything in the National Curriculum and the time pressures this had placed on her had made her feel guilty about experimenting because it 'wasted' the children's time,

In a sense if I don't get it [a lesson] right first time every time I feel inefficient you see. We (the school staff) talked about what I did. I was talking about that you had to take risks as you go along. My deputy head's argument was if you take risks frequently how do we know that the children are getting 'quality' learning. The focus is on getting your planning 'right'. Get it timetabled. You ignore teaching styles, you know what is expected of you. In our school there is a feeling that you've got to be quiet, seated and getting on with your work and that's the one learning style.

She had begun to reflect on the fact that it now seemed that the culture of her school was that only the pupils could learn in the classroom and not her. This feeling was re-enforced when in response to her sharing her experience of this session her colleagues' reactions were to suggest that the task be simplified so that no child would fail!

When I was in the staff meeting I made an analogy between using a recipe book and children doing maths. I said I don't ever want to use a recipe book which I'm dependent on. What I've got to do is learn the process I'm using in each recipe, which I can then adapt and change. I can then make it my own . . . The recipe was important at one stage but then you can throw it out and make it yours . . . What they said was they understood what I had said but they hadn't got the time to do it.

In Sarah's case her transitional image of her own development became clarified by the reflective process because she had already made explicit and problematized her ideal and actual. This relatively inexperienced, interested and committed teacher was now asking herself what impact dealing with the National Curriculum and the culture which surrounded it was having on her professional development and therefore indirectly on the children's learning. The present unachievability of her 'ideal' stops it from becoming the source of any felt tensions. Her more immediate concern, defined during the reflective dialogue was the impact of her 'actuality' on her transitional image, on her construction of herself as a teacher.

Discussion

Schön's (1983) identification of reflection in, and reflection on, action values the professional knowledge of teachers which is embedded in their own interpretations of experience. It is useful but not sufficient as a means of understanding or developing teachers' learning. What this research has shown is that for teachers to understand and act upon their understanding of what they do they need to reflect about the action (Gore and Zeichner, 1991), but first they have to be assisted in locating themselves within their own images of it. Through this, they may not only deconstruct but also reconstruct themselves and their contexts. It is likely that they will have to deal with contradictory images of teaching and themselves as teacher. To do this will involve identifying which image — the actual, transitional or ideal — is dominant. The process in which they engage is both rational, but, more importantly, demands that attention be given to the affective dimensions of their lives. This goes to the heart of a conception of teaching as involving both the head and the heart. It goes beyond even Grimmett's notion of reflection as leading to new understandings of action and self in terms of the cultural contexts of teaching and taken-for-granted assumptions of teaching (Grimmett, 1989, p. 22) by adding self in terms of personal and professional histories, dominant images and the need for critical friend challenge and support. The research so far raises a number of issues concerning research into teacher thinking and teacher learning and development.

Research into Teacher Thinking: Researcher as Interventionist

To date, teacher thinking research may be divided into three strands. The first regards the teacher as operating within a technical rational world context. This cognitive approach studies teachers' information processing and decision-making and largely ignores or filters out environmental and personal effects in its search for, and development of, models of rational decision-making which guide teacher learning and development. This research is characterized by the production of models of mental maps and statistical applications. In contrast, more holistic qualitative research is based on a constructivist premise which asserts that teachers hold personal, practical knowledge which is shaped by life history, narrative, life stories and the social environment. This research is characterized by teacher stories, images, narratives which illustrate the factors which influence teachers in their work. A third strand of teacher thinking research is 'action research'. This represents the 'critical' approach. It is directly concerned with teacher improvement through moving through a cycle of reconnaissance, investigation, experiment and evaluation. Here the researcher takes a 'partisan', interventionist role in collaboration with teachers in a joint research endeavour. This research is characterized by teacher identification of issues and full participation in the learning process if not always its final reporting. Action research is eclectic in that it draws on a range of methodologies appropriate to purpose, it is ethical in that it involves forms of 'contracting' between researcher and teacher, and it is 'practical' in that it results in change to which the participants are committed. At its best, it locates teaching in personal, social and political contexts.

This research differs from the first strand in that it recognizes the rational and non-rational worlds of the teacher. It draws on the other two but goes beyond them. Like action research it is interventionist, like constructivist research, it takes account of personal, historical and environmental factors; and like both, it assumes that teachers need assistance in moving from implicit to explicit models of thinking and action in order to be enabled to examine these and reflect upon their purposes, processes and outcomes in personal, social and broader political contexts. However, it does not assume that all teachers will have the same starting point. Nor does it assume a co-equal collaborative relationship between teacher and researcher. Though certainly the relationship is equitable, the researcher has specific role functions:

1 to assist the teacher in making what is implicit, explicit;
2 to identify with the teacher whether he or she is thinking in an 'actual', 'transitional' or 'ideal' reflective context; and
3 to ensure that the teacher is provided with an opportunity to move between these contexts.

The researcher-interventionist here has a responsibility to assist the teacher in translating between the actual, transitional and ideal worlds through articulated reflection. Dilemmas are multifaceted, there are clear links between personal and professional selves and development (its potential, rate and direction). For example, Sarah's personal world was so overwhelming in its current fragmentation that her professional development world had become dysfunctional. The therapeutic effect of the research enabled this to be identified and for her to move from the actual to the transitional, though not yet to the ideal.

There is much work on reflection and teachers' lives. The identification of different kinds or levels of reflection by Gore and Zeichner (1991), van Manen (1977), Schön (1983) and others over the years is an important step towards explaining the actual and positing the ideal in terms of teacher learning. Feiman Nemser (1990) is closer to the reality of teachers in claiming that reflection should be seen as a 'professional disposition'. The findings of Korthagen (1985) and Korthagen and Wubbels (1991) in working over ten years with mathematics student teachers that there are two student orientations, 'one external and non-reflective, the other internal and more reflective' (cited in Hatton and Smith, 1995) move closer to the central dilemma of the teacher; and Elbaz (1983), Connelly and Clandinin (1990), Ball and Goodson (1985) and others with their work on narrative, story, image and life history have revealed in glorious complexity the factors which shape teachers' lives.

It might be claimed that through these processes, teachers had confronted what Handal and Lauvas (1987) describe as their 'practical theory', described as:

> private, integrated but ever-changing system of knowledge, experience and values which is relevant to teaching practice at any particular time ... a personal construct which is continuously established in the individual through a series of diverse events ... which are mixed together or

integrated with the changing perspective provided by the individual's values and ideas. (Handal and Lauvas, 1987, p. 8)

However, it is clear from both self report and observation that one of the implicit problems which become explicit for the teachers was that of lack of change as a result of development which had been constrained. The constraints were located in personal and professional histories, as well as immediate environmental factors. Reflection upon dilemmas in practice was not in itself sufficient to enable learning and development. This research has identified within the process of reflection the existence of three images held by teachers, and within these different dominant images which inhibit action resulting from reflection unless confronted. The researcher acted as a catalyst for such confrontation. In this sense, the research on relationships between teaching, reflection and change parallels that of Johnston (1994). In this one of the teachers stated:

> I think of a potted plant I have sitting on my front porch. It sat in the same pot for many years neither growing nor dying, just maintaining the status quo . . . Like my potted plant, I sat in my classroom for many years teaching my students as the teachers' manuals directed without much thought as to why I was doing what I was doing. (Johnston, 1994, p. 16)

Its focus, however, is in both uncovering the origins of the potted plant, why it has been neither growing nor dying, how it may recognize the need for growth and how the past might be linked to the future through an identification of the present dominant images.

References

ARGYRIS, C. and SCHÖN, D.A. (1976) *Theory in Practice: Increasing Professional Effectiveness*, New York, Jossey-Bass.

BALL, S. and GOODSON, I. (1985) *Teachers' Lives and Careers*, Lewes, Falmer Press.

BERLINER, D.C. (1988) 'Implications of studies of expertise in pedagogy for teacher education and evaluation', in PFLEIDERER, J. (Ed) *Proceedings of the 1988 ETS Invitational Conference*, Princeton, NJ, Educational Testing Service, pp. 39–67.

BULLOUGH, R. (1989) 'Teacher education and teacher reflectivity', *Journal of Teacher Education*, **40**, 2, pp. 15–21.

BUTT, R. and RAYMOND, D. (1987) 'Arguments for using qualitative approaches in understanding teacher thinking: The case for biography', *Journal of Curriculum Theorising*, **7**, 2, pp. 62–93.

CARTER, R. (1993) 'The place of story in the study of teaching and teacher education', *Educational Researcher*, **22**, 2, pp. 5–12.

CLARK, C. and PETERSON, P.L. (1986) 'Teachers' thought processes', In WITTROCK, M.C. (Ed) *Handbook of Research on Teaching* (3rd ed.), New York, Macmillan, pp. 255–96.

CONNELLY, F. and CLANDININ, D. (1990) 'Stories of experience and narrative inquiry', *Educational Researcher*, **19**, 4, pp. 2–14.

DAY, C. (1981) 'Classroom-based in-service teacher education: The development and evaluation of a client-centred model', Occasional Paper 9, Brighton, University of Sussex Education Area.

DAY, C. (1985) 'Professional learning and research intervention: An action research perspective', *British Educational Research Journal*, **11**, 2, pp. 133–51.

DAY, C. (1991) 'Roles and relationships in qualitative research on teachers' thinking: A reconsideration', *Teaching and Teacher Education: An International Journal of Research and Studies*, **7**, 5, 6, pp. 537–47.

DREYFUS, H. and DREYFUS, S. (1986) *Mind over Machine: The Power of Human Intuition and Expertise in the Era of the Computer*, New York, The Free Press.

ELBAZ, F. (1983) *Teacher Thinking: A Study of Practical Knowledge*, New York, Nichols.

ELLIOTT, J. (1991) *Action Research for Educational Change*, Buckingham, Open University Press.

ERAUT, M. (1994) *Professional Development and Competence*, London, Falmer Press.

FEIMAN-NEMSER, S. (1990) 'Teacher preparation: Structural and conceptual alternatives', in HOUSTON, W.T. (Ed) *Handbook of Research on Teacher Education*, New York, Macmillan.

FOUCAULT, M. (1974) *The Archaeology of Knowledge*, London, Tavistock.

FREEMAN, D. (1994) 'The use of language data in the study of teacher knowledge', in CARLGREN, I., HANDAL, G. and VAAGE, S. (Eds) (1994) *Teachers' Minds and Actions: Research on Teachers' Thinking and Practice*, London, Falmer Press, pp. 77–92.

GOODLAD, J.I. (1991) 'The occupation of teaching in schools', in GOODLAD, J.I., SODER, R. and SIROTNIK, K.A. (Eds) *The Moral Dimensions of Teaching*, San Francisco, Jossey-Bass, pp. 3–34.

GOODSON, I.F. (1991) 'Sponsoring the teacher's voice: Teachers' lives and teacher development', *Cambridge Journal of Education*, **21**, 1.

GORE, J. and ZEICHNER, K. (1991) 'Action research and reflective teaching in pre-service teacher education: A case study from the United States', *Teaching and Teacher Education*, **7**, pp. 119–36.

GRIMMET, P. (1989) 'A commentary on Schön's view of reflection', *Journal of Curriculum and Supervision*, **5**, 1, pp. 19–28.

HABERMAS, J. (1972) *Knowledge and Human Interest*, London, Heinemann.

HABERMAS, J. (1974) *Theory and Practice*, London, Heinemann.

HADFIELD, M. and HAYES, M. (1993) 'A metaphysical approach to qualitative methodologies', *Educational Action Research*, **1**, 1, pp. 153–74.

HANDAL, G. and LAUVAS, P. (1987) *Promoting Reflective Teaching*, Milton Keynes, Open University Press.

HANSEN, B.J. and CORCORAN, T.B. (1989) *Working in New Jersey Public Schools: The Conditions of Teaching*, Trenton, New Jersey School Boards Association.

HATTON, N. and SMITH, D. (1995) 'Reflection in teacher education: Towards definition and implementation', *Teaching and Teacher Education*, **11**, 1, pp. 33–49.

JANESICK, V. (1982) 'Of snakes and circles: Making sense of classroom group processes through a case study', *Curriculum Inquiry*, **12**, 2, pp. 161–90.

JOHNSON, S.M. (1990) *Teachers at Work: Achieving Success in Our Schools*, New York, Basic Books.

JOHNSTON, M. (1994) 'Contrasts and similarities in case studies of teacher reflection and change', *Curriculum Inquiry*, **24**, 1, pp. 9–26.

KAGAN, D. (1992) 'Professional growth among pre-service and beginning teachers', *Review of Educational Research*, **62**, 2, pp. 171–9.

KEINY, S. (1994) 'Teachers' professional development as a process of conceptual change', in CARLGREN, I., HANDAL, G. and VAAGE, S. (Eds) *Teachers' Minds and Actions: Research into Teachers' Thinking and Practice*, London, Falmer Press, p. 233.

KEMMIS, S. (1993) 'Action research', in HAMMERSLEY, M. (Ed) *Educational Research: Current Issues*, London, Paul Chapman Publishing, p. 179.

KORTHAGEN, F. (1985) 'Reflective teaching and pre-service teacher education', in *Journal of Teacher Education*, The Netherlands, Sept-Oct, pp. 11–15.

KORTHAGEN, F. and WUBBELS, T. (1991) 'Characteristics of reflective practitioners: Towards an operationalisation of the concept of reflection', Paper presented at the annual meeting of the American Educational Research Association, Chicago, April 1991.

KWO, O. (1994) 'Learning to teach: Some theoretical propositions', in CARLGREN, I., HANDAL, G. and VAAGE, S. (Eds) *Teachers' Minds and Actions: Research on Teachers' Thinking and Practice*, London, Falmer Press, p. 219.

LANIER, J. and LITTLE, J. (1986) 'Research on teacher education', in WITTROCK, M.C. (Ed) *Handbook of Research on Teaching* (3rd ed.), New York, Macmillan.

LOUIS, K.S. (1991) 'The effects of teacher quality of work life in secondary schools on commitment and sense of efficacy', Paper presented at the Annual Meeting of the American Educational Research Association, Chicago, April.

McLAUGHLIN, M. and MARSH, D. (1990) 'Staff development and school change', in LEIBERMAN, A. (Ed) *Schools as Collaborative Cultures*, New York, Falmer Press, pp. 213–33.

McLURE, M. (1993) 'Arguing for your self: Identity as an organising principle in teachers' jobs and lives', *British Educational Research Journal*, **19**, 4, pp. 311–22.

PINAR, W. (1988) 'Autobiography and the architecture of self', *Journal of Curriculum Theory*, **8**, 2, pp. 7–36.

ROSENHOLTZ, S.J. (1989) *Teachers' Workplace: The Social Organisation of Schools*, New York, Longman.

SCHÖN, D.A. (1983) *The Reflective Practitioner: How Professionals Think in Action*, New York, Basic Books.

SHAVELSON, R. and STERN, P. (1981) 'Research on teachers' pedagogical thoughts, judgements, decisions, and behaviours', *Review of Educational Research*, **51**, pp. 455–98.

SHULMAN, L. (1986) 'Those who understand: Knowledge growth in teaching', *Educational Researcher*, **15**, 2, pp. 4–14.

SHULMAN, L. (1987) 'Knowledge and teaching: Foundations of the New Reform', *Harvard Educational Review*, **57**, pp. 1–22.

SOCKETT, H. (1993) *The Moral Base for Teacher Professionalism*, New York, Teachers College Press.

TABACHNIK, B.R. and ZEICHNER, K. (1984) 'The impact of the student teaching experience on the development of teacher perspectives', *Journal of Teacher Education*, **35**, 6, pp. 28–36.

VAN MANEN, M. (1977) 'Linking ways of knowing with ways of being practical', *Curriculum Inquiry*, **6**, pp. 205–28.

ZEICHNER, K.M. (1994) 'Research on teacher thinking and different views of reflective practice in teaching and teacher education', in CARLGREN, I., HANDAL, G. and VAAGE, S. (Eds) *Teachers' Minds and Actions: Research into Teachers' Thinking and Practice*, London, Falmer Press, pp. 9–27.

13 Applying Constructivist Theory to Multicultural Education Content

*Susan C. Brown, Marcella L. Kysilka
and Maureen J. Warner*

Introduction

Constructivist theory sees the learner as maker of his or her own knowledge. Content being taught is interpreted by the learner in an effort to make sense of the information. Past experiences and present needs and interests influence how the learner views the content. An effective teacher provides content in such a way as to tap into the learner's experiences, needs, and interests. Together teacher and learner use repeatedly the process of discussion and reflection to develop more complete understanding. Participation of other learners with their perspectives and opinions helps to enrich the process and increase the depth of knowledge.

When constructivist theory is applied in the classroom, the teacher's role becomes that of fellow investigator in the continuous process of seeking knowledge. To sustain such a role, the teacher must provide a classroom climate conducive to openness and critical questioning. If the content to be explored is multicultural, then curriculum, instruction, and assessment choices become even more crucial to the process of knowledge acquisition and attitude changing. The teacher must serve as a role model demonstrating the application of multicultural perspectives in his or her classroom.

Two of the authors, a university professor and a high school English teacher, recently taught classes with multicultural education content. In the university multicultural education course, students researched self-selected microcultures in small groups and prepared individual portfolios. The microcultures examined included African American, Native American, biracial children, gifted children, and people in poverty. In the high school 'gifted English class', students researched their own cultural backgrounds and produced individual portfolios with various literary forms expressing their findings. In both classes, students selected their own topics, conducted research, and presented findings to class members. Both groups expressed interest and excitement about their learning during the process of research and portfolio production. At the end of the courses, they also indicated more in-depth understanding and some attitude change concerning multicultural issues when compared with their original expressions of understanding and attitudes.

Student Populations and Course Structures

The university course was offered at a small liberal arts college as an elective to all students in a six-week intensive term. The students ranged from freshmen to seniors, including one non-traditional student. The majority of the twenty students were education majors; the others were mainly speech and hearing or nursing majors. All but one student were European Americans; the one student was Korean American. The primary requirement for the course was a contracted portfolio. Students were instructed to investigate a self-selected microculture in small groups and then interpret the data individually. According to the grade self-selected at the start (A, B, or C), each student performed a variety of investigative projects. Emphasis on the finished products, short written papers explaining what was learned, was deliberately played down in order to center on experiential learning and the growth process. Reflection was stressed in both the written work and the oral discussions. Class time centered around general multicultural themes, using Gollick and Chinn's *Multicultural Education in a Pluralistic Society* (1994) as the main text. Discussions based on outside readings, guest speakers, and student presentations were also essential parts of the course.

The high school course was taught during nine weeks of a year-long English class for gifted students. The eighteen eleventh grade students were very diverse: ten European Americans, two Latinos, two East Indians, two Iranians, one Pakistani, and one Egyptian. Five religions were represented as well as a number of languages. As with the university course, the primary requirement was a contracted portfolio. In this case, however, the portfolio had to contain a number of different types of writing, all reflecting the individual student's own cultural background and heritage. Along with a required research paper, some of the acceptable possibilities were reviews of related contemporary literature, historical short stories, poetry, and scripted video presentations. Each contract was negotiated between the student and teacher. The final grade for the portfolio was based on the grades received for the different parts. Class time was divided between library research and small group collaboration on creative aspects of the writing and presenting. By mid-term, students were beginning to make their presentations and lead discussions about their findings.

Application of Theory

Authors Brooks and Brooks (1993) list twelve descriptors of constructivist teaching behaviors in their book, *In Search of Understanding: The Case for Constructivist Classrooms* (Appendix A). Some of these descriptors seem more like good teaching methods than behaviors specifically related to constructivism. For example, use of wait time after posing questions is a classic technique researched by Rowe (1974) for improving student responses in any teaching situation. The six descriptors selected and listed below seem to best represent tenets of constructivism.

1   Constructivist teachers encourage and accept student autonomy and initiative. This descriptor is perhaps the most comprehensive of the ones chosen and can be seen as an overriding principle. If teachers are serious about student autonomy and initiative, they then must share essential decision-making about the course with their students. More than just allowing students choices involving similar tasks is necessary. Required is a true partnership in learning whereby vital decisions about curriculum, instruction, and assessment are shared. Encouraging and accepting student autonomy and initiative also leads to student empowerment, an important part of multicultural education.

Both instructors shared essential course decision-making with their students. The contracted portfolios, guided by learner decisions, directed weeks of small group and individual work and greatly influenced the curriculum and instruction. The assessment methods provided students with serious choices about their own work and subsequent grades. As one university student remarked, 'This is the first time I have ever chosen a mark. Before, it was always put upon me.'

2   Constructivist teachers allow student responses to drive lessons, shift instructional strategies, and alter content.
Both instructors deliberately allowed the students to decide a large part of the work to be investigated and the content to be covered in class. In addition, both instructors set up class time for the student presentations and student interaction. Student interests, set within broad teacher guidelines, determined a high percentage of the material covered in the classes.

3   Constructivist teachers use raw data and primary sources, along with manipulative, interactive, and physical materials.
Both instructors encouraged the students to develop their own research procedures within stated guidelines. Active student investigation was required. Students traveled to community sites, participated in pertinent activities, interviewed people, and read primary sources. In the university, some kind of community event or activity was a major part of the requirements. For example, one group volunteered at a community soup kitchen while another visited a Native American reservation and interviewed community members, including the school principal.

4   Constructivist teachers engage students in experiences that might engender contradictions to their initial hypotheses and then encourage discussion.
In both classrooms throughout the term, the instructors engaged students in experiential learning. The group research work in the university class and the individual research work in the high school class required investigative approaches which in turn forced closer examinations of beliefs and understandings. Student presentations of diverse viewpoints were starting points for numerous student dialogues.

In the university class, guest speakers also presented diverse viewpoints which challenged preconceived ideas. For example, an African American man described his experiences as a sharecropper's child in the south and how alienated he had felt when he first attended school in the north. Because he was articulate and well-dressed with a Masters degree and a well-paying middle-management position, his comments about institutionalized discrimination were powerfully felt by the students.

In the high school class, the revelations each student made helped to make the others aware of individual differences rather than stereotypical images previously held. Preconceptions were not only cultural or racial but adolescent as well. Teenagers who had previously measured themselves as to how well they fit into a social crowd came to accept and appreciate their own cultural heritages along with those of their peers.

Together for nearly twelve years, the high school students who had previously concentrated on emphasizing their similarities rather than their differences became comfortable delving into various family traditions and religious practices. One East Indian female defended her Hindu beliefs as she explained her participation in an ashram, a retreat for religious meditation. Because of her openness, knowledge, and religious devotion, her classmates who were primarily Christian learned to respect a religious philosophy so distinct from their own.

5   Constructivist teachers inquire about students' understandings of concepts before sharing their own understandings of those concepts.

This descriptor is perhaps the most difficult for teachers to follow consistently when dealing with multicultural issues. Waiting to share personal understandings is not really as much a problem as resisting the temptation to persuade students to adopt the same understandings. As a co-learner in a constructivist classroom, the teacher is now no longer the expert and should not make pronouncements nor expect them to be taken as truths; however, this presents a major difficulty when dealing with issues such as racism and classism. The dilemma for the teacher becomes one of providing appropriate information, while remaining a co-learner in the classroom, about institutions and their power structures that systematically discriminate against individuals and groups. The way the teacher shares information based upon years of experience and knowledge of research is crucial to maintaining the collaborative nature of the classroom. Ahlquist (1992) in her research on multicultural education has recognized and addressed this dilemma as an ongoing instructional problem.

The university course curriculum centered around diverse cultural groups and the problems of racism, sexism, and other forms of discrimination. As the students researched in small groups and presented their information, and as issues from the text were discussed, personal preconceptions and prejudices were revealed. At times, discussions became quite heated. The instructor had to decide on a regular basis whether to contribute personal experience and professional knowledge from research to challenge students' attitudes and beliefs or to maintain a neutral position.

One example of this dilemma in the university class involved a discussion about the caning of an American teenager in Singapore in the spring of 1994. Since the instructor had lived in south-east Asia for a number of years, she was able to share her experiences related to cultural concepts of community and the emphasis of group over individual welfare. Most students then could see some possible merit in a seemingly harsh and cruel punishment when viewed in the context of a small, populous city state. Although the concluding discussion by the students indicated that they by and large still felt the caning was too strict, they were less willing to condemn the Singaporian authorities outright. The one exception was a woman who to the end of the class period continued to cry out, 'But that's mean, that's horrible, that's wrong.'

Since the high school English class involved primarily individual research into personal backgrounds, serious conflicts in opinion did not regularly surface although stereotypical thinking about different cultural groups was challenged. The most significant impact upon the high school group was felt after a Puerto Rican-born female presented her observations on Spanglish, a combination of Spanish and English used conversationally. Her explanation of the hybrid language led her to share her personal experiences in her homeland and the culture and charm of her island and its people. Because this student felt free to speak to her classmates without teacher commentary and because her peers felt free to question her without teacher interruption, the discussion conveyed a tenor of openness and honesty.

The open classroom climate was especially meaningful to the teenagers in this particular high school where the Puerto Rican population of the school community was rapidly increasing and the gulf between European American and Latino students was continually broadening. The interchanges between the female student and her peers, who were the school's leaders, helped set into motion schoolwide multicultural programs led by the students. Such openness among students of different cultural backgrounds has helped to divert the formation of gangs which was problematic in neighboring schools.

6   Constructivist teachers encourage students to engage in dialogue, both with the teacher and with one another.
Dialogue, between student and teacher and student and student, is an essential part of constructivism. Both instructors employed dialogue as a built-in part of the course. In the university, classes were conducted on a discussion basis. Guidelines for topics were provided by the syllabus, the guest speakers, and the student groups. Active participation, in the form of questioning as well as presenting, was expected as part of the course grade. In the high school, the instructor held regular conferences with students on an individual basis throughout the nine-week period. In addition, students were expected to conference with each other for ideas and development of projects. They were also encouraged to question each other's presentations.

In addition to the six principles chosen from Brooks and Brooks' list, we believe that one more principle is an essential part of constructivist theory:

7   Constructivist teachers encourage students to engage in reflective thinking. If students are to construct their own knowledge, they must have time to think about what they are learning, to consolidate that learning, and to expand upon it. Teachers, therefore, must make time in the schedule for their students to reflect, to

analyze their knowledge and beliefs, and to put these thoughts on paper for later examination. As Mathison and Young (1995) point out, constructivist theory supports reflective thinking as a way of working through personal experiences and beliefs that shape attitudes and behaviors. Furthermore, multicultural education demands careful reflection since 'language, cultural values, and cognitive styles all influence one's behaviors, attitudes, and perceptions' (p. 9).

Both instructors used reflection as an essential part of the learning process. In the university class, the design of the portfolio included a reflective part to each component. Students described the selected activity, event, or assignment and discussed what they had learned from it. In addition, the mid-term and final exams consisted of essay questions to stimulate reflection. In the high school, use of the writing process, individual teacher conferences, and peer conferences helped students to think more deeply and more clearly.

Findings

Student self-assessments at the end of the courses indicated an appreciation of the constructivist approach to curriculum, instruction, and assessment. Moreover, their comments demonstrated valuable growth in knowledge, skills, and attitudes. In the university multicultural education class, students responded to final exam questions about the course very positively. They supported the portfolio approach because it expressed 'our own found information as well as our own feelings and attitudes'. They mentioned learning about themselves and needing to work on 'stereotypical attitudes that I was not even aware of'. They showed an appreciation of how they could apply what they knew and could do:

> First I will need to do a tremendous amount of research and then listen to
> my students' feelings, views, and experiences before I can apply anything.
> Then I must come down to their level and work with them, not giving
> them my views but an overall feel for the many microcultures that may
> surround them now or later.

The general reaction of students as well as instructor for the process and products of the course was a positive one. The only negative responses came from the two students who indicated dismay at their own procrastination.

In the high school English class, students generally appreciated learning about what they wanted to know and what to them was 'important'. On an exit survey all but two students viewed this portfolio process as one of their most valuable educational experiences ever. Most believed that they had invested more time and effort in their portfolio than they would have in a project not of their personal selection. All felt that their experience had made them more knowledgeable about themselves as 'cultural human beings' and more willing to accept and appreciate diversity.

Like the university students, only two high school students believed they would have fared better in a more structured environment with more specific, teacher-directed goals. 'I just don't work well with so much freedom', noted one student. 'It's too many choices. I put off my portfolio until it was too late.' The student did, however, admit that 'I got to really know friends I thought I knew for years. It was a good project, but not gradewise good for me.'

Conclusion

Constructivist theory fits well with multicultural education content. The honoring of the individual learner's attempt to make sense of the information presented is also the honoring of that individual, an essential part of multicultural education. The exploration of individual interests and needs through experience, dialogue, and reflection fits both constructivist theory and multicultural education philosophy.

Constructivist theory as applied to multicultural education content establishes the appropriate classroom setting and suitable teaching strategies while offering exciting challenges in the material to be covered. The blending of curriculum, instruction, and assessment in a learner-centered approach stresses the importance of learner-constructed knowledge as it continually expands, deepens, and changes.

Appendix 13.1: Descriptors of Constructivist Teaching Behaviors

1 Constructivist teachers encourage and accept student autonomy and initiative.
2 Constructivist teachers use raw data and primary sources, along with manipulative, interactive, and physical materials.
3 When framing tasks, constructivist teachers use cognitive terminology such as 'classify', 'analyze', 'predict', and 'create'.
4 Constructivist teachers allow student responses to drive lessons, shift instructional strategies, and alter content.
5 Constructivist teachers inquire about students' understandings of concepts before sharing their own understandings of those concepts.
6 Constructivist teachers encourage students to engage in dialogue, both with the teacher and with one another.
7 Constructivist teachers encourage student inquiry by asking thoughtful, open-ended questions and encouraging students to ask questions of each other.
8 Constructivist teachers seek elaboration of students' initial responses.
9 Constructivist teachers engage students in experiences that might engender contradictions to their initial hypotheses and then encourage discussion.
10 Constructivist teachers allow wait time after posing questions.
11 Constructivist teachers provide time for students to construct relationships and create metaphors.
12 Constructivist teachers nurture students' natural curiosity through frequent use of the learning cycle model.

Susan C. Brown, Marcella L. Kysilka and Maureen J. Warner

References

AHLQUIST, R. (1992) 'Manifestations of inequality: Overcoming resistance in a multicultural foundations course', in GRANT, C. (Ed) *Research and Multicultural Education:
From the Margins to the Mainstream*, London, Falmer Press, pp. 89–105.

BROOKS, J. and BROOKS, M. (1993) *In Search of Understanding: The Case for Constructivist Classrooms*, Alexandria, VA, Association for Supervision and Curriculum
Deveopment.

GOLLICK, D. and CHINN, P. (1994) *Multicultural Education in a Pluralistic Society* (4th ed.),
NY, Merrill.

MATHISON, C. and YOUNG, R. (1995) 'Constructivism and multicultural education: A mighty
pedagogical merger', *Multicultural Education*, **2**, 4, pp. 7–11.

ROWE, M. (1974) 'Relation of wait-time and rewards to the development of language,
logic, and fate control: Part one — wait time', *Journal of Research in Science Teaching*, **11**, 2, pp. 81–94.

14 Arts-based Educational Research: Making Music[1]

C.T.P. Diamond, C.A. Mullen and M. Beattie

Research as Improvising and Framing

Each moment I live, I must think where to place my fingers, and press them down with no confidence of hearing a chord. (Updike, 1966, pp. 189–90)

A musical chord consists of a group of notes sounded together. We position our-selves as 'co-educators' in each other's transformations (Connelly and Clandinin, 1995), moving from the eye, the hand, and the ear. We seek to tell a shared story of how educational research can be re-imagined as an improvisatory and also framed form of art. Like Sarason (1990), we define artistic research as 'the choice and use of a particular medium to give ordered expression to internal imagery, feelings, and ideas that are in some way unique' (p. 1). Along with Bateson (1990), we wonder what insights and contributions come from the experience of perform-ance in a 'complex weave of collaboration' (p. 10).

By releasing intuition and imagination, arts-based forms engage and deepen our understanding of teacher education and provide a method of the inside. We ask: 'What artistic forms are appropriate to an arts-based metaphor of inquiry and development?' Although music and drama exist as scripts, they live only when they are interpreted in performance (McCutcheon, 1982). Just as slightly different cadenzas are heard when individual performers play the same concerto, even the same actor plays a different Hamlet each night. The distinctive features of arts-based texts are actively brought out in different readings (Barone and Eisner, 1995). We later present our performance as an arts-based, illustrated trio.

Arts-based educational research is both a document and a performance. In our collaborative work, we are seeking to rescript and to enact an alternative form of research. We also wish to restory ourselves as artistic teacher educator-researchers. We have previously used the devices of self-narrative (Beattie, 1995b, Diamond, 1995; Mullen, 1994a, 1994b); duography or shared narrative (Diamond and Mullen, 1995a, 1995b; Mullen and Diamond, 1995); and musical imagery (Beattie, 1995a, 1995c). In this paper, we first elaborate our argument as to why traditional research scores need to be reorchestrated and then we stage our joint performance.

Our way of finding art's place (Paley, 1995) is enacted and illustrated as a 'mono-logue articulated through multiple voice and response' (p. 185). We are all authors of this paper but we write together without presupposing unity of experience or expression.

We are improvising with a form of arts-based research that enhances self-knowledge within the resonating context of shared story and joint performance. Through self-study exploration, we catch our reflections in the others' understandings of how we frame and exhibit those qualities and forms which are central to our individual work. We ask: 'What is our experience as practicing teacher educator-artists in the academy?', and 'What are our experiences of collaborative production in composing and performing arts-based texts?' In this paper we share our re-sponses to both of these questions. By attempting to push the boundaries of what is known in our field, we strive to work in critical, reflexive relation to each other's practices and to those of our field (e.g., Day, Pope, and Denicolo, 1990; Elbaz, 1990). Changing the dominant chord, whether in teacher education or in music, is analogous to transformation of perspective. We introduce a new model of arts-based educational research using the elements of IICO (Intuition, Imagination, Collaboration, and Orchestration) to guide our theorizing and practice. We each have our favorite or preferred mode for improvising and framing art: the eye, hand, and ear, respectively.

A Construct of Artistic Research

We have designed IICO (Intuition, Imagination, Collaboration, and Orchestration) as a four-part notion of artistic research that consists of personal knowing, compos-ing, improvising, and framing. This is not so much a linear sequence as a multiple lens for the study and enactment of arts-based collaborative research. 'Intuition' encourages the release of imagination. Through the artistic media of metaphors, visuals, and stories, 'imagination' in turn frees up meanings. 'Collaboration' forges new relationships among these processes, experience and knowledge, self and other, art and research, and the academy and the arts. 'Orchestration' is a collabor-ative, arts-based shaping and performance as in the workshop production of music, drama, poetry, collages, and self- and group-portraits. Improvising and framing through stories and metaphors shows us interesting places to go as we watch our-selves and each other at work.

We imagine IICO as a way of representing our developing understanding of those emotional and cognitive dimensions of research that connect us to our artistic selves and each other. As teacher educator-researchers, we seek the fuller meaning of experience which is, in itself, an artistic process that can be rendered through playing with form and technique (as in the trio below). Artistic form is consistent with the qualities of direct, mental, and emotional life. Works of art are projections of such experienced life into visual, musical, spatial, temporal, and poetic struc-tures. Art expresses and presents emotions to our understanding, formulating feel-ing for our consideration and structures that give it ordered expression.

To remedy the sensuous deficit in traditional research, we ask: 'How have we already used intuition, imagination, collaboration, and orchestration in our educational research?' and 'What choices have we made to give ordered expression to the individual images, fantasies, feelings, and ideas that are inside of us?' We also ask: 'How can educational research be undertaken to give form to inner meaning?', and 'How might the experience of collaboration give shape to other forms of knowing?' We have found that we must 'do' art to get at it. We document our 'doing' of art as the joint narrative of our using story, visual, and metaphor to develop our underlying chords or themes.

A Method of the Inside

Intuition requires an inner self-awareness that, through arts-based educational research, becomes willed self-consciousness. All our present understandings and interpretations are then subject to revision or replacement. Teacher educator-researchers do not need to be hemmed in by either prevailing paradigm or current categories of our own habitual thinking. We can entertain the possibilities entailed in making the lines of our own divisions fall into different places.

Diamond (1991) has described transformation of perspective as being triggered by re-imagining. To experience a reversal of perspective, Mullen (1994b) located herself within a prison and its rehabilitative programs, learning how to connect with imprisoned others through story. Instead of positioning herself as a 'powerful journalist/researcher presuming to speak on behalf of the downtrodden' (Barone, 1994, p. 96), she sought to extend the quality of her experience within the context of prisoners' lives, stories, and published texts (see, e.g., Caron, 1978; Harris, 1986; MacDonald and Gould, 1988). This inside approach contrasts with outside, abstract accounts of prisoners (Davies, 1990; Harlow, 1987; Lovitt, 1992). Like Mullen (1994a), Beattie (1995a) told her own story as a teacher and researcher before she told that of her participant in the research. The teacher described their collaboration as 'playing together' whereas for Mary it was 'finding the music'. Our developing arts-based research is marked by reflexivity, responsiveness, and reciprocity. Such changes in the perception and evaluation of familiar meanings in research enlarge our understandings as we find new, artistic ways of proceeding. The reconstruction of professional knowledge takes place when image and imagination are linked and is heightened when understood and pursued as art.

Arts-based research offers a way of fine-tuning what we are seeing, feeling, and imagining. We can orchestrate these perceptions into clusters which are then available to be framed and sculpted into content. Intuition, which unfetters our imagination, constitutes 'the primary means of forming an understanding of what goes on under the heading of "reality"; imagination may be responsible for the very texture of experience' (Greene, 1991, p. 30). Once we remove the subjective from the shadow of the objective, the inside from the outside, appearance from reality, we are able to place imagination at the core of our understanding and engage with the different art forms. When we realize that experience offers us composites and that we always need to construe their intersections afresh, we can learn to think of events as mobile, narrative sequences. Arts-based educational research helps us to spring into a wider meaning world of multiple and moving perspectives. Such research also helps us escape from the constricting ensnarements of traditional, one-point perspective.

Moving towards Artistic Collaboration

As researchers experimenting separately with artistic approaches to inquiry, we had each previously felt alone. Now that we have connected we are able to derive insights from our different versions of practice. We are learning to accept that, by launching the filaments of inquiry out of ourselves, we can together form a keyboard. We have developed IICO as a specialized series of terms for describing the practice of artistic research. Through sharing our guiding metaphors, visuals, and narratives, we show that educational research can be usefully understood and pursued as art. By reviewing our different compositions from this fresh perspective, the melody and qualities of each of them can be revealed and enhanced.

We strive through collaboration to structure and reconfigure our consciousness and so to strike a chord for work already done. We then hear a song against which to improvise. If Patrick's way of finding and playing with the tune is that of the hand, Carol's is that of the eye, and Mary's is that of the ear. Patrick's favored modalities are visual and literary; Carol's are dream-based and mythological; and Mary's are musical and literary. These understandings enable us to watch ourselves more closely at work; to be more aware of our underlying themes (Oldfather and West, 1994); and to re-imagine ourselves as collaborative educator-artists. To show how arts-based research can deepen personal experience, we share below the stories of what we have done in our different ways to practice it. Like jazz musicians, we are using a basic tune to keep us together. Its repeated chords and structure keep us on track. We now take turns to solo, each managing a part of the performance through our self-narratives, re-imagined as improvisatory and framed art.

Patrick's Eye

Working with teachers, I invite their re-invention of self. I now realize that I too need to become a self-researcher, telling my own stories as a teacher educator. I also need personal, reflexive writing to deepen my understandings. I am using the writing and visualization tools that I suggest to my teacher colleagues in order to promote my development. Self-narrative is drawing my attention to the formal, taken-for-granted constructions through which I have learned to view research. I am reconstructing my self as a process of becoming which is enlarged through intertextual writing and reading, and collaboration. I have used visual (Norman Rockwell's mirroring self-portraits) and literary examples (Philip I and Philip II in

THE
MÖBIUS
STRIP:

MAKING MUSIC
TOGETHER

Figure 14.1:   The Möbius strip: Making music together

Roth's (1993) *Operation Shylock: A Confession*) to illustrate the struggle to recompose self. In my first self-referential work (Diamond, 1993), I originally wrote a letter to self ('Dear Pat, . . .') to reconsider an earlier attempt at self-narrative. In the second self-narrative, I mapped my education along four intertwined paths (Diamond, 1995). These conceptual and romantic tales have led me to my present position. I am still learning that I can trust the previously neglected resources of personal intuition and imagination.

My current eye-based metaphor for the joint exploration of arts-based research is that of a Möbius strip. The spiral is formed by taking a short strip of paper, twisting it once before taping its ends together. One can begin anywhere on the surface, drawing a continuous line along it. The first return will always be on the other side of the paper. Only on the second go round is the beginning of the line rejoined. Bateson (1994) describes the journey along the other side of the strip as not only a return over the same ground but also as the next level of a spiral (see Figure 14.1). This as an analogue of my work with Carol and Mary. When a draft section can be traversed without a break, it may seem one-sided. However, there are always two linked sides and the whole consists of a three-dimensional spiral.

Much of our writing and researching together as educational researchers consists of taking ideas that are webbed around others, circling endlessly. Transformation requires us to return from the end to the beginning, revisiting the past from the present (previously its future). Working together by producing and performing a tripartite text allows us to re-encounter our individual understandings through those of the others. This is like 'returning on a second circuit of a Möbius strip and coming to the experience from the opposite side' (Bateson, 1994, p. 31). When seen from Carol and Mary's contrasting points of view, my familiar patterns become accessible for revisioning. With yet another return, what seemed so different is shown to be shared.

Carol's Hand

Although jazz can be defined as the way of the hands (Sudnow, 1993), my hands have never actually shaped and shared art works. However, I can remember playing with clay in class and asking why. I also remember accidentally potato printing my clothing during an art lesson in elementary school and ruefully thinking, 'I'd rather be writing'. During tense and inspiring moments with loved ones and colleagues, I always want to record and reconstruct the text of my own life-experiences and dreams. The notion of literary writer as artist was missing from my early education and growing up — and later from my initial graduate studies. I was left dreaming on the margins. But it was here, on the edges, that I focused on my hands. They would shape the texts that voice and communicate my perceptions and experiences of research, and in my own terms. Unknowingly engaged in a process of self-education, I followed my intuitive sense. This enabled me to resource my imagination to conjure up possibilities for intellectual and emotional survival.

When I reflect on the IICO sequence shared in this paper, I realize that I have existed intuitively on the fringes of both the art world and the field of teacher education. Here, I am focusing on my hands as they shape the texts that release my artist self. I offer accounts of my individual and collaborative mythology about my engagement in educational contexts which promote location through dislocation. Stories which investigate marginalized lives in school and prison (e.g., Feuerverger and Mullen, in press) have the potential to awaken the 'shadowed zones' (Paley, 1995) of mainsteam academic knowledge. Without self-narrative, I would be left the prisoner of undisclosed, structural systems. I would then stare into the eyes of the gatekeeper, mirroring that closed world. But I choose instead to stare into my own eyes — and those of others' through my own. However, even my own constructs can operate as vigilant controls.

The restrictions on personal writing in prison reminded me of the academy with its seeming suspicion of creative thinking and intimate forms of knowledge. My encounters with authority intensified: I was advised to control my impulses to do creative work and to rethink my direction. My participants or student-inmates experienced criticism and censorship of their stories prepared for our creative writing newsletter; my poetry was banned from it too; and my research proposal was initially rejected as too personal.

My imagination kept the intuitive alive for me within both sets of institutional constraints. The teacher educator-researcher must learn to see art even in that which oppresses its expression and form. Just as the inmates and I wrote to break free as 'frozen ponies on a carousel halted in mid-gallop' (Mullen, 1994b, 1995), I have re-imagined teacher education and research as a merry-go-round of paradigmatic and institutional restrictions. When inmates are valued and recognized as artists, they can invent and try more productive ways of living and working. Like the conductor who shapes the overall movement of a performance, the process of working collaboratively allows me to watch many hands at work.

Mary's Ear

The School Orchestra

I remember the sound of massed strings in the early morning.
The flashes of the red-brown wood of the instruments
And drawing my chair in close, to restore the ear's primeval power.
I remember the controlled movements of hands and eyes.
The bows going and the co-mingled sounds
The feeling of being wrapped in a timeless sound-space,
before the ticking of work-time.
The joyous co-created sound going up like a mass concelebrated.
Then that time when the music faltered and my own solitary violin held on
Until the sound grew strong and we raised the roof with our ending.
'You are like the Rock of Gibraltar,' smiled the young nun, shaking her
head.
'Solid as a rock'.
Nearly three decades later, I now know that rocks hold onto sound.
Mass-rocks seeped with whispered prayers,
Silent and secretive stone-walls,
Mountains whose power is in the stories folded into the seams.
And me still listening beyond the silence.
Strings vibrating to stray wisps of song.

I wrote 'The School Orchestra' in 1994 to try to express what I know about shared creative activity, and to try to make sense of this urge in my life. I am conscious of the distinction I make between solitary as opposed to shared creative work. I believe that my life is enriched by both and that something is missing when I am engaged in only one of them. My participation in artistic activity takes place mainly through words. Words and music share many of the same qualities for me, but I have greater facility for creation with the language of words than with the notes of music.

The major principles of arts-based teaching and collaborative research mirror those of violin playing. Here too the creation of spaces, of rhythms and forms, and of making music together, are possible. In both teaching and research, the spaces created allow voices to resonate, narratives to interact, and approaches to vary. There is no standardized B or C — each one played is different. Like the space created on a violin, the teaching and the research spaces are settings for meanings to be made and to co-exist at any one time. In music, the middle levels of vibration are heard as tones with discernible pitch. Modifying and changing the rhythm and quality of these tones are waves of vibration underneath which comprise subtle surgings, vibratos, and ornamentations, all of which make up the style and expressiveness of an individual player. The listener then has his or her own way of hearing and feeling the music.

The metaphor of how the right hand of the violinist expresses itself also applies to teaching and research. The qualities of attentiveness to rhythms and timing, of sophisticated listening and empathetic understanding of the other, of 'reaching out and holding back in relationship' (Beattie, 1995a), and of creating, shaping, and giving form to what is being made are essential in teaching and research. When things do not go well, there is cacophony. When they do, there is music. In violin playing, as in teaching and in collaborative artistic research, successful 'music-making' has to do with being connected to one's own, and to others' intuition and imagination, with finding forms and structures to express ideas and emotions. I find myself constantly making choices and decisions, as well as adapting, modifying, and expanding on them. I imagine new variations while shaping the elements into a coherent and aesthetic whole.

In collaborative 'music making experiences', I have experienced the rewards of collaborative research — of entering into the other's reality, of being inspired and transformed through the process. I bring a sense of optimism and a longing for authentic collaboration. I listen for resonances that 'strike a chord' in me. I search for the wholeness, the coherence, and the unity of what can be created together. I wrote 'The School Orchestra' during my work with Pat and Carol, both of whom I knew from previous shared contexts.

Conclusion

In artistic research, we turn back upon ourselves, tracing the course of our insights and limitations. Through improvising with language and other art forms, we go in search of our own images and visions of things. We are freed to become more present to experience and ourselves. This leads to a participant, relational way of knowing in which we are no longer constrained by established convention. We define ourselves as arts-based teacher educator-researchers who attend to imaginative constructions and representations of research. We ask, 'Who are the teacher educator-researchers doing artistic work?' And, we also ask, 'What artistic processes and chords underlie such work?' We agree that artistic forms of research still need to be more fully brought into narrative and educational research through self-reflective and shared storying, and through metaphor-making (Beattie, 1995a; Diamond, 1991; Mullen, 1994b).

Just as Jackson (1992) described a new way of helping teachers to develop as that of art, wonder, and of altered sensibility, we are exploring art as an alternative way of doing research. Even as there is no clear and unequivocal language for describing the process of what happens when a person confronts or makes a work of art, we are experimenting with language and form, and the creation of context-rich graphic displays (see Kealy and Webb, in press). We study our individual and shared understandings of experience and interpretation in an effort to reconstrue and promote new kinds of development and educational research. We have offered a four-part construct of artistic inquiry (Intuition, Imagination, Collaboration, and Orchestration) which we enacted as a trio. In a responsive set of exchanges with each other, meaning is further developed and even transformed. By entertaining and performing alternative versions of the same sequence, that is, of theories and practices in teacher development using arts-based approaches to research, our attention has been focused and renewed.

Experience spirals through all our life cycles, presenting similar insights from different angles. Development involves making meaning with those who share at least partly overlapping understandings. To escape the imprisoning framework of assumptions learned within a single paradigm, our habits of attention and interpretation need to be stretched and circled back upon themselves. Such experiences are too complex for any single encounter. They require the garnering of doubling, tripling, and even contrary visions. Through our musical structure, we build a 'a double helix of [shared] and personal growth' (Bateson, 1994, p. 44), but strung as a three-dimensional performance.

As collaborating researcher-artists at the computer keyboard, we are now more confident about learning the music of research. Even the first fingerings load each note with the double meaning of text and performance. However, as for a beginning pianist also at the keyboard (see our dual keyboard image in the graphic in Figure 14.1), such expressive attempts are:

> difficult and complex . . . How great looms the gap between the first gropings of vision and the first stammerings of percussion! Vision timidly becomes percussion, percussion becomes music, music becomes emotion, emotion becomes — vision. (Updike, 1966, p. 186)

We are slowly learning to sustain our imaginative but orderly inquiries, laying other melodies over the underlying chords, and playing on the changes. In arts-based research, we choose those forms to improvise and in the collaborative performance become immersed in the remaking of selves. We have made arts-based applications to many contexts, including university-level faculty development; preservice and inservice teacher education; and other, perhaps less conventional, schooling contexts such as prisons. Our text- and performance-based trio provided us with a form for shaping, designing, and releasing the energies of artistic educational research. Artistic work provides a joint setting within which we can each learn to stage our transformations.

Note

1 We wish to thank William A. Kealy, Assistant Professor, College of Education at Texas A&M, for the contribution of his context-rich graphic display to our paper.

References

Barone, T. (1994) 'On Kozol and Sartre and educational research as socially committed literature', *The Review of Education/Pedagogy/Cultural Studies*, **16**, 1, pp. 93–102.

BARONE, T. and EISNER, E.W. (1995) 'Arts-based educational research', in JAEGER, R. (Ed) *Complementary Methods of Educational Research*, Washington, DC, AERA.

BATESON, M.C. (1990) *Composing a Life*, New York, Penguin Books.

BATESON, M.C. (1994) *Peripheral Visions: Learning along the Way*, New York, Harper Collins.

BEATTIE, M. (1995a) *Developing Professional Knowledge in Teaching: A Narrative of Change and Learning*, New York, Teachers College Press, and Toronto, OISE Press.

BEATTIE, M. (1995b) 'New prospects for teacher education: Narrative ways of knowing teaching and teacher education', *Educational Research*, **36**.

BEATTIE, M. (1995c) 'The making of a music: The construction and reconstruction of a teacher's personal practical knowledge through inquiry', *Curriculum Inquiry*, **25**, 2, pp. 133–50.

CARON, R. (1978) *Go-Boy!*, Toronto, McGraw-Hill Ryerson.

CONNELLY, F.M. and CLANDININ, D.J. (1995) 'Narrative and education', *Teachers and Teaching: Theory and Practice*, **1**, 1, pp. 73–85.

DAVIES, I. (1990) *Writers in Prison*, Toronto, Between The Lines.

DAY, C., POPE, M. and DENICOLO, P. (Eds) (1990) *Insights into Teacher Thinking and Action*, Lewes, Falmer Press.

DIAMOND, C.T.P. (1991) *Teacher Education as Transformation: A Psychological Perspective*, Milton Keynes, Open University Press.

DIAMOND, C.T.P. (1993) 'Writing to reclaim self: The use of narrative in teacher education', *Teaching and Teaching Education*, **9**, 5, 6, pp. 511–17.

DIAMOND, C.T.P. (1995) in NEIMEYER, R.A. (Eds), *Advances in Personal Construct Psychology III*, Greenwich, CT, JAI Press.

DIAMOND, C.T.P. and MULLEN, C.A. (1995a) 'Studying the self: Narratives of two arts-based researchers', Unpublished manuscript.

DIAMOND, C.T.P. and MULLEN, C.A. (1995b) 'Roped together: A duography of supervision and post-mentorship', Unpublished manuscript.

ELBAZ, F. (1990) 'Knowledge and discourse: The evolution of research on teacher thinking', in DAY, C., POPE, M. and DENICOLO P. (Eds) *Insights into Teacher Thinking and Action*, Lewes, Falmer Press.

FEUERVERGER, G. and MULLEN, C.A. (in press) 'Portraits of marginalized lives: Stories of literacy and collaboration in school and prison', *Interchange*.

GREENE, M. (1991) 'Texts and margins', *Harvard Educational Review*, **61**, 1, pp. 27–39.

HARLOW, B. (1987) *Resistance Literature*, New York, Methuen.

HARRIS, J. (1986) *Stranger in Two Worlds*, New York, Kensington Publishing.

JACKSON, P.W. (1992) 'Helping teachers develop', in HARGREAVES, A. and FULLAN, M.G. (Eds), *Understanding Teacher Development*, New York, Teachers College Press, pp. 62–74.

KEALY, W.A and WEBB, J.M. (in press) 'Contextual influences of maps and diagrams on learning', *Contemporary Educational Psychology*.

LOVITT, C. (1992) 'The rhetoric of murderers' confessional narratives: The model of Pierre Rivière's memoir', *Journal of Narrative Technique*, **22**, 1, pp. 23–34.

MACDONALD, M. and GOULD, (1988) *The Violent Years of Maggie MacDonald*, Toronto, McClelland-Bantam.

MCCUTCHEON, G. (1982) 'Educational criticism: Reflections and reconsiderations', *Journal of Curriculum Theorizing*, **4**, pp. 170–74.

MULLEN, C.A. (1994a) 'A narrative exploration of the self I dream', *Journal of Curriculum Studies*, **26**, 3, pp. 253–63.

MULLEN, C.A. (1994b) 'Imprisoned selves: A narrative inquiry into incarceration and education', Unpublished doctoral dissertation, University of Toronto, Toronto.

MULLEN, C.A. (1995) 'Carousel: Researching lives in prisons and teacher education', Unpublished manuscript.

MULLEN, C.A. and DIAMOND, C.T.P. (1995) 'Narratives of marginality: From imprisonment to transformation', Unpublished manuscript.

OLDFATHER, P. and WEST, J. (1994) 'Qualitative research as jazz', *Educational Research*, **23**, 8, pp. 22–6.

PALEY, N. (1995) *Finding Art's Place: Experiments in Contemporary Education and Culture*, New York, Routledge.

ROTH, P. (1993) *Operation Shylock: A Confession*, New York, Simon and Schuster.

SARASON, S.B. (1990) *The Challenge of Art to Psychology*, New Haven, CT, Yale University Press.

SUDNOW, D. (1993) *Ways of the Hand: The Organization of Improvised Conduct*, Cambridge, MA, MIT Press.

UPDIKE, J. (1966) *The Music School: Selected Stories*, New York, Knopf.

15 Teacher Knowledge Development in a Social and Individual Context[1]

Elisabeth Ahlstrand, Görel Carlsson,
Sven G. Hartman, Anders Magnusson,
Lars Næslund and Annika Rannström

Abstract

Studies carried out by a group of researchers studying different aspects of teachers' knowledge are introduced through the main lines of history in teaching, and school reforms in Sweden. History provides rich variation in teachers' knowledge as different groups cultivate different types of professional knowledge. In addition, there is an equally rich individual variation which develops throughout life. The researchers studied these variations in teachers' knowledge against a background of history of professions and school reforms. In the subsequent pages some examples are given from the ongoing studies. The following themes are focused:

- teacher students' pre-understandings of their future teacher knowledge;
- variations in teachers' knowledge and professional identity;
- the voice of a reflecting teacher; and
- teacher values in retrospect.

Homogeneity and Variation: Some Historical Preconditions for the Development of Teachers' Knowledge in Sweden

Research colleagues from abroad sometimes describe encounters with Swedish school systems and educational theory as a visit to a very large, extended village. Not because we are particularly isolated or undeveloped — at least this is what they say — but because most teachers have relatively similar frames of reference, work under the same conditions, often share the same values and, they often know one another even if they work far apart. The same goes for pedagogical research: even with much variation in the theoretical approach and the way of work, there is more to unite than to separate.

This kind of first impression of the Swedish educational world captures much of

Centralism
Dominating state control

1   2

Uniform culture   **Pluralism**
Predominant Lutheranism   Growing secularization

3   4

Decentralism
Dominating local control

Figure 15.1:   Four different social standpoints for the formulation of school policy

the basic preconditions for pedagogical work in Sweden as there has always been a large component of central control and homogeneity in the Swedish educational system. But there has also been a fundamental difference that has permeated schools. In the tension between these two poles, the teacher develops his knowledge.

Homogeneity and Variation

The Swedish educational system has its roots in a society of great uniformity (Hartman, 1994). The elementary school was established in a fairly compact, Lutheran, uniform, culture. Even when secularization lessened the influence of the Church, the culture was still fairly closed. Since the Second World War, however, pluralism has grown at an ever-increasing rate. For the school system this has meant that certain basics have changed. A school class of the 1940s looked entirely different from a typical class of the 1980s. Greater social mobility, more secularization, and increased immigration partly explain the new situation.

The model sketched in Figure 15.1 illustrates this change. It indicates a shift from position 1 to position 2, from a centrally governed school system to one that, while it is still centralistic regarding content at least, must operate in a pluralistic society. This change certainly went on for a long time, but was not fully visible until after the Second World War.

Changes in Swedish educational policy during the past four or five years have been in the direction of increased local autonomy. In addition during this period there has been a start on applying a very generous policy towards independent schools. Up until the beginning of the 1990s private or independent schools were very rare in Sweden. These changes would seem to imply a shift from position 2 towards position 4 in the model.

The changes are certainly linked with the international neoliberal trend and the awareness of the market that have been visible in international educational development in recent years. The centralistic school policy becomes expensive to administer and increased local control, it was assumed, would lead to greater variation, greater freedom of choice and thus better quality (Miron, 1993; Englund, 1994).

New trends in Swedish educational policy created new conditions for teachers' career development. Since the middle of the nineteenth century the two distinct teacher groups have successively seen their professional status enhanced with the help of the state bureaucratic apparatus and through laws and regulations. This is how the teacher groups' professional claims *vis-à-vis* parents and the clergy were asserted once upon a time. Now the State was saying that much of the work of the school was to be governed on the basis of the teacher groups' own professionalism and with cooperation between local educational authorities and the teaching body. This was no longer the job of the State and the Parliament.

Thus teachers' autonomy with reference to central authority has increased, while at the same time the dependence of their position relative to school managers and local educational politicians has grown. Nevertheless the possible remaining conflicts of interest between the two large teacher groups must be handled at local level.

Two Different Teaching Systems Merge into One

One of the peculiarities of Swedish education is that it long consisted of two mutually independent teaching systems: one for elementary education and one for higher studies where the clergy and officials were educated. Even though the Church had a strong influence on both, the systems were kept separate from the middle ages until the time of the Second World War.

This division into two has permeated educational discussion in Sweden. Different views and traditions developed in the separated systems. The way of looking at teaching and knowledge, pupil and teacher roles, school and society was different.

Popular Education, Folkskolan: The Elementary School

In 1992 the 150th anniversary of the Swedish elementary school was celebrated, but it was not with the 1842 elementary school statute that popular education started. There was a well-developed system of popular education much earlier. Nor was it the case that the elementary school was all ready once the elementary school statute was adopted. Swedish popular education has very deep roots.

Most simply stated, through the Reformation Christianity became a book religion. The sermon became the central element in the cult and the church books, primarily the psalm book and the catechism, carried very great weight. The program popular education was filled out. It was stressed more and more that it was not enough to know the catechism by heart, one also had to be able to *read* 'and see with thine own eyes what God in His holy word offers and commands'.

The 1686 Ecclesiastical Act was an important milestone for Swedish popular education. It indicated effective methods of checking that the population fulfilled the obligations prescribed by the educational program. The Act made parents and masters responsible for teaching their children and servants to read. It charged the clergy to check and record, by means of oral examinations at parish catechetical meetings, that parents were performing their teaching duties with approved results.

This early popular education was based on the double principle of the family head's duty to instruct and the clerical official's duty to examine. To be able to read and to know one's catechism became required previous knowledge for preparation for confirmation and first holy communion, this in turn was a condition for being accepted into the adult community (Johansson, 1995; Rodhe, 1994).

The system proved to be effective. As early as the eighteenth century Swedes were a reading people, as were Nordic neighbors. Parents' obligation to instruct became an important family matter which in time was to be defended when the authorities produced new regulations demanding that teaching should be managed by professional teachers. This meant that the elementary school teachers, with the support of the authorities, were obliged to wrest their professional territory from the parents and to some extent from the Church.

The adoption of the 1842 elementary school statute implied two important decisions of principle. First, the decision meant that popular education assumed the character of an educational task and not a matter for the poor-house. Secondly, the popular education was to be kept entirely separate from education for the public class, that is, the school form that was to be designated *läroverk* and which corresponded most closely to 'grammar school' (Richardson, 1992). In this way, much of the professional development of the teaching body was determined. This was to take place along two separate lines.

Läroverket: The Grammar School

Schools for the education of the clergy and public officials had the longest history, with roots in the middle ages. But neither these schools, the teachers or the *djäknar*, the grammar-school pupils, had a specially high status to begin with. Indeed to get anyone at all who was willing to assume the hateful occupation of teaching in a grammar school, a system was introduced whereby one could count two years of service for each academic year's schoolteaching. In this way teachers could qualify rapidly for service outside the school.

But in the middle of the nineteenth century a change took place. Society's demand for more specialized studies began to make itself felt. The tendency became that the classical languages gradually lost ground to scientific subjects.

During this period the social status of the *läroverk*, grammar school, improved markedly. In contrast to how the grammar-school pupils had been viewed previously, it was now thought possible to distinguish among the grammar-school boys the country's hopes for the future. It was they who would head authorities and firms. It was not that the grammar school gave them the education they needed for their future working lives, but that their school days afforded them a social position which could lead directly or indirectly to leading positions. The grammar school students were looked upon as superior to their contemporaries in the town. During the nineteenth century the *läroverk* became increasingly a school for the boys of the well-to-do. Even boys from the very highest level in the country could now be sent to the grammar school (Florin and Johansson 1993).

This development also affected the position of grammar-school teachers in a positive direction. Their social status improved markedly, and so did their salaries. Their professional position was strengthened through the introduction of new teaching subjects and in other ways, the educational level was raised and they became more independent of the Church.

Grundskolan: The Comprehensive School

In time the grammar-school teachers position was upset by the elementary-school teachers' professional claims. The elementary school teachers worked for coordination of the separate educational systems and for a common course of studies for all children, a basic school, for the first six years of schooling. This issue dominated educational discussion in Sweden from the 1880s until the foundation of the Swedish comprehensive school in 1962. The 1940s and 1950s were the decades of the committee and the pilot scheme. The requirements for a new content in school activity and for a new organization were investigated and debated. The idea of a basic school was to be implemented at last.

The comprehensive school reform involved combining previously parallel school forms. The upper part of the elementary school termed the continuation school, the lower secondary school, the girls' school and parts of former vocational schemes now became, in a combined form, the upper grades of the comprehensive school. Compulsory schooling was lengthened from seven years to nine. This involved a great increase in the volume of the school sector. More teachers were needed and new school premises. This in turn required the merging of municipalities to provide a sufficiently large economic base. Educational development and municipal development went hand in hand.

In the structure of the new school traces of the earlier systems can be seen clearly. The comprehensive school was to be one school, but it got three levels, with three teacher categories corresponding to what had existed in different school forms at the beginning of the century. The designation of the different teacher groups was changed but the question is whether ways of working changed to the same extent.

Large sections of the former parallel school system were incorporated into the comprehensive school system. This is evident from *Lgr 62*, the first Comprehensive School Curriculum. The upper level was differentiated with various study choices in the ninth year. The options largely corresponded to the choices that had been available in the old parallel school system. The detailed syllabus seems to have been inspired by the former lower secondary school. However, the methods prescribed in *Lgr 62* agree with the notions of the activity teaching approaches. Five principles were to apply to teaching: it was to be characterized by Motivation, Activity, Concretion, Individualization and Cooperation. The acronym of its Swedish initials MAKIS became the methodological formula for teaching in the comprehensive school (OECD, 1980). The distinction built into the comprehensive school also existed in teacher training, which offered entirely different programs for the three teacher categories.

Not until 1988 did there start a new program of teacher education with the purpose of creating a mixed-ability educational system and a single teacher category for the comprehensive school. The problems we have been struggling with since then have consisted of getting different teacher training traditions to work together and getting the two to become one (Askling and Jedeskog, 1993).

Two Separate Teaching-houses

Educational systems and their ideological views have often been compared to intellectual edifices or teaching-houses. In Sweden teacher knowledge has been developed, both figuratively and literally, in different houses. The basic structure of the buildings has been the same, that is, a foundation of practical teaching skill has been successively reinforced with a floor of particular values and then given a scientific superstructure. But the fittings on the three floors and the devices over the facade have differed in the teachers' different knowledge-houses (Hartman, 1993).

Education and subjects were focused in the house that the school-for-learning, (i.e., the grammar school tradition, built for its teacher knowledge). It was thus the care and the handing-on of knowledge that were long considered the main task of grammar-school and university teachers, not research. This view was current until well into the twentieth century. General education had a higher priority than subject specialization, and was in fact considered a condition for specialization. Broad inter-subject studies were a compulsory part of university examinations well into the twentieth century. Studies of this kind were, in turn, compulsory for authorization to teach in universities and grammar schools.

During the latter part of the nineteenth century, research was increasingly carried on in the universities. This is how the modern university came about. A new body of knowledge grew up and expanded at an increasing tempo. This entailed changes in the professional profile, the teaching-house was altered with new rooms. It was no longer necessary to 'know everything', you had to specialize within some particular discipline and 'know your subject'. A more enclosed concept of knowledge was to gain ground.

In the grammar schools this change in the protracted struggle between 'Latin domination' and the new natural science subjects was noticed. An educational, integrative, subject perspective was slowly replaced by, or supplemented with, a more confined, specialty-oriented and particularizing discipline perspective.

Training was the device that, figuratively speaking, was written over the other house, the teaching-house where teachers were trained for the needs of the elementary school. The professional skills of the first elementary teachers were aimed at the ability to handle teaching and large and clearly separated pupil groups. Children of the people together and children of the better-off together. Routines and means of control had to be acquired that allowed the teacher to control giant classes: classes long remained very large.

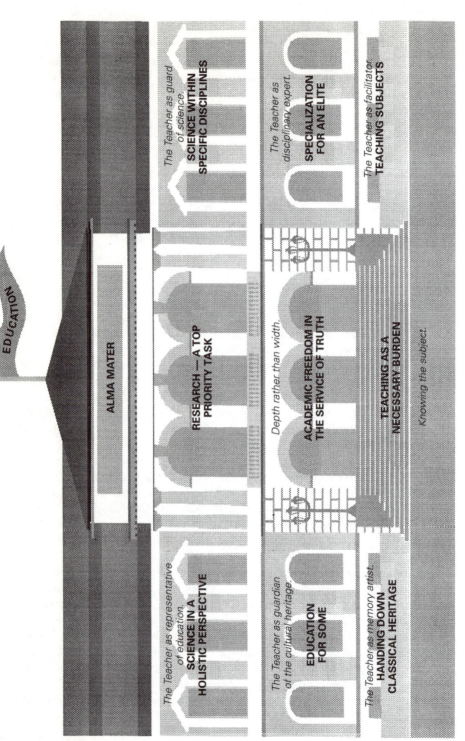

Figure 15.2: Teacher-knowledge according to the ideals of university tradition

In Figure 15.2 the picture shows the first house of teacher-knowledge, the one that was built according to the ideals of university tradition. A series of typical concepts and positions have been grouped on the three floors: the basic teaching practice floor, the values floor, and the research superstructure floor. In the background can be seen the outlines of the principle building of Uppsala University. It was inaugurated in 1887. There is a time dimension in the picture: the developmental tendency suggested in the sketch runs from the bottom upwards and from left to right.

Starting in the 1880s the elementary teachers' union organization worked largely for an educational policy that would promote the idea of a bottom school common for all children. The educational tendency to separate was increasingly replaced by an integrating one. Every child was to receive the first formal education in a common school. Integration required that the teachers could meet individual pupils. This required smaller groups, but also the teacher's ability to individualize. This came to be counted an important element within the teaching profession. Emphasis on the teacher's ability to individualize the teaching did not mean that the ability to manage the whole class became less important; rather, the teacher's skills had been developed and differentiated through this.

One line saw teaching as a social task and the teacher as an important agent for social development under controlled conditions. The other line placed the psychological aspects of teaching in the center and considered the teacher as a pedagogically and psychologically schooled supervisor of his pupils' school work. Both positions were successful in how they viewed practical and value-forming aspects of the teaching profession.

In the second teaching-house, as in the first, attempts were made to create a scientific superstructure. Teaching was to be made scientific. In time, the scientific perspective also gained a profile of its own. Within the various disciplines that conduct research into education and teachers' work some concentrate on social and societal aspects and others concentrate on more psychological dimensions.

In Figure 15.3 the picture shows the second house of teacher-knowledge, the one that was built according to the ideals of the teacher training college tradition. A series of typical concepts and positions were grouped on the three floors: the basic teaching practice floor, the values floor, and the research superstructure floor. In the background can be seen the outlines of the teacher training college building erected in Linköping in 1869. There is also a time dimension in the picture: the developmental tendency suggested in the sketch runs from the bottom upwards and from left to right.

Dimensions of Teacher Knowledge

I consider that, using these examples from the educational history , one can observe three steps in the growth of the teachers' professional field (Goodson, 1994). First, practical knowledge predominates, then a special value basis develops in the two teacher groups and gradually a scientific perspective is introduced in and on teachers'

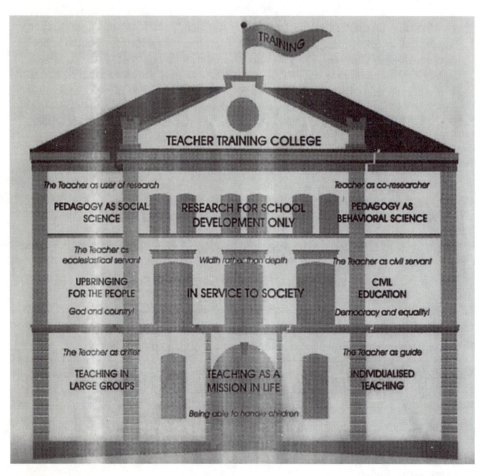

Figure 15.3: Teacher-knowledge according to the ideals of teacher training college tradition

work. I consider this as three separate perspectives within which teachers' knowledge has developed. The way in which one develops one's knowledge determines its character.

Knowledge that has grown up in a certain perspective and which has proved valuable is not always applicable in a different perspective. This is not so much because of the borders of a particular preserve as it is because of the conditions for observations and conclusions differ in kind with the different contexts. Whoever oversteps the boundary of 'his' perspective on knowledge risks drawing untenable conclusions. The practitioner's unique knowledge is based on *well-tried experience*. One has learned what works best in different contexts. One knows what best suits oneself, the subject matter and the pupils one is working with. One knows what needs to be done for something to function at all. The individual teacher's well-tried experience cannot be generalized to all situations. Knowledge is both person-dependent and situation-bound.

This kind of knowledge is often hard to formulate in such a way that it can be communicated to others. This is why well-tried teaching experience often cannot be subjected to rational assessment. The knowledge base of the evaluative perspective consists of *convictions* of people, groupings or traditions. Differing positions regarding view of knowledge, humanity and society are often justified on the basis of overall systems of explanation that are chiefly religious or political. The limitations that this entails mean that the arguments upon which the values are based are valid primarily in more or less ideological contexts. Such arguments can be tested only against their own preconditions in terms of values. They cannot replace scientific or experientially based testimony on educational issues; but they are no less valuable on that account; rather the reverse. What is founded on conviction contains qualities that neither practical experience or science possess. Without the ardor of conviction an educational debate is half dead before it has begun. For this reason a mistake sometimes made is to conceal the ideological arguments and clothe them in the scientist's white coat for greater weight.

The value base of teachers' knowledge has been noted in international educational research, in different contexts and different constellations of concepts. There has been mention of the moral dimensions of teaching. Teaching ethics and teaching philosophy can imply more theoretical perspectives in the same area. This perspective can also be seen as a special portion of reflective teachers' knowledge, sometimes as a parallel to a more scientific reflection. A peculiarity of the Swedish debate is, in my opinion, that the value premises for teacher's work have seldom been discussed. The scientific perspective comprises a very special type of teachers' knowledge. In saying that it is based on *science*, one has also said it is general in character. It usually concerns general circumstances at a fairly theoretical level. It is mostly knowledge 'at a distance', with a relatively abstract, if not chilly, approach to reality.

This character also determines the limitations of the scientific perspective. It is impossible on the basis of the general observations science makes to draw any quick conclusions about individual practical teaching problems. The traditional method of deductive inferences from general to specific circumstances can be applied

Two Teaching Houses

Dimensions of teacher knowledge	Subject focused education	Teaching focused training
science	I	II
values	III	IV
practice	V	VI

Figure 15.4:   Traditions and dimensions of teacher knowledge

within one knowledge perspective, but it is very complicated to try and apply this method between different knowledge perspectives. My thesis is that much of the confusion one meets within the educational sector comes from not making any distinctions between different perspectives of knowledge. Teaching-methodological standpoints clash with ideological and scientific as if it were a matter of inter-changeable types of knowledge. This is why it has not even been possible to agree on what one is disagreeing about.

The history of education, then, has created a fairly differentiated profiling of teachers' fields of professional knowledge. A way of further clarifying this spread is to combine the traditions from the two separate teaching-houses with the three-fold division of the bases of teachers' knowledge. The ensuing schedule has six main categories, that could be further specified into subcategories.

Let us assume that all the variants of teachers' knowledge that I mention in my schedule can be deployed on the one hand and made into objects for reflection on the other. In the latter form all kinds of teachers' knowledge would then be communicable in some sense, and hence possible to relate to each other.

One ought perhaps to distinguish between the teacher-knowledge actors and its authors. It is doubtless the case that the majority of the representatives of teachers' knowledge remain anonymous precisely because they are the actors who do the job in the classroom in developing ideas or in the research workshop. It is the authors who get noticed, since it is they who have taken upon themselves the task of gathering and conveying knowledge about what the others do.

The studies summarized in this paper have been carried out in a research group engaged in the study of various aspects of teacher knowledge. We have found that also studies in the history of teacher professions and school reforms can add interesting aspects to research in teaching. The historical development has led to a rich variation in teachers' knowledge. Thus, different groups cultivate different types of professional knowledge. In addition, there is an equally rich individual variation, which, to all appearances, develops throughout life. In our research group we attempt to study teachers' knowledge in a life-long perspective based on the history of professions and school reforms.

At present we are working on the following themes:

- teacher students' pre-understandings of their future teacher knowledge;
- variations in teachers' knowledge and professional identity;
- the voice of a reflecting teacher; and
- teacher values in retrospect.

We will give some examples from our research dealing with young and old actors and authors on the professional field of teaching. They demonstrate different aspects and stages of teachers' knowledge in a life-long perspective.

Student Teachers' Pre-understandings of Their Future Professional Knowledge

It can be difficult to express what teachers' professional knowledge really comprises, and this is demonstrated in existing descriptions of teachers' knowledge. To develop teachers' professional knowledge can imply that:

1 they deepen their knowledge of the subjects they teach (Shulman, 1987);
2 they get a chance to reflect on what they do (Zeichner and Liston, 1987);
3 they develop their knowledge through working in a context, that is, in a teaching situation (Elbaz, 1983); and
4 they may develop their personalities, each thus following a development of personal, practical knowledge of self (Clandinin, 1986). If a student teacher imagines his or her forthcoming professional knowledge, what does this involve?

The present paper draws on the results of an inquiry into newly accepted student teachers' conceptions about their forthcoming professional knowledge, in order to get a picture of new students' invisible 'filter' (Rannström, 1995). The researchers who have studied students' conceptions about training and teachers' work have approached the problem in three different ways. They study what *character* the conceptions have, how they may be *influenced* by training, and, finally, what *significance* the preconceptions have for what actually reaches the students.

When researchers have sought descriptions of conceptions about teachers' professional knowledge from non-teachers, they have done so primarily from students in teacher-training courses. They have also tried to investigate whether there are any differences between experienced teachers', new student teachers' and newly qualified teachers' conceptions, so as to see whether the nature of teachers' knowledge can be surveyed by means of such comparisons.

At the start of his or her training, a student teacher has conceptions about different phenomena. Their significance as a 'filter' for new knowledge has been remarked by several researchers. In their attempts to understand the character of a 'filter', Schmidt and Kennedy made an investigation in 1990 to get more knowledge of how they could influence students' 'filters'. The difficulties in making the 'filter' visible through such comparative studies have been confirmed by the research of Mertz *et al.*, (1992) who showed that no homogeneity could be determined in student teachers' cognitive structures.

From such studies, it is possible to conclude that structures once formed are resistant to change and may be likened to a 'filter' through which all new information must pass. Many researchers agree that the structures are stable and permanent. Conceptions about teaching and learning are consequently stable, which can cause difficulties in learning about teaching (Calderhead, 1991a; Feiman-Nemser and Buchmann, 1987).

The group that has been investigated comprised twenty-seven recently accepted students who were interviewed during the first two weeks of their training. The following questions functioned as 'background prompts', for me as an interviewer.

- What do newly accepted student teachers' conceptions about being a teacher consist of?
- What do they imagine they need to learn to become teachers?
- What do students understand by the concept of teaching? What do students think they need to learn so as to be able to teach?

In the material there were two different ways of conceiving a teacher's professional knowledge. First, the students expressed the view that there was knowledge from without — handed over to them, for example in the form of certain facts. This seemed to be knowledge that could be taught and was thus to some extent precise and delimited, which is here called Formal knowledge (F). This kind of knowledge refers to the content of knowledge, i.e., what is learned. Three subcategories of F-knowledge were found; knowledge of the subject, of methods and of children.

The second kind of knowledge depended on the person involved in its acquisition — the Experiential knowledge (E). This includes how the individual is as a *person* and what *experience* he or she has. In addition, the knowledge the students described had a feature that was somewhat difficult to identify.

When in the interviews the conversation turned to teachers' knowledge, the students expressed the view that knowledge of a subject, especially factual knowledge, was important for a teacher; this was the dominant conception. The character of subject knowledge proved to concern both quantity and quality. Quantity was how much subject knowledge a teacher needed and was often expressed in college or university credits. The quality of subject knowledge related to the teacher's ability to treat the subject in a way suited to the pupils to be taught.

Most of the interviewees also expressed views on the importance of knowledge about children. This concerned both affective knowledge and cognitive knowledge. When the students expressed views about methods the most common idea was that the method the teacher should employ is that of imparting his or her subject knowledge. In this context, it became clear that many students believe that some methods of teaching are more correct than others. The image of a teacher's knowledge becomes more complex; apart from the F-knowledge already described, there is also informal knowledge (here referred to as experiential knowledge) to be defined and described.

This was expressed as something invisible and unclear but also stressed as an essential part of what a teacher must know. It can be knowledge a student acquires on a course but may just as well be knowledge obtained in some other way. It can also be characterized as intuitive knowledge that everyone formulates from individual experience, both in everyday life and in school. It includes an aspect, hard to define, which the students, nevertheless, tried to describe.

To learn through *experience*, which is a dimension of E-knowledge, concerns learning that is more random, and includes the individual as a significant factor. When trying to describe E-knowledge, one enters, perhaps, an area that is in some ways unresearched, in that it contains events, facts and phenomena that individuals have experienced but not yet conceptualized (Kroksmark, 1992). This accords with the image that emerges when students wish to describe something they know but cannot express in words. The subcategories here became personality, experience and something I would designate as 'hard to identify'.

If we proceed from the result of the present study, what can we do about the student teachers' assumed 'filters'? That a student's 'filter' is decisive for how, during training, that student will accept or reject different messages has been expressed by researchers, including Weinstein (1988). The conceptions student teachers bring to their training become the basis on which their teacher training begins. Thus, I feel it is important for active teacher trainers to understand what is really happening. Research ascribes such great significance to the 'filter' that it seems reasonable to work consciously on students' conceptions, or their complex 'filters'. For this to be possible, the character of the 'filter' should be possible to describe, a feature to which the present study can perhaps contribute.

But if one considers that all the aspects defined in this study exist as individual 'filters', and can occur in a group of students beginning their teacher training, then this really is an example of a complex pattern. Now if we also consider that, say, thirty students begin their teacher training with various 'filters', then the 'filter' really does represent a frame factor for how well the training can succeed in conveying what it has to offer.

Many students thus perceive, at the beginning of their studies, that there exists this something that is hard to identify. What were the present students' descriptions about when they mentioned a sort of knowledge that was hard to identify? Were they describing a process, a relationship for example between teachers and pupils, or something other than facts? Did it have to be something experienced but not possible to formulate?

That knowledge is hard to identify does not necessarily imply it cannot be consciously appreciated or named. If we assume that a recently accepted student begins teacher training in the belief that there exists knowledge that comes with time, this knowledge is so far unformulated but the student begins an unconscious, unassisted search for something. Making this something visible in the ensuing training can be a condition for the student to be able to ponder about seemingly simple, sometimes self-evident conduct, and even gain access to his or her own development of competence.

The main conclusion to be drawn from this study is that the results can be seen as examples of a conceptual 'filter' which teacher educators have to consider in the planning of teacher training as well as try to influence during training.

Variations in Teachers' Knowledge and Professional Identity

The purpose of the present study is to elucidate the relationship between personal and professional development in the Swedish educational context and from a Swedish perspective. In this paper I do this by discussing some preliminary findings and conclusions as to how teachers view teacher identity, teacher knowledge and the development of teacher knowledge. The study is part of a collaborative research project that is based mainly on English material produced under the leadership of Professor Chris Day.

The change in the Swedish context of teachers' professional development can be described in terms of top–down and bottom–up models of control. Until the mid-1950s, we had a bottom–up situation characterized by great professional-teacher involvement through the professional associations. From the mid-1950s until 1990 a top–down situation emerged, despite step-by-step decentralization and deregulation characterized by state initiatives and little professional involvement except from the central professional unions. From 1978, as a part of this process, efforts were made to implement a collective code in teacher work. The present phase started in 1990 and was reinforced in 1994 by implementation of the new National Curriculum with almost total decentralization and deregulation. This may be described as a purely bottom–up situation.

When considering teachers' professional development (Hoyle, 1982) it is of great importance to know what kind of knowledge is to be developed. What do we mean by teachers' professional knowledge? How can we recognize it? An interesting question for the study is whether the teachers consider their knowledge as individual or collective, i.e., how they position themselves regarding individual or collective autonomy.

An explorative, qualitative, case study method was used. Ten teachers were interviewed. While the goal was access to teachers' often unformulated thoughts and conceptions of what it is to be a teacher, a method was needed that would allow me to approach teachers from different directions and to use what came up in the situations. The result will be discussed in relation to the outlined context and the theoretical framework of two dimensions, professional-autonomous and control-philosophical. To make a deeper understanding of the individual character possible I present two cases, Bengt and Michael.

Bengt

Bengt is a happy and very enthusiastic person with thirty-five years' teaching experience. His attitude to inservice training is very positive and he has gone on many courses over the years. '. . . I think you could say this is characteristic of me as a person, that I've always been on the way somewhere and I have a horror of feeling that I'm stagnating.' He spoke much of enthusiasm and the importance of experience, and of his own and his pupils' development. He intended his work to develop his pupils and he felt great satisfaction in this. He said he was a gardener and he loved to see plants grow both in the classroom and at home in his garden: he exhibited great enthusiasm when talking about this. He did not remark specially on his subjects' functions as bearers of knowledge: I felt he saw them more as means for his pupils' development. He said his personality was his chief tool in the classroom and he appeared keen to develop his personality in the inservice courses he went on. He read a great deal in his free time; newspapers, books and much philosophy.

It appeared from his answers that he was governed more by an inner conviction than by factors in his surroundings that would normally, directly or indirectly, influence his teaching. Bengt gained his strength, his conviction and thus his driving force from within and this naturally influenced his way of looking on his teachership and its development. He appeared to suck up new knowledge and could describe how parts of every inservice activity had stuck, forming new layers of teacher knowledge.

Michael

Michael's main job as a teacher was to teach knowledge, but he was fully aware that knowledge can be transferred in different ways and he varied his teaching to make his pupils' learning easier. He stressed that learning had to be interesting and fun. Being a teacher, for Michael, meant chiefly being a supervisor. He also compared his work to that of a guide, a modern tourist guide:

> Well it means I know a great deal and if anyone has a question like this for me which we are going to get to naturally, er, at the same time I have my goals clear in my mind, sort of, I can give tips in a good way and guide (. . .) I mean a modern guide is actually a person who gives you tips about where you can go, I'm more like that, and sometimes I'm a guide who guides if there's some slippery path somewhere, I can help them along it, well I suppose there's always someone breaks a leg . . .

Michael stated that he sat at home and 'fiddled' with his lessons, meaning he collected material, structured it, decided what items to include, what his pupils should get out of it, etc. He appeared keen to develop teaching methods to make the contents available and interesting.

Michael gave the impression of wishing to produce a technically perfect lesson and appeared to enjoy developing methods of variation. He emerged as a mixture of teaching technologist, craftsman and artist and to have an approach to his work which I recognize from many intermediate-level teachers. At the same time he had elements of the traditional senior-level teacher in that he placed his subject knowledge first and did not noticeably question what was to be taught.

The 'portraits' are condensed and stylized by the following aspects:

Aspects	Bengt	Michael
Approach	Artist	Craftsman
Self-image	Gardener	Guide
Form of communication	Iconic	Analytical
Development project	Cultivation	Education
Objective	The good	The perfect
Tool	The personality	The method
Ethos	Individual	Collective
Orientation	From within	From without
Mission	Existential	Social

These two teachers were selected because they illustrated the variations in the material in a concentrated manner. Yet there were many similarities between the two teachers described. The most interesting difference was where they developed their knowledge. While Bengt read and indulged in everyday philosophy and developed his personality on his own and on various inservice courses, Michael developed together with colleagues and in his own practical work.

Ben and Mike vary in how they view their teacher knowledge and professional identity. While Ben as a senior teacher fits into the individual and bottom–up strategy known from the early half of the century, Mike as a junior teacher fits into the collective and top–down strategy we know from the Deweyan peak in Swedish reform history in the early 1980s. A tentative assumption is made that the variations can be explained by the fact that teachers' viewing of their teacher knowledge and professional identity depends on how their individual career is related to the reform history.

It is possible or even probable that an intervention towards personal development contributes to reveal variations in teachers' identity, knowledge and knowledge development. In view of the dramatic changes in Swedish education and policymakers' implicit assumptions of teachers' readiness and willingness to revise and develop their professional knowledge, it is of great importance to take these variations into account.

The Voice of a Reflecting Teacher

The focus of this explorative study was how teachers cope with weak readers. The study took place in a Swedish school where many of the pupils had immigrant backgrounds. The sample consisted of six female teachers working at comprehensive school intermediate level with pupils between 10 and 12. First each teacher was observed in the classroom for two to four lessons. This was followed by a taped interview of 30–90 minutes. One of the teachers used different language and had a higher inclination to reflect than teachers commonly do. Alexandersson (1994), Griffiths and Tann (1992), van Manen (1977, 1991), differentiate the concept 'reflection' by defining four levels for use in analysis.

Level 1 Comprises common sense. Action is routine.

Level 2 The teacher focuses on various practical methods to try and reach fixed goals.

Level 3 The reflection is more complex and takes note of the relation between principles for practical reality and the practical reality it self.

Level 4 Reflection is here turned inwards upon one's own awareness. This means both noting *what* one is reflecting about in one's work and *how* one is reflecting about it.

Now back to the teacher. I noticed her unusual use of language in the middle of the interview and burst out 'You don't sound like other teachers.' When the teacher asked me to explain myself I had to improvise an answer, something about her describing her work in analytical terms in a way researchers do rather than teachers. The teacher (call her Maria) was amused, perhaps slightly flattered, but the exchange was rather a digression, since the interview continued as before. Yet the discovery raised many questions:

- What (specially) characterized Maria's use of language?
- Did Maria's pattern of reflection mirror the highest level (level 4) in van Manen's categorization?
- Were there circumstances in Maria's career that explained the difference?

While listening to the interview and writing it out I tried to reconstruct some special features of Maria's way of talking. It turned out that her eloquence was not only at the phonetic level, even though the calm tempo and clear diction contributed to a 'finely chiseled' character. Three features that stand out even in a transcription could be distinguished.

1 Teachers' answers to interview questions are often in the form of fragments which the researcher has to synthesize to produce wholes. In this interview, however, I got more connected discourses when the questions were answered.

2 Many teachers describe their working conditions and the way their tasks are organized by depicting concrete situations. Maria, however, gave more generalizing descriptions, but also illustrated them with descent into concrete examples.

3 The majority of teachers use everyday words to describe their practice. Maria's speech included many abstract words of concept status.

Referring to Basil Bernstein's linguistic sociology, one might say that Maria's language evinced an 'elaborated code', which is common among the middle class; while the normal teacher's comprises a 'restricted code' usually associated with the working class (Bernstein, 1977). When Maria diagnosed one of her pupils she did so in the following terms:

— And then we have NN, the boy I was talking to in the front. He's not an expressive soul, but persistent, with some kind of an urge to learn. Or perhaps he sees the necessity of it, I don't know which — he can manage texts.

— Where's he from?

— Iran. I also notice when we're doing maths and working on what we call 'reading numbers'. This calls for an ability to 'break the code', and you can see directly if someone hasn't done this.

Special feature 1, connected discourse, appears clearly in this passage. Maria is not content with clipped answers to my questions, she leads the interview through her finely chiseled one. The second special feature, generalizing descriptions, emerges when her diagnosis of the pupil's language ability is facilitated by her choosing a situation (reading numbers in maths) and formulating the criterion that supports her conclusion (the ability to perceive or 'break the code'). Expressions such as 'expressive soul' and 'break the code' have the status of concepts and are part of scientific vocabulary.

Somewhat later in the interview another pupil was commented upon as follows:

Then there's OO, one of the ones who reported. She's made a 'qualitative leap' and really developed enormously. She has stable Spanish and she uses it. She's doing Spanish as a home language and they speak Spanish at home. I think it's somehow that she's stored up understanding which she can now draw on by using the language actively.

The statement is elaborate (special feature number 1) and expressions such as 'qualitative leap' and 'stored up understanding' are metaphors with a conceptual-theoretical content (special feature number 3). Special feature 2 appears when Maria combines an observation (sudden development) with a basis of interpretation (the significance of home language for language development in Swedish) which gives a reasonable explanation of what is going on. This inclination towards reflection also appears clearly in the following exchange:

— What frames of reference do you sense?

— None but my own. *Say I make a wrong diagnosis about a pupil , for example I misinterpret the boy's writing hang-up or the girl's sudden development* [Maria is referring to two cases described earlier in the interview]. *Then I wonder: am I observant enough and receptive, am I drawing the right conclusions, can I reassess them later? and so on. It's easy to say it but harder to do. In the classroom I get on with it: outside I reflect.*

— In the bath and places like that?

— Afraid so. It should be with the other teachers, discussing, because then I can 'try things out'.

— Is this because there isn't time, because you can't make the effort or because the other teachers haven't seen your class?

— All three. You're tired because you're on your own. In teaching you're working with twenty-seven pupils in 40-minute units.

The italics in the foregoing section show the part of the teacher's statement that more than anything else corresponds to the definition of reflection at level 4. The reflection turned inward onto her own awareness and Maria focused on both the content and the forms.

There was nothing in the interview to show that Maria's formal education differed from that of the average teacher. However, she had in two connections tried educational roles other than the teacher's. For a year, she had trained upper-level teachers in the methods that were in line with the intentions of the present National Curriculum. Also, she was chairman of an educational association that combines the views of philosophy/ethics, depth psychology and educational theory. The association is basically a national one but the majority of members, according to Maria, live in the Stockholm area.

It is easy to conclude, perhaps, that being well versed in the world of theory is less important for Maria (and others?) than the habit of formulating, as a self-imposed demand, issues related to one's work in terms more general than the very obvious. But this conclusion is not self-evident, for some allusions in Maria's testimony indicate that her wide reading could be significant even though she had no 'certificates' of this repertoire. Her wide reading seemed more centered on the border area between depth psychology and the existential field, while the interview excerpts quoted are about her pupil's learning and the conditions for her teaching. Does one conclude from all this that theoretical awareness in one area is catching in another so that the tendency to theorize becomes a general one even where the theories and concepts remain specific to certain areas? The questions are many but the answers are by no means self-evident.

Seniority and Values: A Study with a Life-history Approach

The purpose of this section of the chapter is to describe and analyze how two older teachers formulate their professional knowledge in a life-history perspective. Two teachers, a woman and a man (Elsa and Peter) were asked to talk about their long professional lives. Using this approach we intend to arrive at how professional knowledge has grown and developed both in connection with the persons' lives and experience and with the historical and societal context. The period during which the two teachers have been active has been marked by a struggle towards a more democratic school in many respects. In addition, educational reform has been initiated and controlled very much from the center. Via the teachers interviewed, therefore, there are possibilities of gaining insight into how social and educational changes have been perceived and dealt with, and how the reform program has been experienced and understood.

Our analysis is also based on Hartman's (1995) three aspects of teachers' knowledge; practically based, value-based and scientifically based. We will be especially interested in the basis of values underlying teachers' work. Regarding underlying values, in this concept we include how in their accounts the two teachers express their views of man, knowledge and society. One reason for this choice of focus is that values have received far too little attention in teacher training and educational research. Another reason is that in Sweden questions of basic values in teachers' work have become topical now that the premises for school work have been changed. Partly, society has changed from a uniform one to a pluralistic one, partly, control of the school has shifted from the center to the local level.

Some Results: A Preliminary Analysis

A first section attempts to show how the reforms of the Swedish school system have been reflected in the two teachers' accounts. A second section describes some features of these teachers' knowledge.

Forces for Change in the Educational Field During the Teachers' Active Professional Lives

While Elsa and Peter were professionally active a number of educational reforms were carried out in Sweden. The two teachers' stories reflect these changes, each in its own way. The reflection lies partly in how the persons interviewed spent their own schooldays and partly in how, in their professional lives, they were involved in, and affected by, the implementation of these reforms.

Elsa, for example, tells how, where she grew up, there was only the elementary school. To go further, she had to board in a town far from her home and her parents could afford neither this nor the actual costs of textbooks, and so on. In Sweden there was at the time a parallel school system which meant that only a few economically, socially and geographically favored children had access to the *läroverken* — grammar schools. For the other children only the teaching of the elementary school was available. Elsa herself experienced both in her own life and in the encounter with pupils what consequences an undemocratic educational system can have. She worked actively for the introduction of a democratic system. Among other things she undertook to teach pupils who did not 'fit in' in school and attempted to arrange her teaching so that these pupils, too, were able to develop.

An idea, which was implemented in the Swedish comprehensive school in 1978, originated in the Committee on Inner Work of the School. The notion was to create smaller units within the school each consisting of several classes. The teachers were to plan teaching for the unit collectively. In this way, several teachers could share the responsibility for a class. This system, in Peter's view has been a burden on his working week since much time is spent on teachers' meetings of various kinds, despite fewer teaching hours. Peter shares this view with many Swedish teachers (Ahlstrand, 1995). Peter prefers a higher teaching obligation in a class with fewer pupils rather than sharing responsibility with colleagues for a larger class.

Features of Teachers' Knowledge and How It Is Formulated

Elsa develops her knowledge largely through her experience in her own practical work. Pupils are an important source of knowledge for her, both the great variation there is within a class and the special difficulties pupils may have. She says:

> You can never generalize, for it's always here and now. Here you are and there are the children and there's a now with masses of circumstances and frames — not least time, and other things to consider. And you have to decide what you're going to do and how you're going to use the time somehow — we have to do that from day to day and moment to moment — sort of what's best just now.

Elsa's account has many examples of her great creativeness and inventiveness. One can follow how, for her, a job expands after she has found solutions and seen the consequences. The task grows. She sees how new needs in her pupils can be met and how good conditions for learning can be created.

Peter uses teachers he has met as models and patterns for his own ideals of what a good teacher is. He reports in detail about a teacher he met during his very first stand-in period as a teacher. In his role as educator Peter has also been influenced by another teacher whom he describes as a very conscientious and orderly person. Doing one's work properly, being on time, keeping one's things in order, having good handwriting are parts of the educator role Peter emphasizes. The daily round and work are important parts of Peter's view of society and he takes great responsibility for this in his own actions. Lessons can be broken up for the pupils when they are to leave the classroom to go to the special teacher. Peter gets inspiration for his work through good models. Elsa exploits practical teaching situations and accepts the challenge of solving them, and then taking them further. Imitation here is set against improvisation.

A view of knowledge is emphasized when Elsa says you must recognize that 'you cannot' — and where can I find people who can? Who can I ask? Who can I, or do I think I can, cooperate with and who is prepared to cooperate with me? Elsa is keen to seek for knowledge and its sources, e.g., in persons she imagines master various areas, as well as in literature. Peter says that teachers should have a sound knowledge of their subject. For children to be able to develop their curiosity the teacher has to be able to answer their questions, meet them and give them further stimulation. Peter argues that teaching has changed as a consequence of social change while the core of the profession has remained the same: the ability to meet children, to look them in the eye, to be able to capture their interest. Here we feel we can perceive the two teachers' *view of knowledge*. Teachers' knowledge is also linked to how they wish to create learning situations for their children. Elsa represents an investigative approach. Through an investigative way of working in which pupils acquire experience and knowledge in different ways, Elsa feels she also created better opportunities of getting to know her pupils and seeing different ways in which they needed support and stimulation. By conveying his sound subject knowledge Peter can be the authority on facts he wishes to be. Peter represents an instructional teaching approach.

Linguistic Form

Elsa's account is, to quite a large extent, built up by associations — sometimes thematic ones. It is a mixture of narrative and exposition. Her presentation often centers round episodes or small narratives. This approach reinforces her close ties with the classroom situation, from where she draws the inspiration to develop her teacher knowledge. Peter's account is based largely on a series of general statements: on how teaching has changed, on the circumstances of young families, on what children are like these days, on what they watch on TV and video. Reporting with general impressions is here termed descriptions. Thus, Peter uses these more general descriptions but exemplifies with small events from the classroom and the encounter with children, narratives. If Elsa's and Peter's accounts are compared with respect to structure, Elsa represents a thematic-associative structure and Peter a chronological one. In describing and interpreting teachers' ways of developing their expositions we have been inspired by Fritz Schütze (Workshop in Magdeburg, May 1995).

Conclusion

The two teachers who told us about their professionally active lives showed that teachers' knowledge is communicable. Moreover, it varied between the two teachers. The two teachers' strategies can be expressed in two phrases:

- 'Hoist the sails'
  Elsa feels we have come a long way towards a good school. If the teacher accepts the challenge to create good conditions for learning there is a chance for all children in our schools today.
- 'Still the storm'
  For Peter it is important in an all too turbulent world to give the children alternative images. The teacher has a great responsibility to offer a good example, to give the children much knowledge and guidance.

We assume that the underlying system of values, expressed partly in views of knowledge, society and man, emerges in both teachers' accounts. It looks different but it is there. They both struggle for a democratic school and are loyal to the school system. But 'a democratic school' has different meanings to them. Concerning the view of knowledge you can say that Elsa is a teacher representing the philosophy of Dewey and Peter represents more traditional values. The teachers in this study have experiences of long lives and rich professional knowledge and are inclined to express their integrated values. We view the life-history approach as a possible avenue to get knowledge of the underlying values.

Note

1   This chapter represents an integrated set of papers originally presented as a symposium at ISATT 1995.

References

AHLSTRAND, E. (1995) 'Lärares samarbete — En verksamhet på två arenor. Studier av fyra arbetslag på grundskolans högstadium (Teachers' co-operation — An activity in two arenas. Studies of four teacher-teams in lower-secondary school)', *Linköping: Studies in Education and Psychology*, **43**, Linköping University, Department of Education and Psychology.

ALEXANDERSSON, M. (1994) 'Metod och medvetande (Method and Consciousness)', *Studies in Educational Sciences*, **96**, Acta Universitatis, Gothoburgensis, Göteborg.

ASKLING, B. and JEDESKOG, G. (1993) 'Some notes on the teacher education programme in Sweden', *Teacher Education Quality Study: The Teacher Education Study*, OECD/ CERI.

BERNSTEIN, B. (1977) 'Towards a theory of educational transmissions', *Class, codes and control*, **3** (2nd ed.) London, Routledge and Kegan Paul.

CALDERHEAD, J. (1991a) 'The nature and growth of knowledge in students', *Teaching and Teacher Education*, **7**, 5, 6, pp. 531–35.

CLANDININ, D.J. (1986) *Classroom Practice: Teacher Images in Action*, Lewes, Falmer Press.

ELBAZ, F. (1983) *Teacher Thinking: A Study of Practical Knowledge*, New York, Nichols Publishing Company.

ENGLUND, T. (1994) 'Útbildning som "public good" eller "private good" — Svensk skola i omvandling?', *Kampen om Lärohusen — Studier Kring Statsmakt och Föräldrarätt i Nordisk Skolutveckling*, Stockholm Almquist and Wiksell International.

FEIMAN-NEMSER, S. and BUCHMANN, M. (1987) 'When is student teaching teacher education', *Teaching and Teacher Education*, **3**, 4, pp. 255–73.

FLORIN, Ch. and JOHANSSON, U. (1993) 'Där de härliga lagrarna gro . . .', *Kultur, Klass och Kön i Det Svenska Läroverket 1850–1914*, Stockholm, Tiden.

GOODSON, I.F. (1994) *Studying Curriculum: Cases and Methods*, NY and London, Teacher College Press.

GRIFFITHS, M. and TANN, S. (1992) 'Using reflective practice to link personal and public theories', *Journal of Education for Teaching*, **18**, 1, pp. 69–84.

HARTMAN, S.G. (1993) 'On what teacher know', Paper presented at the ISATT conference in Gothenburg.

HARTMAN, S.G. (1994) 'Children's personal philosophy of life as the basis for religious education', *International Journal of Comparative Religious Education and Values*, **6**, 2, Winter 1994.

E. Ahlstrand et al.

HARTMAN, S.G. (1995) 'Lärares kunskap. Traditioner och idéer i svensk undervisningshistoria', *Skapande Vetande*, **27**, Linköping University.

HOYLE, E. (1982) 'The professionalization of teachers: A Paradox', *British Journal of Educational Studies*, **XXX**, 2, pp. 161–71.

JOHANSSON, E. (1995) 'Orality, reading and writing in the history of literacy', *Alphabeta Varia Album Religionum Umense*, **1**, Umeå.

KROKSMARK, T. (1992) 'Metodikämnet i grundskollärarutbildningen', in KROKSMARK, T. and STRÖMQVIST, G. (Eds) *Undervisnngsmetodik*, Lund, Studentlitteratur.

MERTZ N.T. and MCNEELY, S.R. (1992) 'Preexisting teaching constructs: How students "see" teaching prior to training', Paper presented at the annual meeting of the American Educational Research Association, San Fransisco.

MIRON, G. (1993) 'Choice and the use of market forces in schooling: Swedish education reforms for the 1990s', *Studies in Comparative and International Education*, **25**, Stockholm University.

OECD (1980) 'Educational policy and planning: Goals for educational policy in Sweden', A Status report on Compulsory Schooling and Higher Education.

RANNSTRÖM, A. (1995) *Teacher Students' Conceptions of Their Future Professional Knowledge*, Department of Education and Psychology, Linköping.

RICHARDSON, G. (1992) *Ett Folk Börjar Skolan: Folkskolan 150 år 1842–1992*, Allmänna förlaget, Stockholm.

RODHE, B. (1994) 'Offentligt och fristående i svensk utbildning under två århundraden', *Kampen om Lärohusen: Studier Kring Statsmakt och Föräldrarätt i Nordisk Skolutveckling*, Stockholm, Almquist and Wiksell International.

SCHMIDT, W.H. and KENNEDY, M.M. (1990) *'Teachers and teacher candidates' beliefs about subject matter and about teaching responsibilities'*, Research report, Published by The National Center for Research on Teacher Education, Michigan State University, East Lansing.

SHULMAN, J. (1987) 'From veteran to novice teacher: A case study of a student teacher', *Teacher and Teacher Education*, **3**, 1, pp. 3–27.

VAN MANEN, M. (1977) 'Linking ways of knowing with ways of being practical', *Curriculum Inquiry*, **6**, 3, pp. 205–28.

VAN MANEN, M. (1991) 'Reflectivity and the pedagogical moment: The normativity of pedagogical thinking and acting', *Journal of Curriculum Studies*, **23**, 6, pp. 507–36.

WEINSTEIN, C.S. (1988) 'Preservice teachers' expectations about the first year of teaching', *Teacher and Teacher Education*, **4**, 1, pp. 31–40.

ZEICHNER, K. and LISTON, D. (1987) 'Teaching student teachers to reflect', *Harvard Education Review*, **57**, 1, pp. 1–22.

16   Representing Teachers: Bringing Teachers Back In[1]

Ivor Goodson

The Representational Crisis

Educational study is undergoing one of those recurrent swings of the pendulum for which the field is noted. But as the contemporary world and global economies are transformed by rapid and accelerating change such pendulum swings in scholarly paradigms seem to be alarmingly exacerbated.

Hence we see a response to a specific structural dilemma in which educational study has become enmeshed; but alongside this the field is becoming engulfed (though more slowly than in many fields) by a crisis of scholarly representation. A specific structural dilemma now becomes allied with a wider representational crisis. Jameson (1984) has summarized the latter crisis succinctly as arising from the growing challenge to 'an essentially realistic epistemology, which conceives of representation as the production, for subjectivity, of an objectivity that lies outside it' (1984, p. viii). Jameson wrote this in the forward to Lyotard's *The Postmodern Condition*. For Lyotard (1984) the old modes of representation no longer work. He calls for an incredulity towards these old canonical metanarratives and says: 'The grand narrative has lost its credibility, regardless of what mode of unification is used, regardless of whether it is a speculative narrative or a narrative of emancipation' (1984, p. 37).

Returning to the field of educational study we see that in response to the distant, divorced and disengaged nature of aspects of educational study in universities some scholars have responded by embracing the 'practical', by celebrating the teacher as practitioner. My intention here is to explore in detail one of these movements aiming to focus on teachers' knowledge — particularly the genre which focuses on teachers' stories and narratives. This movement has arisen from the crises of structural displacement and of representation briefly outlined — hence the reasons for this new genre are understandable, the motivations creditable. As we see the representational crisis arises from the central dilemma of trying to capture the lived experience of scholars and of teachers within a text. The experience of other lives is, therefore, rendered textual by an author. At root this is a perilously difficult act and Denzin (1993) has cogently inveighed against the very aspiration.

> If the text becomes the agency that records and represents the voices of the other, then the other becomes a person who is spoken for. They do not talk, the text talks for them. It is the agency that interprets their words, thoughts, intentions, and meanings. So a doubling of agency occurs, for behind the text as agent-for-the-other, is the author of the text doing the interpreting. (Denzin, 1993, p. 17)

Denzin then is arguing that we have a classic case of academic colonization, or even cannibalization; 'The other becomes an extension of the author's voice. The authority of their "original" voice is now subsumed within the larger text and its double-agency' (p. 17).

Given the scale of this representational crisis one can quickly see how the sympathetic academic might wish to reduce interpretation, even collaboration and return to the role of 'scribe'. At least in such passivity sits the aspiration to reduce colonization. In this moment of representational crisis the doors open to the educational scholar as facilitator — as conduit for the teacher, to tell his or her story or narrative. The genuine voice of the oppressed subject, uncontaminated by active human collaboration. Teachers talking about their practice — providing us with personal and practical insights into their expertise. Here maybe then a sanctuary, an inner sanctum, beyond the representational crisis, beyond academic colonization. The nirvana of the narrative, the Valhalla of voice; it is an understandable and appealing project.

The Narrative Turn/The Turn to Narrative

So the turn to teachers' narratives and stories is at one level a thoroughly understandable response to the way in which teachers have tended to be represented in so much educational study. The teacher has been represented to serve our scholarly purposes.

Given this history, and the goal displacement of educational study noted, it is therefore laudable that new narrative movements are concentrating on the teachers' presentation of themselves. This is a welcome antidote to so much misrepresentation and representation in past scholarship and it opens up avenues of fruitful investigation and debate. The narrative movement provides then a catalyst for pursuing understandings of the teacher's life and work.

In many ways, the movement reminds me of the point raised by Andrews (1991) in her elegant study of elderly political activists. She summarizes the posture of those psychologists who have studied such activists:

> When political psychology has taken to analysing the behaviour of political activists it has tended to do so from a thoroughly external perspective. That is to say, that rarely have their thought processes been described, much less analysed, from their own point of view. Yet it is at least possible that a very good way to learn about the psychology of political

activists is to listen to what they have to say about their own lives. (Andrews, 1991, p. 20)

What Andrews says can be seen as analogous to a good deal of our scholarly representation of teachers where they are seen as interchangeable and essentially depersonalized. In 1981 I argued that many accounts presented teachers as timeless and interchangeable role incumbents. But that:

> The pursuit of personal and biographical data might rapidly challenge the assumption of interchangeability. Likewise, by tracing the teachers' life as it evolved over time — throughout the teachers' career and through several generations — the assumption of timelessness might also be remedied. *In understanding something so intensely personal as teaching it is critical we know about the person the teacher is.* Our paucity of knowledge in this area is a manifest indictment of the range of our sociological imagination. (Goodson, 1981, p. 69)

The argument for listening to teachers is therefore a substantial and long overdue one — narratives, stories, journals, action research, phenomenology, have all contributed to a growing movement to provide opportunities for teacher representations. In the case of stories and narratives Carter (1993) has provided a valuable summary of this growing movement.

> With increasing frequency over the past several years we, as members of a community of investigator-practitioners, have been telling stories about teaching and teacher education rather than simply reporting correlation coefficients or generating lists of findings. This trend has been upsetting to some who mourn the loss of quantitative precision and, they would argue, scientific rigor. For many of us, however, these stories capture, more than scores or mathematical formulae ever can, the richness and indeterminacy of our experiences as teachers and the complexity of our understandings of what teaching is and how others can be prepared to engage in this profession.
>
> It is not altogether surprising, then, that this attraction to stories has evolved into an explicit attempt to use the literatures on 'story' or 'narrative' to define both the method and the object of inquiry in teaching and teacher education. Story has become, in other words, more than simply a rhetorical device for expressing sentiments about teachers or candidates for the teaching profession. It is now, rather, a central focus for conducting research in the field. (Carter, 1993, p. 5)

Story and History

The new emphasis upon teacher stories and narratives then encouragingly signifies a new turn in presenting teachers. It is a turn that deserves to be taken very seriously for we have to be sure that we are turning in the right direction. Like all new genres stories and narratives are Janus-faced; they may move us forward into new insights or backwards into constrained consciousness, and sometimes simultaneously.

This uncertainty is well-stated in Carter's summary of 'The place of story in the study of teaching and teacher education'.

> Anyone with even a passing familiarity with the literatures on story soon realises, however, that these are quite turbulent intellectual waters and quickly abandons the expectation of safe passage toward the resolution, once and for all, of the many puzzles and dilemmas we face in advancing our knowledge of teaching. Much needs to be learned about the nature of story and its value to our common enterprise, and about the wide range of purposes, approaches, and claims made by those who have adopted story as a central analytical framework. What does story capture and what does it leave out? How does this notion fit within the emerging sense of the nature of teaching and what it means to educate teachers? These and many other critical questions need to be faced if story is to become more than a loose metaphor for everything from a paradigm or worldview to a technique for bringing home a point in a lecture on a Thursday afternoon. (Carter, 1993, p. 5)

But what is the nature of the turbulence in the intellectual waters surrounding stories and will they serve to drown the new genre? The turbulence is multifaceted but here I want to focus on the relationship between stories and the social context in which they are embedded. For stories exist in history — they are in fact deeply located in time and space. Stories work differently in different social contexts and historical times — they can be put to work in different ways. Stories then should not only be *narrated* but *located*. This argues that we should move beyond the self-referential individual narration to a wider contextualized collaborative mode. Again, Carter hints at both the enormous appeal, but then the underlying worry, about narrative and story. At the moment the appeal is substantial after long years of silencing, but the dangers are more shadowy. I believe that unless those dangers are confronted now narrative and story may end up silencing or at least marginalizing in new ways the very people to whom it appears to give voice:

> For many of us, these arguments about the personal, storied nature of teaching and about voice, gender, and power in our professional lives ring very true. We can readily point to instances in which we have felt excluded by researchers' language or powerless in the face of administrative decrees and evaluation instruments presumably bolstered by scientific evidence. And we have experienced the indignities of gender bias and presumptions. We feel these issues deeply, and opening them to public scrutiny, especially through the literature in our field, is a cause for celebration.
>
> At the same time, we must recognise that this line of argument creates

a very serious crisis for our community. One can easily imagine that the analysis summarised here, if pushed ever so slightly forward, leads directly to a rejection of all generalisations about teaching as distortions of teachers' real stories and as complicity with the power elite, who would make teachers subservient. From this perspective, only the teacher owns her or his story and its meaning. As researchers and teacher educators, we can only serve by getting this message across to the larger society and, perhaps, by helping teachers to come to know their own stories. Seen in this light, much of the activity in which we engage as scholars in teaching becomes illegitimate if not actually harmful. (Carter, 1993, p. 8)

Carolyn Steedman (1986) in her marvellous work *Landscape for a Good Woman* speaks of this danger, she says: 'Once a story is told, it ceases to story: it becomes a piece of history, an interpretive device' (p. 143). In this sense a story 'works' when its rationale is comprehended and its historical significance grasped. As Bristow (1991) has argued. 'The more skilled we become at understanding the history involved in these very broadly defined stories the more able will we be to identify the ideological function of narratives — how they designate a place for us within their structure of telling' (Bristow , 1991, p. 117). In reviewing Steedman's (1986) work and its power to understand patriarchy and the dignity of womens' lives, Bristow (1991) talks about her unswerving attention to

the ways in which life writing can bring its writers to the point of understanding how their lives have already been narrated — according to a prefigurative script, Steedman never loses sight of how writers may develop skills to rewrite the life script in which they find themselves. (Bristow, 1991, p. 114)

This I think focuses acutely on the dangers of a belief that merely by allowing people to 'narrate' that we in any serious way give them voice *and* agency. The narration of a pre-figurative script is a celebration of an existing power relation. Most often, and this is profoundly true for teachers, the question is how to 'rewrite the life script'. Narration then can work in many ways but clearly it can work to give voice to a celebration of scripts of domination. Narration than can both reinforce domination or rewrite domination. Stories and narratives are not an unquestioned good: it all depends. And above all it depends on how they relate to history, and to social context.

Again Molly Andrews' (1991) work on the lives of political activists captures the limitation of so much of the developmental psychologists' study of lives and it is analogous to so much work on teacher narratives:

In Western capitalist democracies, where most of the work on development originates, many researchers tend to ignore the importance of the society — individual dialectic, choosing to focus instead on more particularised elements, be they personality idiosyncrasies, parental relationships, or cognitive structures, as if such aspects of the individual's make-up could be neatly compartmentalised, existing in a contextual vacuum. (Andrews, 1991, p. 13)

The version of 'personal' that has been constructed and worked for in some western countries is a particular version, an individualistic version, of being a person. It is unrecognizable to much of the rest of the world. But so many of the stories and narratives we have of teachers work unproblematically and without comment, with this version of personal being and personal knowledge. Masking the limits of individualism such accounts often present 'isolation, estrangement, and loneliness . . . as autonomy, independence and self-reliance' (see Andrews, 1991, p. 13). Andrews concludes that if we ignore social context we deprive ourselves and our collaborators of meaning and understanding. She says:

> it would seem apparent that the context in which human lives are lived is central to the core of meaning in those lives. Researchers should not, therefore, feel at liberty to discuss or analyse how individuals perceive meaning in their lives and in the world around them, while ignoring the content and context of that meaning. (p. 13)

This I believe has been all too common a response among these educational researchers working with teachers' stories and narratives. Content has been embraced and celebrated, context has not been sufficiently developed. Cynthia Chambers (1991) has summarized this posture and its dangers in reviewing work on teacher narratives:

> These authors offer us the naive hope that if teachers learn 'to tell and understand their *own* story' they will be returned to their rightful place at the centre of curriculum planning and reform. And yet, their method leaves each teacher a 'blackbird singing in the dead of night'; isolated, and sadly ignorant of how his/her song is part of a much larger singing of the world. If everyone is singing their own song, who is listening? How can we hear the larger conversation of humankind in which our own history teacher is embedded and perhaps concealed? (Chambers, 1991, p. 354)

Likewise Salina Shrofel (1991) in reviewing the same book highlights the dangers. Focus on the personal and on practice does not appear to lead practitioners or researchers/writers to

> analyse practice as theory, as social structure, or as a manifestation of political and economic systems. This limitation of vision implicit in the narrative approach serves as a constraint on curriculum reform. Teachers will, as did the teachers cited by Connelly and Clandinin, make changes in their own classroom curricula but will not perform the questioning and

challenging of theory, structure, and ideology that will lead to radical and extensive curriculum reform.

It can be argued that the challenge of running a classroom fully occupies the teachers and that questions of theory, structure, and ideology don't affect the everyday lives (practical knowledges) of teachers and are relegated to 'experts'. However, there are many dangers in separating practice from these other questions. First, as Connelly and Clandinin point out, it ignores the dynamic relationship of theory and practice. Second, it ignores the fact that schools are intricately and inextricably part of the social fabric and of the political and economic system which dominates. Third, because curriculum reform is implemented in the classroom by teachers, separating teachers from these other aspects might negatively affect radical and widespread curriculum reform. To avoid these dangers, either the narrative method will have to be extended, or it will need to be supplemented with a process that encourages teachers to look beyond the personal. (Shrofel, 1991, pp. 64–5)

In summary should stories and narratives be a way of giving voice to a particular way of being, or should the genre serve as an introduction to alternative ways of being. Consciousness is constructed rather than autonomously produced, hence giving voice to consciousness may give voice to the constructor at least as much as the speaker. If social context is left out this will likely happen.

The truth is that many times a lifestory-teller will neglect the structural context of their lives or interpret such contextual forces from a biased point of view. As Denzin (1989) says: 'Many times a person will act as if he or she made his or her own history when, in fact, he or she was forced to make the history he or she lived' (p. 74). He gives an example from his 1986 Study of Alcoholics: 'You know I made the last four months by myself. I haven't used or drank. I'm really proud of myself. I did it.' A friend, listening to this account commented:

You know you were under a court order all last year. You didn't do this on your own. You were forced to, whether you want to accept this fact or not. You also went to A.A. and N.A. Listen Buster, you did what you did because you had help and because you were afraid and thought you had no other choice. Don't give me this, 'I did it on my own crap'.

The speaker replies, 'I know. I just don't like to admit it.' Denzin concludes:

This listener invokes two structural forces, the state and A.A., which accounted in part for this speaker's experience. To have secured only the speaker's account, without a knowledge of his biography and personal history, would have produced a biased interpretation of his situation. (Denzin, 1989, pp. 74–5)

The great virtue of stories is that they particularize and make concrete our experiences. This, however, should be their *starting point* in our social and educational study. Stories can so richly move us into the terrain of the social, into insights into the socially constructed nature of our experiences. Feminist sociology has often treated stories in this way. As Hilary Graham says: 'stories are pre-eminently ways of relating individuals and events to social contexts, ways of weaving personal experiences into their social fabric' (see Armstrong, 1987, p. 14). Again Carolyn Steedman (1986) speaks of this two-step process. First the story particularizes, details and historicizes — then at second stage, the 'urgent need' to develop theories of context.

> The fixed townscapes of Northampton and Leeds that Hoggart and Seabrook have described show endless streets of houses, where mothers who don't go out to work order the domestic day, where men are masters, and children, when they grow older, express gratitude for the harsh discipline meted out to them. The first task is to particularise this profoundly a-historical landscape (and so this book details a mother who was a working woman and a single parent, and a father who wasn't a patriarch). And once the landscape is detailed and historicised in this way, the urgent need becomes to find a way of theorising the result of such difference and particularity, not in order to find a description that can be universally applied (the point is *not* to say that all working-class childhoods are the same, nor that experience of them produces unique psychic structures) but so that the people in exile, the inhabitants of the long streets, may start to use the autobiographical 'I', and tell the stories of their life. (Steedman, 1986, p. 16)

The story then provides a starting point for developing further understandings of the social construction of subjectivity. If the teachers' stories stay at the level of the personal and practical we forgo that opportunity. Speaking of the narrative method focusing on personal and practical teachers' knowledge. Willinsky (1989) writes: 'I am concerned that a research process intended to recover the personal and experiential (aspects or not?) would pave over this construction site in its search for an overarching unity in the individual's narrative' (p. 259).

Personal and practical teachers' stories may, therefore, act not to further our understandings but merely to celebrate the particular constructions of the 'teacher' which have been wrought by political and social contestation. Teachers' stories then can be stories of particular political victories and political settlements. Because of their limitation of focus teachers' stories, as stories of the personal and practical, are likely to be limited in this manner.

A Story of Action within a Story of Context

This section comes from a phrase often used by Lawrence Stenhouse. Stenhouse (1975) who was concerned in much of his work to introduce a historical dimension to our studies of schooling and curriculum. Whilst himself a leading advocate of the teacher as researcher, and pioneer of that method, he was worried about the proliferation of practical stories of action, individualized and isolated, unique and idiosyncratic, as our stories of action and our lives are. But as we have seen lives and stories link with broader social scripts — they are not just individual productions they are also social constructions. We must make sure that individual and practical stories do not reduce, seduce and reproduce particular teacher mentalities and lead us away from broader patterns of understanding.

Let us try to situate the narrative moment in the historical moment — for the narrative movement itself could be located in a theory of context. In some ways the movement has analogies with the existential movement of the 1940s. Existentialists believed that only through our actions can we define ourselves. Our role, existentialists judged, was to invent ourselves as individuals then as in Sartre's trilogy *The Roads to Freedom*, we would be 'free', free especially from the claims of society and the 'others'.

Existentialism existed at a particular historical moment following the massive trauma of the Second World War, and in France, where it developed most strongly, of the protracted German occupation. George Melly (1993) judges that existentialism grew out of this historical context.

> My retrospective explanation is that it provided a way of exorcising the collective guilt of the occupation, to reduce the betrayals, the collaboration, the blindeye, the unjustified compromise, to an acceptable level. We know now that the official post-war picture of France under the Nazis was a deliberate whitewash and that almost everyone knew it, and suppressed the knowledge. Existentialism, by insisting on the complete isolation of the individual as free to act, but free to do nothing else, as culpable or heroic but *only* within those limits, helped absolve the notion of corporate and national ignominy. (Melly, 1993, p. 9)

Above all then an individualizing existentialism freed people from the battle of ideologies, freed them from the awfulness of political and military conflict. Individualized existentialism provided a breathing space away from power and politics.

But the end of the Second World War did not provide an end to politics — only a move from hot war to cold war. As we know ideologies continued their contest in the most potentially deadly manner. During this period narratives of personal life began to blossom. Brightman (see Sage, 1994) has developed a fascinating picture of how Mary McCarthy's personal narratives grew out of the witch-hunting period of Joe McCarthy. Her narratives moved us from the 'contagion of ideas' to the personal 'material world'. Mary McCarthy she says could 'strip ideas of their abstract character and return them to the social world from whence they came' (p. 5), as in Irving Howe's memorable phrase 'ideology crumbled, personality bloomed' (quoted in Sage, 1994, p. 5).

And so with the end of ideology, the end of the cold war, we see the proliferant blooming of personality not least in the movement towards personal narratives and stories. Once again the personal narrative, the practical story, celebrates the end of trauma of the cold war and the need for a human space away from politics, away from power. It is a thoroughly understandable nirvana, but it assumes that power and politics have somehow ended. It assumes, in that wishful phrase, 'the end of history'.

In educational bureaucracies, power continues to be hierarchically administered. I have often asked administrators and educational bureaucrats why they support personal and practical forms of knowledge for teachers in the form of narratives and stories. Their comments often echo those of the 'true believers' in narrative method. But I always go on, after suitable pause and diversion, to ask 'what do you do on your leadership courses?' There it is always 'politics as usual' management skills, quality assurance, micropolitical strategies, personnel training. Personal and practical stories for some, cognitive maps of power for others. So whilst the use of stories and narratives can provide a useful breathing space away from power it does not suspend the continuing administration of power; indeed it could well make this so much easier. Especially as over time teachers' knowledge would become more and more personal and practical — different 'mentalities', wholly different understandings of power would emerge as between say teachers and schoolmanagers, teachers and administrators, teachers and some educational scholars.

Teachers' individual and practical stories certainly provide a breathing space, however, at one and the same time they reduce the oxygen of broader understandings. The breathing space comes to look awfully like a vacuum, where history and social construction are somehow suspended.

In this way teachers become divorced from what might be called the 'vernacular of power' — the ways of talking and knowing which then become the prerogative of managers, administrators and academics. In this discourse politics and micropolitics are the essence and currency of the interchange. Alongside this, and in a sense facilitating this, a new 'vernacular of the particular the personal and the practical' arises which is specific to teachers.

This form of apartheid could easily emerge if teachers' stories and narratives remain singular and specific personal and practical, particular and a political. Hence it is a matter of some urgency that we develop stories of action within theories of context — contextualizing stories if you like — which act against the kinds of divorce of the discourses which are all too readily imaginable.

Kathy Carter (1993) had begun to worry about just such a problem in her work on the 'Place of Story' in the study of teaching.

> And for those of us telling stories in our work, we will not serve the community well if we sanctify story-telling work and build an epistemology on it to the point that we simply substitute one paradigmatic domination for another *without challenging domination itself*. We must, then, become much more self conscious than we have been in the past about the issues involved in narrative and story, such as interpretation, authenticity, normative value, and what our purposes are for telling stories in the first place. (Carter, 1993, p. 11)

Some of their worries about stories can be explored in scrutinizing the way in which powerful interest groups in society actually promote and employ storied material.

Note

1 Ivor Goodson's chapter is drawn from his closing keynote address at ISATT 1995.

References

ANDREWS, M. (1991) *Lifetimes of Commitment: Aging, Politics, Psychology*, Cambridge, UK and New York, Cambridge University Press.

ARMSTRONG, P.F. (1987) 'Qualitative strategies in social and educational research: The life history method in theory and practice', *Newland Papers*, **14**, The University of Hull, School of Adult and Continuing Education.

BRISTOW, J. (1991) 'Life stories: Carolyn Steedman's history writing', *New Formations*, **13**, Spring, pp. 113–30.

CARTER, K. (1993) 'The place of story in the study of teaching and teacher education', *Educational Researcher*, **22**, 1, pp. 5–12, 18.

CHAMBERS, C. (1991) 'Review of teachers as curriculum planners: Narratives of experience', *Journal of Education Policy*, **6**, 3, pp. 353–4.

DENZIN, N.K. (1989) 'Interpretive biography', *Qualitative Research Methods Series*, **17**, Newbury Park, London and New Delhi, Sage Publications.

DENZIN, N.K. (1993) 'Review essay: On hearing the voices of educational research', Mimeo, University of Illinois, Urbana-Champaign.

GOODSON, I.F. (1981) 'Life history and the study of Schooling', *Interchange*, **II**, 4, p. 69.

JAMESON, F. (1984) 'Forword', in LYOTARD, J.F. (1984) *The Postmodern Condition: A Report on Knowledge*, Minneapolis, University of Minnesota Press, pp. vii–xxi.

LYOTARD, J.F. (1984) *The Postmodern Condition: A Report on Knowledge*, Minneapolis, University of Minnesota Press.

MELLY, G. (1993) 'Look back in *Angst*', 13 June, *The Sunday Times*, p. 9.

SAGE, L. (1994) 'How to do the life: Review of C. Brightman's *Writing Dangerously: Mary McCarthy and Her World*', *London Review of Books*, p. 5.

SHROFEL, S. (1991) 'Review essay: School reform, professionalism, and control', *Journal of Educational Thought*, **25**, 1, pp. 58–70.

STEEDMAN, C. (1986) *Landscape for a Good Woman*, London, Virago Press.

STENHOUSE, L. (1975) *An Introduction to Curriculum Research and Development*, London, Heinemann.

WILLINSKY, J. (1989) 'Getting personal and practical with personal practical knowledge', *Curriculum Inquiry*, **19**, 3, pp. 247–64.

Notes on Contributors

Elisabeth Ahlstrand, Görel Carlsson, Sven G. Hartman, Anders Magnusson, Lars Nœslund and Annika Rannström are members of the LARK Teacher Knowledge project in which Sven Hartman is the scientific supervisor. They are from the Department of Education at Linkoping University in Sweden.

Mary Beattie is an associate professor at the Faculty of Education, University of Toronto (FEUT), in the Policy and Foundations Department. She also has a cross-appointment to the JCTD. She is a co-investigator with Patrick in a three-year SSHRC funded project on preservice teacher education.

R. Terrance Boak is dean of the Faculty of Education at Brock University. He has a long standing interest in teacher thinking, and adult and distance learning and has been active in writing and research in these and other fields.

W. Richard Bond is an assistant professor at the Faculty of Education of Brock University, Department of Graduate and Undergraduate Studies. He has coordinated programs, developed policy analysis, and has taught exclusively in institutes of higher education. His interests include policy and politics in higher education and distance education.

Susan C. Brown is an assistant professor of education at Elmira College, NY. She has lived in Lebanon, Australia, the Philippines, Indonesia, Italy, Canada, and the United States. Her educational experiences overseas ranged from principal of a Pakistani school to parents advisory board chair of a British-curriculum school.

Ingrid Carlgren is an assistant professor of education at Uppsala University, Sweden. She is currently involved in the construction and implementation of the new Swedish National Curriculum and grading system for compulsory school. Her research is mainly focused on the relation between the theoretical and the practical in teachers' work and education, as well as classrooms as social practices.

D. Jean Clandinin is professor and director of the Center for Research for Teacher Education and Development, University of Alberta. She is the author of many books and research articles in the area of teacher knowledge, classroom practice and narrative inquiry. Her most recent book, authored with F. Michael Connelly, is entitled *Teachers' Professional Knowledge Landscape* (Teachers' College Press, 1995).

F. Michael Connelly is Professor and Director of the Joint Centre for Teacher Development at the Ontario Institute for Studies in Education (OISE) and the University of Toronto. He is editor of *Curriculum Inquiry* and is the author of several books and many book chapters and articles. He has developed a long-term program of research in the area of research in teacher knowledge. His ongoing collaboration with teachers, administrators, and other colleagues has contributed to his understanding of teacher education and curriculum studies.

Karyn Cooper is from the Faculty of Education at The University of Alberta, Edmonton, Canada.

Christopher Day is professor of education, chair of the School of Education and head of Advanced Studies, University of Nottingham. His particular concerns center upon the professional development of teachers, teachers' thinking, leadership and school cultures. Recent publications include *Insights into Teachers' Thinking and Action* (1990, co-edited with Maureen Pope and Pam Denicolo); *Research on Teacher Thinking: Towards Understanding Professional Development* (1993, co-edited with James Calderhead and Pam Denicolo), and a series for Open University Press entitled 'Developing teachers and teaching'. He is secretary-treasurer of ISATT and chair of the editorial board for the ISATT journal *Teachers and Teaching*.

Pam Denicolo, having held senior positions at Surrey University, has recently taken up a post in the Faculty of Education and Community Studies at Reading University. Here she hopes to pursue interests of developing supervision skills, in a variety of professional contexts, research methodologies and practice in education.

C.T. Patrick Diamond is a professor and dissertation supervisor of arts-based educational research at the Joint Center for Teacher Development (JCTD) of the Ontario Institute for Studies in Education of the University of Toronto (OISE/UT), Canada. He is Acting Director of the JCTD and an associate editor for *Curriculum Inquiry*.

Don Dworet is an associate professor in the Faculty of Education at Brock University. Don is a former Chair of the Preservice Department and has interests in special education, volunteers in schools, social issues and teacher thinking.

Elliot Eisner is a professor of education at Stanford University. He has a long-standing of excellence and insight into teachers' thinking and practices. Among his many writings is *The Enlightened Eye.*

Ivor Goodson is professor of education, University of Western Ontario, London, Ontario, and the Frederica Warner Scholar in the Graduate School of Education and Human Development at the University of Rochester. At Western, he is a member of the Faculties of Graduate Studies, Education, Sociology and The Center for Theory and Criticism. In England he taught at two innovative comprehensive schools before moving to the University of Sussex in 1975, where he became the Director of the Schools Unit. He is the author of a range of books on curriculum and life history studies, as well as the founding editor and North American editor of *The Journal of Education Policy* and the national editor of *Qualitative Studies in Education.*

Mark Hadfield is a researcher at the School of Education, University of Nottingham. His interest in teachers' thinking research is based on his work on how teachers deal with controversial issues within the curriculum. He is currently working with the Chinese University of Hong Kong on a comparative study of the 'dilemmas' teachers face in the classroom.

Michael Kompf is an associate professor in The Faculty of Education at Brock

University, St Catharines, Ontario, Canada where he teaches and researches issues related to distance learning, adult learning and teaching, life and career-span development, and personal construct psychology. Michael is an associate editor of the ISATT journal *Teachers and Teaching*.

Marcella L. Kysilka has taught undergraduate and graduate classes in the Educational Foundations Department of the University of Central Florida for twenty-five years. She is recognized for her work in the areas of curriculum, teaching, and thinking skills development. She is current editor of *The Educational Forum*, the journal for Kappa Delta Pi, an International Honor Society in Education.

Per F. Laursen is an associate professor in the Institute of Education, Philosophy and Rhetoric at the University of Copenhagen, Denmark. His main research interests are teacher thinking, curriculum theory and physical education.

Janice Martin is a doctoral candidate at the Ontario Institute for Studies in Education (The University of Toronto). She completed her Master of Education at Brock University and is an educational practitioner and consultant in a large metropolitan school board.

Carol A. Mullen is an Assistant Professor using arts-based methods of instruction and research in the Department of Educational Curriculum and Instruction (EDCI) at Texas A&M University (TAMU). She is Principal Investigator of a study exploring Hispanic preservice teachers' expressions of cultural self-identity.

Margaret R. Olson is an assistant professor with Queen's University working in the Trent-Queen's Concurrent Teacher Education Program at Trent University. Her teaching focuses on educational contexts. Her research focuses on teacher education, particularly personal/professional development of teachers in diverse educational contexts.

Maureen Pope is the dean of the Faculty of Education and Community Studies at the University of Reading, UK. She has published a large number of articles on personal construct psychology as applied in an educational context. She is founding member and ex-chair of ISATT. In addition to her research on student teacher thinking she is currently investigating the role of interprofessional education and interprofessional working amongst community health nurses and social workers. She has conducted a large number of workshops within the UK and abroad on aspects of her research, research methodology and staff development of university teachers. In addition to her duties as dean of the faculty, Professor Pope has a large number of doctoral students and is an external examiner and consultant to a number of research projects. Professor Pope is also an associate editor for the ISATT journal *Teachers and Teaching*.

Cecilia Reynolds is an associate professor in the Faculty of Education at Brock University, Department of Graduate and Undergraduate Studies. She has taught for over seventeen years in both elementary and secondary schools and is a former director of the undergraduate Women's Studies Program at Brock. Currently, she is working on studies of women as educational leaders.

Joan Tucker is in the Faculty of Education, Department of Teacher Education Development at the University of The West Indies.

Maureen J. Warner teaches Gifted and Advanced Placement English in Oviedo,

Florida, a suburb of Orlando experiencing increased student diversity. She has served on a county committee facilitating the inclusion of minority students in the Gifted Program. She previously taught in inner city and suburban schools in Cleveland, Ohio.

K.W. Yeung completed his MA in counseling under Professor Maureen Pope's supervision. He is currently a lecturer at the Hong Kong Technical Teachers' College and acts as a counselor within the Counseling Service at Hong Kong University. He is about to submit his PhD thesis on the 'Impact of teaching practice on student teachers' development of self-esteem, professional self-esteem and teaching efficacy.'

Index

Abbott, A., 51
Abernathy, S., 104, 113
action stories, 218–21
active learning, 64
activity-planning, 27
administrators, 73, 86
Ahlstrand, E., 2, 133, 186–210
Alberta University, 70, 142
Alexandersson, M., 202
Andrews, M., 212–13, 215–16
anti-intellectualism, 62
anxiety, 105
apartheid, 61, 220
Apple, M.W., 60
apprehension, 28–9
apprenticeships, 31, 33–6, 52, 54
Aries, P., 84
art, 6–7, 120–30, 175–85
assessment, 13, 15–16, 82, 94,
    172–3
assignments, 38, 42, 104, 113
assumptions, 43, 93
Atwood, M., 81
awareness, 17, 27, 39, 40, 58, 203

Ball, S., 163
Barnes, D., 60, 61
Bateson, M., 175
Beattie, M., 2, 133, 175–85
Beethoven, Ludwig van, 11
behavior problems, 93, 99, 113
behaviorism, 49, 79–80, 83
Belenky, M., 87
Bell, J., 59
Ben-Peretz, M., 105
Bennet, C., 120, 127–8
Berliner, D.C., 151
Bernstein, Basil, 203

best practice, 90
Beyerbach, B.A., 94
Bird, John, 3
Blase, J.J., 105
Boak, R.T., 3, 131–5
Bond, W.R., 5–6
Bost, J.M., 93
Bourdieu, Pierre, 71
Brightman, 219
Bristow, J., 215
Britain see also United Kingdom, 50
Britzman, Deborah, 74
Brock University, 1, 3, 57
Brooks, J., 168
Brooks, M., 168
Brown, L.M., 35
Brown, Alan, 1
Brown, Susan, 2, 133, 167–74
Bryan, L., 61–2
budgets, 59–60
Buitink, J., 105

Campbell, N.J., 93
Canada, 70, 73, 85
caning, 170–1
cannibalization, 212
capitalism, 13, 18, 215
Capra, F., 79
careers, 120–1, 124–6
Carlgren, Ingrid, 1, 6, 20–32, 76
Carlsson, G., 2, 186–210
Carter, K., 60, 213, 214–15, 220
centralism, 187
Chambers, Cynthia, 216
change, 21–2, 206–7
child development theory, 83
child identity, 83–5
Chinn, P., 168